On Economic Knowledge

TOWARD A SCIENCE OF POLITICAL ECONOMICS

Approximative thought is the only creator of reality.—The real is not entirely rational, nor is the rational entirely real.—The irrational imposes limits on the rational which, in turn, gives it moderation.

—Albert Camus, *The Rebel*

On Economic Knowledge

TOWARD A SCIENCE OF POLITICAL ECONOMICS

ENLARGED EDITION

Adolph Lowe

M. E. SHARPE, INC., PUBLISHER　　WHITE PLAINS, NEW YORK

This book was originally published as Volume XXXV of WORLD PERSPECTIVES, planned and edited by Ruth Nanda Anshen, by Harper & Row Publishers, Inc.

This edition is published by arrangement with the author.

Library of Congress Catalog Card Number: 77–72365
International Standard Book Number: 0–87332–107–3

Printed in the United States of America.

Contents

PART FOUR

ASPECTS OF A SCIENCE OF POLITICAL ECONOMICS

PART FIVE

A POSTSCRIPT

Preface to First Edition

This book is the fruit of forty years of reflection about the subject matter and the method of a science of Economics. As is only natural my ideas have undergone considerable changes during this time, and it may facilitate the understanding of what follows if I briefly sketch the major stages in this development.

I started out as a convinced partisan of the traditional approach as formulated in neo-classical equilibrium theory. At the same time, some work in business cycle research, in which I was then engaged, made me realize the serious gap that separated all equilibrium models from an economic reality which was subject to wide fluctuations in employment and output. However, I thought it possible to bridge this gap by extending the stationary framework of prevailing analysis into a "dynamic" model that would account for the periodic deviations of the economic process from a steady path.[1] Above all, I shared the orthodox opinion that economic theory had to be a self-contained body of generalizations, independent of socio-political considerations and valid for all types of economic systems.

A second stage was reached when I abandoned this latter dogma. In other words, I began to recognize that classical, neo-classical, and Marxian theories of the market, not to mention the later blueprints of a socialist economy, depicted different forms of social and technical organization.[2] But I still believed that industrial market systems, now understood as inclusive socio-economic phenomena, exhibited regularities of motion sufficiently strict to be formulated in laws of coexistence and succession.

[1] See my "Wie ist Konjunkturtheorie ueberhaupt moeglich?" (The Feasibility of Business Cycle Theory), *Weltwirtschaftliches Archiv*, Vol. 24, 1926, pp. 165–97.

[2] See my *Economics and Sociology*, London, 1935.

It is this belief which subsequent experience and reflection have shattered for good, exposing me once again to the fundamental question whether Economics is a proper subject for a theoretical science. Part One of this book sets forth what appear to me the strongest arguments against a feasible economic theory. At the same time it will be shown that in the absence of such an intellectual tool we may be unable, in Keynes' words, to avoid "the destruction of existing economic forms in their entirety."

How it is possible to overcome this dilemma is the topic of Part Two. There the outlines are presented of an analytical procedure— instrumental inference—which seems to me capable of satisfying our theoretical as well as our practical needs.

These observations should make it clear that the ultimate concern of this book is not methodological. If a critique of conventional procedures and suggestions for their revision are in the foreground, the reason is the novel function which scientific thinking has acquired for the guidance of economic practice. In particular I hope to demonstrate that successful public control has by now become a prerequisite not only for the stability and growth of industrial systems but also for their scientific interpretation. Only with the help of such control shall we succeed in bestowing on the economic states and processes of the real world that degree of orderliness which is a precondition for theoretical generalization.

For this reason Political Economics, as I have named the body of empirically relevant theorems within our reach, is the result of a continuous interplay between thought and action. This is my principal thesis to be elaborated in Chapter 5, but already indicated in the title of the book. In speaking there of economic *knowledge* rather than of economic *theory*, I wish to point to a scientific approach in which observation and cogitation—the conventional tools of science—are supplemented by "participation"—actual intervention in the course of events.

Much of what will be said below is critical of conventional techniques of analysis. But nothing is further from my mind than a summary rejection of prevailing practice. Rather it will be the task of Part Three to show that, in gradually extricating themselves from an inherited frame of reference, leading theorists have for quite some time been moving in what seems to me the right direction. Still, largely unaware of the change in trend thus initiated, they have been doing so in piecemeal fashion. In what follows I have tried to make this trend explicit, and to present some test cases in which the new analytical technique is applied. This is the main content of Part Four.

Hard as was the struggle for clarification, I found it almost as difficult to tackle the problem of communication. Among the addressees of this study are, of course, my fellow economists and graduate students with a venturesome turn of mind. But in the course of this work my conviction has deepened that Economics is a social science in more than a trivial sense. Therefore I am anxious not to repel our comrades-in-arms from the other social sciences or natural scientists and humanists concerned with the foundations of scientific knowledge by an esoteric manner of presentation. This is even more valid for so-called lay readers who are willing to spend some intellectual effort on the issues here discussed.

This is the reason why I have used technical language sparingly, relegating it whenever possible to footnotes. For the rest I ask the patience of economists and non-economists alike for sometimes laboring what to the former is the obvious, and for at other times skipping over what for the latter may still be a problem.

* * *

It is in the nature of a long-drawn-out effort that it becomes more and more difficult to sort out that which is one's own from what others have, knowingly or unknowingly, contributed. Moreover those helpmates who have influenced my general outlook—they include not only colleagues in practically every field of the sciences and humanities, but also generations of students in three countries —are far too numerous to be mentioned here by name. But in evoking the memory of Karl Mannheim, Franz Oppenheimer, Kurt Riezler and Alfred Schuetz I wish to acknowledge an intellectual debt which a lifetime is too short to pay.

In the treatment of some special problems I have benefited from the critical comments of Murray Brown, Aron Gurwitch, Hans Jonas, Hans Neisser, Hans Staudinger, Paul Tillich, and Geoffrey Vickers, none of whom of course bears any responsibility for the text. I am grateful to Ernest Lustig for enlightening me about model construction in the physical sciences.

No word of acknowledgment can do justice to the contribution which Robert L. Heilbroner has made to the form as well as to the content of this book. Every section has been discussed with him and, more often than not, has been redrafted in line with his suggestions. In particular, to his empathy as a reader and brilliance as a writer must be credited any success of mine in communicating my ideas to the non-specialist. I heartily welcome the opportunity to acknowledge this intellectual companionship as one of the most precious gifts which life in America has bestowed on me.

I also pay grateful tribute to Ruth Nanda Anshen, who plans and edits *World Perspectives*. Five years ago she suggested to me the general idea of a book which would deal with those fundamentals of Economics that transcend merely specialist concerns. Her encouragement and patience have greatly supported me during the difficult stages of gestation.

In thanking my wife I express more than the conventional matrimonial apology. Not only has she transcribed with meticulous care four illegible drafts into workable text but her assistance in reading proofs and preparing the index has proved invaluable. The final typescript is the work of Miss Violet Serwin, performed with great intelligence and superior technical skill.

More than a decade ago the Lucius N. Littauer Foundation awarded me a grant for research into some of the problems discussed in this book. I am happy to demonstrate my appreciation visibly even if belatedly.

I cannot conclude this very incomplete account without a word of gratitude and praise for the intellectual and human environment in which I have been privileged to work during the past decades: the Graduate Faculty of the New School for Social Research inspired by its venerable founder, Alvin Johnson. Its traditional concern with interdisciplinary problems and with the humanistic aspects of all technical work in social science has, I hope, found some reflection in what is stated in this book.

Much of the writing was done during several summers at Kandahar Lodge, Vermont, a haven for any scholar stimulated by pleasant natural and personal surroundings.

ADOLPH LOWE

Thanksgiving, 1964
New York

Preface To Enlarged Edition

This book appeared originally in 1965 as Volume 35 of *World Perspectives,* a series planned and edited by Ruth Nanda Anshen and published by Harper & Row. It was reprinted in 1970 as a Torchbook paperback. It is now reissued under a new imprint and brought up to date by a Postscript that deals with a number of factual and theoretical issues which have come to the fore during the last decade.

Some of these issues have already been discussed in an earlier publication in which appear the proceedings of two symposia devoted to the original book, held in 1968.[1] Furthermore, the ideas and analytical techniques sketched in Chapter 11 of the original text have now been fully elaborated in a recently published volume.[2]

In view of these subsequent publications, the reader may wonder why the original text is presented here once more rather than a revised version of it. An obvious answer is that such a revision

[1] See *Economic Means and Social Ends, Essays in Political Economics,* edited by Robert L. Heilbroner, Prentice-Hall, Englewood Cliffs, 1969 (henceforth cited as *Emase).* See especially my introductory summary of the main theses of *On Economic Knowledge,* and my Rejoinder to the controversies raised.

[2] See Adolph Lowe, *The Path of Economic Growth,* Cambridge University Press, London, New York, Melbourne, 1976.

would have posed serious technical problems to both the author and the publisher. But the real reason concerns the substance of the book—a revised edition would in all essentials look like the original. To be sure, minor shortcomings could be dealt with by shifting certain emphases, by softening the tone of some critical comments, and by stressing even more strongly than before the convergence of my approach with that of certain branches of modern theory, such as Activity Analysis and Decision Theory. Still, my basic propositions would remain unchanged.

At the same time, a number of thoughtful objections have convinced me that some theoretical issues and, especially, some points of method are in need of further clarification. Moreover, the chain of turbulent events that marks our recent experience has induced me to reexamine the practical goals which a Political Economics can and should pursue in the coming decades. These second thoughts, I felt, could best be dealt with in an afterword that reflected back on the original text. Accordingly, it is with these issues that the Postscript is mainly concerned.

I wish to express my sincere thanks to Mr. Arnold C. Tovell, Editorial Director of M. E. Sharpe, Inc., and his staff for their work in preparing this new edition.

Thanksgiving 1976   A. L.
New York

PART ONE

---◆---

CAN ECONOMICS
BE A SCIENCE?

1

Man-Matter-Society

1. A Setting for the Problem

Looking through the record of Man's thinking about economic affairs is a puzzling experience. Since the dawn of prehistory Man has been an "economizing" animal, and during the millennia now past no other activity has claimed so many of his waking hours. Yet systematic reflection about this foremost of his preoccupations dates back no further than to the seventeenth century.

Of course, natural science as we understand it today is not much older, but this analogy misses the point. Even if he is highly critical of the physical and biological speculations of a Democritus or an Aristotle and of their followers up to the Renaissance, no modern scientist will dispute the didactic intent and methodical style of these intellectual pursuits. Nor can the want of an equivalent ancient or medieval Economics be ascribed to a general lack of interest in the study of Man and Society. The nature, origin, and function of government and the role of the individual in a civilized community have been perennial topics of Western philosophy for more than two thousand years. In fact, what comments on economic matters have been handed down to us from distant ages are to be found in those very discourses on Politics and Natural Law.

Even more startling, however, than the lag in its historical development is the scientific turn which Economics took after it emerged, around the middle of the eighteenth century, as a separate branch of social inquiry. Within a century it had purged itself of

3

all the philosophical, political, and sociological residues of its origin, to present the most extreme case of specialization among all the sciences dealing with Man. Moreover, in the choice of its research technique—the so-called hypothetico-deductive method—it went furthest in emulating the exact sciences dealing with Nature. Like them, Economics tries "to discover and to formulate in general terms the conditions under which events of various sorts occur . . . by distinguishing and isolating certain properties in the subject studied and by ascertaining the *repeatable patterns of dependence in which these properties stand to one another.*" Along with his fellow worker in Physics, the modern economist will not rest content until "with the help of a small number of explanatory principles an indefinitely large number of propositions about these facts can be shown to constitute a logically unified body of knowledge."[1]

Not that this scientific trend has gone unopposed. Since the early nineteenth century periodic resistance movements have arisen—the best known being the German Historical School, American Institutionalism, and the Functionalist branch in contemporary Sociology—stressing taxonomic, historical-descriptive, or "structural-functional" approaches to the subject matter of Economics.[2] Furthermore, the practitioners of other social sciences such as Politics, Sociology, and Anthropology, even if not entirely unaffected by the pattern of economic theory, have looked and still look at its constructs with a mixture of jealous awe and skeptical doubt. How is it possible, most of them ask, that the tools of the exact sciences can be applied to the analysis of one type of social relations, when the other types with which they are familiar prove the epitome of multiformity and mutability?

These critical voices have not been given a sympathetic hearing within the fold of theoretical Economics, and the past generation has moved with even greater determination in the direction of scientific exactitude. The protagonists of classical and neo-classical

---

[1] There is far-reaching agreement among philosophers and methodologists as to what constitutes a fully developed "science." The above definitions have been taken from Ernest Nagel, *The Structure of Science* (New York, 1961), p. 4. (italics added)

[2] For details see chap. 4, sec. 1 and sec. 8, note 40.

Economics were still satisfied with what has aptly been called armchair-theorizing. They did not feel bound—nor did they have the appropriate research techniques—to submit either the hypotheses on which their theorems were based or these theorems themselves to empirical tests. Common-sense observations of data and conclusions and cogent inference appeared to them as sufficient proof. It is these remnants of a speculative past which are progressively eliminated in the work of modern Econometrics. It submits the constants and variables figuring in its theoretical constructs to precise measurement, and incorporates the results in ever more complex models to be employed in the forecasting of short- and long-term movements of the parts and aggregate of the economic process.

However, consistent as this development may appear, it poses a puzzle when we try to evaluate the results of these sophisticated procedures by the only relevant yardstick—their correspondence with observable facts. To put it bluntly, our ability to explain and to predict has not improved in proportion to the exactitude of the methods applied.

In order to exclude any bias which might color this verdict, we refer to the testimony of a pioneer and generally recognized authority in the field of Econometrics. Summarizing a survey of recent research he concludes: "We must face the fact that models using elaborate theoretical and statistical tools and concepts have not done decisively better, in the majority of available tests, than the most simple-minded and mechanical extrapolation formulae."[3] One reason for this perplexing conclusion has been found in the fact that we "do not know which basic assumptions about the behavior of the strategic decision-making units are empirically relevant. Until we do, model-building will be a branch of mathematics and logic rather than a powerful tool for an empirical science."[4] What this amounts to can best be shown by an analogy. Since the decision-making units represent the "forces" in the universe of economic motion, ignorance about the relevant behavior patterns can be com-

[3] See T. C. Koopmans, *Three Essays on the State of Economic Science* (New York, 1957), p. 212.

[4] *Ibid.*, p. 209, a quotation from a memorandum of another econometrician, Professor James Tobin.

pared with the state of mind of a physicist who tries to predict planetary motion without knowing the strength and direction of the force of gravitation.

All builders of mathematical and econometric models are not equally self-critical. The inquisitive bystander is usually invited, and properly so, to control his impatience for quick results of an enterprise only lately begun. So it seems quite legitimate to re-examine in the meanwhile the foundations on which this ultra-science of modern Economics rests. In doing so we ask ourselves: *what must we know in order to gain systematic understanding of the economic activities of a human group,* and *by what intellectual techniques can such "economic knowledge" be obtained?* In our search for this knowledge the peculiar features of traditional Economics alluded to—its late development, the affinity of its methods with those indigenous to the exact sciences, and the limited if not diminishing relevance of its findings—will serve as signposts for the next step to be taken. It will be a step toward reintegrating Economics with Social Science at large while maintaining its concern with "repeatable patterns of interdependence."

2. *The Realm of Economic Activity*

Our first issue is the true relationship that exists between Economics and the exact sciences. In fact, a strong argument can be made in favor of a quite intimate relationship. It bases itself on the presence of a nucleus in all economic activities which relates Man to Matter rather than Man to Man. As a consequence Economics, irrespective of all its social aspects, poses first of all a problem in Applied Natural Science.

Though it is not always stated so bluntly, this view is quite compatible with orthodox definitions of economic activity as "that part of individual and social action which is closely connected with the attainment and with the use of the material requisites of wellbeing" (A. Marshall) or as "the creation and use of Wealth" (J. B. Clark).[5] This does not deny that the concrete form in which this

[5] Even more explicit is Walras in his definition of the "theory of industry,"

relationship between Man and Matter manifests itself has always been shaped by the prevailing relationship between Man and Man, that is, by the order of Society. But whereas social organizations differ in space and time, economic activity as carried on in any one of them shows an invariant core, a core for which the biological processes of metabolism offer a good analogy.

Just as the survival and growth of any living organism is conditional on the steady absorption of external matter, so Homo sapiens depends for many of his pursuits on the materials and forces of his environment. Economic activity is the procedure by which he tries to cope with this dependence. At primitive levels of civilization he mainly does so by seizing material resources in their natural state; at higher stages he converts matter as offered by Nature into forms which he regards as more suitable to the satisfaction of his wants. Thus the basic problems for actor and observer alike are two: how are the available inputs to be transformed into suitable outputs and how are the outputs themselves to be disposed of by needy Man—problems which are dealt with in the textbooks under the headings of Production and Distribution.

In order to penetrate to the economic gist of these issues, we shall avail ourselves of a methodological device which has a long history in economic analysis: the fiction of an isolated man. This will permit us to abstract the Man-Matter relationship from all social implications and to lay bare the essential features of this association. Thus considered, any economizing act presents itself as a specific manner in which certain means are applied to the attainment of certain ends. What means—to what ends?

It is generally agreed that the ultimate end or goal of economic activity is the satisfaction or, more pointedly, the maximum satisfaction of human wants. Plausible as this notion appears at first sight, it tells us less than we need to know. Satisfaction of wants or

which is supposed to study the "relations between persons and things." But he contrasts this "applied science or art" with an allegedly "pure theory" of Economics which is to deal with the "natural phenomenon" of exchange. (See Leon Walras, *Elements of Pure Economics*, trans. by William Jaffé [Homewood, Ill., 1954], pp. 63, 69, 71.)

the so-called utility of the means from which such satisfaction derives is "a treasure locked in each man's mind, and we have no key that will enable us to bring these treasures out . . . we must find a concept which is perhaps less ultimately significant for the individual, but which is more measurable than utility. This we may find to some extent in an index of physical output."[6]

In taking this hint we can define as the end of the economic activity of our Robinson Crusoe the "basket of goods" whose procurement directs his productive efforts. But we must be aware that, in substituting the physical results of production for the psychological benefits which want-satisfaction in general yields, we have done more than simply replace an unmeasurable concept by a measurable one. We have, in fact, narrowed down the range of phenomena which are to be labeled "economic." The act of consumption itself and the state of satisfaction thus achieved are excluded from the economic sphere, and this sphere has thus become a realm of activities rather than of states of mind, the proximate goal of these activities being the *provision of the material means* required for the realization of those states.

In so defining economic activity we have introduced an important limitation. But we had better first bring out some of the implications of this definition itself. In particular, can we make any general statement about the size and the composition of the basket of goods which is the economic goal of our Robinson Crusoe?

Its composition will of course be related to the specific wants he experiences, and will thus reflect the final goals he wishes to attain. These goals then are ultimate data both for Crusoe and for any observer who tries to analyze his behavior. But what about the size of his basket? There is certainly an upper limit to this size which is determined by another datum—the stock of his resources.

At this point it has become a sort of convention to interpose a lament about the imperfection of Man's estate, revealed by the irremediable *scarcity* of his resources. Scarcity is understood here as a relative concept, relative, namely, to Man's final goals. The supposition is that the latter are indefinitely manifold, and are means-

[6] See K. E. Boulding, *Economic Analysis* (New York, 1948), p. 649.

requiring far beyond any conceivable scope of actual resource supply. But though this fact is deplored as an obstacle to the fulfillment of human desires, the curious fact is that both for the economic actor and for the scientific observer looking for a principle of orientation it seems to turn into a blessing in disguise. For not only does scarcity offer a rationale for all economic activity, but it also appears to be the key to the solution of all the basic problems of Economics.

For instance, does not scarcity of resources imply an obvious answer to the question of the size of his basket which our Crusoe is going to choose? Remembering our earlier reference to maximizing satisfaction, the implication seems to be that Crusoe, unable to satisfy all his wants, will always prefer a larger to a smaller basket, and will therefore aim at maximizing his output. Still, at second thought some doubts arise. Can we be sure that reducing his sleep to the physiological minimum and spending all his waking hours on the production of goods will maximize Crusoe's satisfaction? He may prefer to lie half the day in the sun or to puzzle out a mathematical problem or to stroll along the beach for physical exercise or for aesthetic pleasure.

As expositors of the "praxiological" school of modern Economics, Professors von Mises and Robbins[7] would say that such "leisure time" activities or passivities also claim scarce resources, namely, Crusoe's physical and mental energy and (or) time. As a consequence they define economic activity as including the application of any conceivable scarce means to any conceivable ends. To them the "production of philosophy" has an "economic aspect" as has the "production of potatoes," and "there are no limitations on the subject matter of Economic Science" save one: the activity considered must "involve the relinquishment of other desired alternatives" (Robbins)—which all human activities are bound to do since they have a time dimension.

This grandiose expansion of Economics into a general "logic of

---

[7] See L. von Mises, *Human Action*, A Treatise on Economics (New Haven, 1949), and Lionel Robbins, *An Essay on the Nature and Significance of Economic Science* (London, 1946), chap. I.

choice" brings into the open a second limitation which our earlier definition of the goal of economic activity has introduced. It can be stated quite simply if we divide the aggregate of resources available to our Crusoe into "internal," or "immaterial," resources—energy and time—and into "external," or "material," resources—the basic materials and forces which Nature offers. Then by stressing the provision of material means our definition *restricts economic behavior to those activities which always claim, in addition to the use of immaterial resources, the use of some material resources.*

To argue about definitions is, in principle, an unproductive undertaking unless it can be shown that, by circumscribing the scope of a given phenomenon in one way rather than another, its essential features are thrown into relief. This we are trying to do now for our narrow definition of economic activity as the provision of material means.

The advantage of our definition is twofold. First, it singles out from the universal "logic of choice" a well-circumscribed realm of specific activities. Second, it highlights the merely historical—rather than intrinsic—role which "scarcity of natural resources" plays in the shaping of such activities. This is so because the wants which require material means for their gratification are by no means intrinsically limitless, nor are, within conceivable limits, all required resources intrinsically scarce. In contrast with this it is those human ends which can dispense with material means—henceforth called immaterial ends—that are truly limitless, and the immaterial resources required to their attainment—human energy and time—are irremediably scarce.

What this amounts to can easily be grasped when we turn to that minority which in every society of the past has escaped the harsh constraints that scarcity of material resources has indeed imposed on the majority. From the beginning of history the presence of such a minority has held out a promise which over the last century has been progressively fulfilled by the advance of technology and social organization. It is the promise that the strata capable of rising above minimum subsistence will steadily expand, devoting increasing quantities of their immaterial resources to what is badly described as "leisure time activities"—a term which implies, however, the existence of another realm of activities congruent with what we defined as the economic realm.

Especially significant in this development is the changing role which the material resources themselves play in it. Far from freezing the satisfaction of output-requiring goals at any fixed level, this continuous shift of immaterial resources to the attainment of immaterial ends has been accompanied by a vast expansion of the provision of material means. This has been possible because modern technology is steadily multiplying the supply of natural resources, and is likely to break through all known barriers by progressively substituting the ultimate natural resource—the unlimited and ubiquitous elements of Chemistry—for the scant and localized products of a slow geological and biological evolution—the inorganic and organic creations of the mineral, vegetable, and animal kingdoms.

One may still maintain that neither nuclear fission or fusion, nor automation nor all the discoveries and inventions still to come will ever provide mankind with the material means necessary to gratify all imaginable whims. But we must remember that means are scarce only relative to the ends for which they are desired. And we can certainly conceive of many states of material provision above the threshold of mere subsistence, in which the prevailing cultural value system would limit the scale of wants requiring material means to the point where the available stock of natural resources would no longer be an obstacle to their full satisfaction.

It is true, even such abundance of natural resources will not change the resulting material means into "free goods" like atmospheric air, the light and warmth of the sun in daytime, and water (Walras). This is so because there is no known technology or method of organization which could render the complementary *immaterial* resources equally abundant. But once the threshold of mere subsistence has been passed, the unalterable scarcity of the latter is no longer grounded in the economic realm of means provision. Rather Man's immaterial resources are and will remain scarce relative to the unlimited scope of his *total* pursuits, among which means provision is likely to claim a steadily diminishing share. It is in his striving for immaterial goals, culminating in creative activity or mystical contemplation, that Man's condition proves existentially dismal, namely, beset with the agonies of Tantalus, whom fulfillment forever evades. Not even return to the Garden of Eden, where all the material means are there for the taking, would deliver him from this evil, unless he was transformed at the same time into an all-powerful, immortal god.[8]

The upshot of all this is the insight that *unqualified scarcity of resources cannot be made the criterion for economic activity.* First, by blurring essential differences the notion misses those features of "economizing" that since time immemorial have vexed actors and observers alike. Second, it misrepresents the true function of economic activity by placing it side by side with all other human activities, such as love and charity, the striving for power and the concern for the common good, the search for truth and the contemplation of the beautiful and the holy, and even with the acts of consuming material goods. All these activities carry their meaning and "value" in themselves, their ultimate goals being intrinsic to them. Nothing of this is true of economic activity. It is supplementary to all the others, coming into play only if, and to the extent to which, the realization of their goals is conditional on prior provision of material means. Economizing is no more than a special technique without any inherent value attached to it, a mode of procedure with the help of which genuine substantive goals extrinsic to such manipulation can be attained more successfully. Its one intrinsic end—procurement of material means—is merely intermediary and provisional.[9] Only the perverted mind of a miser to whom amassing of means as such yields satisfaction can raise it to a final goal.

[8] These considerations will prove relevant when we subsequently examine the "utility principle." See chap. 8, sec. 5.

[9] That this holds even for the goal of "unlimited accumulation" prevalent in a certain stage of capitalist development will be shown in chap. 3.

In thus assigning to economic activity a mere "modal" signifi-cance we only accept the negative verdict which so many ancient myths, most political utopias of modern times, and above all, the lamentations of the common men in all civilizations have passed on it.[10] This verdict protests against a world in which most of the potentialities of a good life devoted to the realization of meaningful ends must be sacrificed to the toil and trouble required for procur-ing means. And no appeal to the "instinct of workmanship" or the educational value, not to say the pure joy springing from such toil, has stifled the hope that a time may come when Man finds himself liberated from these fetters. Even today, of all the struggles for emancipation none commands such universal assent as does the Promethean revolt of modern technology against Adam's curse. An Economics which centers on the notion of unconditional scarcity turns a deaf ear to the promise of this revolt—the eventual de-thronement of what is modal by what is final through the conquest of the stinginess of Nature.[11]

3. The Technological Core of Economic Activity

It was the question of how to determine the size of Crusoe's out-put basket that led us to a closer scrutiny of the notion of scarcity. What answer can we derive from our findings?

The two sets of data so far considered—Crusoe's list of final goals and his stock of resources—do not offer any definite answer. This is at least so if his stock of resources is large enough to permit him freely to choose between catching another fish or sleeping an hour longer. To arrive at a decision he requires an additional cri-terion which tells him how to divide his "surplus" of resources and,

[10] See Ernst Bloch, *Das Prinzip Hoffnung* (Frankfurt am Main, 1959), esp. Part Four. Also Herbert Marcuse, *Eros and Civilization* (Boston, 1955), chaps. 7 and 9.

[11] It is quite a different problem whether any form of social organization known to us today is fit to use these potentialities, once they have become realities, "for the benefit of mankind" (see Norbert Wiener, *The Human Use of Human Beings* [Garden City, N.Y., 1954]). This problem far transcends the boundaries of "economic knowledge," and can be touched in this book only incidentally.

in particular, his surplus of energy and time between providing more material means and satisfying more of his immaterial wants.

Since it is to direct his actions, this criterion can only be another goal. In trying to define it we must realize that there is a certain objective hierarchy of final goals. Pride of place belongs to the absolute wants on the satisfaction of which survival depends. Now it is a fact of life—indicated in the analogy of economic with metabolic processes—that these absolute wants cannot be gratified without material means. Therefore within these limits economic activity is bound to precede all other activities, and the new goal or action directive for which we search must be concerned with those resources which are to be devoted to the procurement of material means beyond what is necessary for sheer survival.

In contrast with the final goals encountered hitherto, we meet here with *modal* goals which, in the sphere of individual decision-making, reflect the modal purpose of the economic realm at large. As such their attainment is conditional on quantitative rather than qualitative decisions, decisions, namely, about the aggregate amount of resources to be applied to means provision and about the ratios in which the individual resources are to be combined.

Of course, such a modal goal presupposes prior decisions on final goals, that is, on the qualitative composition of the desired basket of output. This is to say, Crusoe must first make up his mind that he prefers, say, milk to fish and berries to snails. But once he has listed the potential items in his consumption basket he must, in addition, determine the quantities of milk and of berries to be obtained. We know that the upper limit of these quantities is fixed by the total stock of his resources, material and immaterial, relative to the resource requirements per unit of the various outputs. However, the actual quantities to be produced and, thus, the aggregate size of his basket depend on the proportion of his total resources he is willing to mobilize for current production.[12]

---

[12] The first to emphasize the distinction between final and modal goals and its relevance for economic analysis was Franz Oppenheimer, *System der Soziologie* (Jena, 1923), vol. 3, pp. 17–21. We shall see later that, though modal goals are the source of quantitative decisions, their own "focal point" may well be qualitative. See chap. 5, sec. 5.

In determining this proportion Crusoe can choose between many alternatives. By applying all his disposable energy and time to the seizure and transformation of natural resources he can "maximize" his output. Or he may choose input quantities compatible with any other level of output between such a maximum and the minimum of subsistence. And he may do so by quite different combinations of the various inputs, e.g., by being lavish with the expenditure of energy or of time while being parsimonious with natural resources, or conversely. But assuming that he does achieve what he wants to achieve, pursuit of any such modal goal establishes a state of *optimum* provision—the mere fact that he freely selects this one among other possible alternatives proving that in this quantitative combination his qualitative outputs yield him maximum satisfaction.

At first sight this seems to be a rather trivial conclusion. Yet it contradicts an assumption which underlies practically all conventional reasoning about economic behavior. Classical as well as modern economists have singled out one particular state of provision as the true optimum, reserving the attribute "economic behavior" for those and only those actions which aim at that particular state. In fact, it is the state which was described above as maximum provision. In the current formulations this state appears as the result of allegedly "rational" actions which conform to a so-called economic principle, actions which achieve a maximum aggregate output through minimizing input per unit of output. The attempt has even been made to derive from this economic principle verifiable laws of economic behavior "with apodictic certainty and incontestability" as the consequence of the "logic of choice."[13]

When we proceed to the study of economic societies we shall come to understand the reason why traditional Economics has been so much concerned with the establishment of definite patterns of economic behavior and, in particular, with the "rational" pattern defined above. But so long as Crusoe prefers his habitual ways of utilizing resources and the ensuing state of provision to any other mode of behavior and productive result, no objective principle can be invoked to convince him that his ways are "wasteful." Even if

[13] See L. von Mises, *op. cit.*, p. 39.

by sacrificing his present leisure time for making a net he can reduce the energy and time required for his daily catch and thus increase his future leisure time, he may refuse to do so. Perhaps he
belongs to that human breed so severely censured by the late Professor von Boehm-Bawerk,[14] who "underestimates the future" and
prefers two hours of leisure today to four hours of leisure next week.

To summarize, in choosing his modal goal or action directive
Crusoe is as free as he is in choosing the items which are to go into
his basket. Nor should we expect him to adhere to the same action
directive all the time. He can maximize his input today and minimize it tomorrow, prefer a "labor-intensive" mode of production
now and a "material-intensive" some other time. Like the set of
final goals and the stock of available resources, the modal goal and
its modifications over time represent variable data for both actor
and observer. Neither is the modal goal implicitly contained in his
final goals,[15] nor is there—so long as we judge economic activity
by the ultimate satisfaction it yields to the actor—a categorical
economic imperative which could once and for all proclaim any
particular action directive as intrinsically right.

Even so, we have not yet exhausted the list of independent determinants of Crusoe's economic activity. His final and modal goals
together form the *purposive* factors which shape his dispositions.
However, his purpose remains blind unless it is enlightened by
knowledge of his environmental conditions. In order to be able to
choose one level of output and one combination of inputs rather
than others, he must be aware of the stock of his resources and the
various ways in which they can be joined.

In referring to this *cognitive* determinant of economic action we
shall henceforth speak of the common-sense knowledge of the actor
as distinguished from the scientific knowledge of the observer. This
qualification is to stress that, as a rule, the actor's knowledge is
neither systematic nor necessarily in accord with the facts. It is the

[14] See Eugen von Boehm-Bawerk, *Positive Theory of Capital* (New York,
1891), Book IV, sec. 1.
[15] The professional reader will notice that this statement contradicts the
prevailing interpretation of the "utility principle." More about this in chap. 8.

result of fragmentary experience and information, of speculation and hunches, and—in the social context presently to be studied—of communication with others. Since most economic dispositions extend into the future, such knowledge culminates in *expectations,* the nearest equivalent to predictions on the common-sense level.

These purposive and cognitive determinants form the compound of motivations from which overt behavior springs. What is this behavior itself concerned with?

Given his final and modal goals Crusoe allocates his available resources—his inputs—among the intended outputs and distributes the realized outputs in accord with his pre-established purposes. Are there definable rules—repeatable patterns of interdependence—to which such allocations of inputs and reallocations of outputs must conform? There certainly are, and maximum want satisfaction no matter how understood by Crusoe is conditional on his strict adherence to these rules.

On the level of production these rules refer to the manipulations through which natural resources are physically transformed into finished goods ready for use. Such use itself consists, first of all, in replacing the reproducible inputs, in particular energy spent in production and the wear and tear of any tools applied. If Crusoe aims at improving rather than maintaining his material condition he must cut down temporarily on those outputs which serve his present consumption in favor of other outputs normally bearing the character of tools suitable to raise his future consumption.

Thus the transformation of inputs into outputs and the distribution and consumption of the outputs themselves are linked in a circular process in which today's inputs consist of yesterday's outputs—with one important exception, which concerns irreproducible natural resources. Their utilization occurs in a linear process ending in consumption, be it acts of satisfaction of final wants or the "productive" consumption which tools undergo in the acts of output creation. It then depends on Nature's bounty and the technical inventiveness of the user of natural resources how often this linear process and, as a consequence, the more comprehensive circular process of production and distribution can be repeated, that is, the time span over which provision can extend.

All the rules referred to are *engineering rules* in the widest sense of the term. They are themselves based on laws of nature—laws which govern the growth of plants, the breeding of animals, and the mechanics of artisanship. In other words, given his final and modal goals and his stock of resources, the core of Crusoe's economic activity is *technological,* namely, application of his common-sense knowledge of the laws of nature and the rules of engineering to the production and distribution of output.[16]

4. *The Socialization of the Technological Core Processes*

We begin to understand in what sense there is a "scientific" foundation of Economics. However, what happens to our findings when we apply them to the conditions under which a social economy operates? On the surface not much seems to change. Consider the situation of a householder in any type of socioeconomic organization, be it a primitive tribal system or a modern market economy or an order ruled by collectivist planning. He possesses a stock of resources, to be applied to the provision of a basket of specific goods in accord with his final and modal goals, and to be disposed of in the light of his common-sense knowledge. It is true that the particular forms in which these activities take shape—as traditional

[16] Attempts have been made—going back to Max Weber—to establish a basic distinction between technical activity and the Man-Matter core of economic activity. For instance, Professor Robbins insists that "the problem of technique arises when there is one end and a multiplicity of means, the problem of economy when both the ends and the means are multiple" (see *Nature and Significance* . . . , chap. II, sec. 4). The implication is that in the latter case a choice must be made not only among the means but also among the ends. But this is contradicted by the fact that to the economic decision-maker the ends are always *given,* and not as a random sample but as a hierarchy, and that the degree of satisfaction of each member in this hierarchy is predetermined by the given modal goal. As we shall presently see, this technological core of economic activity is modified only when it is placed in a social context, so that the Man-Man relationship must be taken into account. The same position as in the text is taken by Oscar Lange, *Political Economy* (New York, 1963), vol. I, pp. 148–150, 238–239.

conduct or as a freely entered contract or as response to central command—differ as drastically from Crusoe's behavior as they do from one another. And even our original data—the content of the goals and the stock of resources—can no longer be traced back exclusively to Nature and the biopsychological endowment of the individuals concerned. They are now modified, if not positively created, by the prevailing social order, as is the manner in which the aggregate output is distributed among the producing members.

But all these modifications do not alter the technological requirements of the core process. Whether a social group preferring missiles to butter lives under American Capitalism or Soviet Communism or whether another group's desire for breakfast cereals springs from physiological needs or from the appeal of television commercials, the circular processes through which inputs are transformed into outputs and the outputs are reallocated as inputs remain in principle the same. And those processes must conform to definite engineering rules based on knowledge of the laws of nature.

Still, Crusoe meeting Friday and deciding to set up housekeeping with him cannot help realizing that something fundamental has changed in his economic dispositions. The only constraints with which he had to contend while living in isolation were Nature's stinginess, the limitations of his physical and mental energy and of his time, and the laws of nature. Now another constraint has been added, namely, the behavior of a fellow man who unwittingly and —more important—wittingly interferes with Crusoe's activities. What are the consequences of this additional constraint?

What is at stake can be best illustrated on the basic organization of socioeconomic production—the division and cooperation of labor. This represents, first of all, a technological phenomenon, namely, the spatial and temporal splitting up of each process of input transformation into a number of discrete steps, the sequence of which is strictly determined by the engineering rules pertinent to the intended output. But, and this adds the social to the merely technological aspect, in principle each step is entrusted to a different member of the economic society in question. Therefore the productive success—the attainment of the intended output—depends on a sequence of technologically adequate decisions capable of inter-locking the actions of many individuals at every stage and between successive stages.

Take a modern market society and assume that my goal is pro-vision of a loaf of bread. Assume further that I possess plenty of resources symbolized by money—will this assure me of the satis-faction of my want? It will do so only if my money offer stimulates the baker, the miller, the farmer, the maker of ovens, of trucks, of millstones and grinders, etc., and all those who must operate these tools, to perform actions which will complement one another in such a manner that the technical result is a loaf of bread. In a col-lectivist society the initiating stimulus is different—central com-mand rather than decentralized demand—but the linkage of the behavioral responses must be equally strict.

Primitive as the level of provision of our Crusoe may be, he ob-viously enjoys a great advantage over the members of a social economy. If his technological knowledge is adequate and he ap-plies it within the limits of his resources, attainment of his produc-tion goal is assured. Alas, no member of an economic society can draw such assurance from his own goal-adequate behavior. The symbiosis of the Man-Man relationship with the Man-Matter re-lationship poses quite a new problem: how can *patterns of behavior* be created and maintained that make the actions of each one com-patible with those of all the others, and also with the attainment of the final goals of all?

Patterned behavior differs from random behavior in that each individual act, and any sequence of such acts, is consistent with some purpose. In this sense also Crusoe's economic behavior must be patterned if it is to be successful; it must be technologically con-sistent with his final and modal goals relative to his stock of re-sources. What happens to goals and resources in a social economy that now requires individual behavior to be consistent not only with the purposes of the actor himself but also with those of his fellow actors?

It is a structural change in the object of the provisioning process that makes the consistency conditions more stringent. The object is now society at large or rather—to avoid any misleading reification —the aggregate of its members. This makes it necessary to reconcile the claims of individuals and subgroups on the available stock of resources in a socially approved state of satisfaction of all. The content of the collective basket of goods thus established can be described as the *final macro-goal* to the attainment of which the activities of the members are devoted. But as is the case with an isolated man, the qualitative order of the macro-goal must be supplemented by quantitative criteria or *modal macro-goals* to make the productive and distributive processes determinate. In other words, maximum aggregate output or some other level between that maximum and the minimum of subsistence must be postulated as the *production optimum,* to be obtained through specific resource combinations. Furthermore, a particular standard according to which aggregate output is to be shared out among the members must now be added as the *distribution optimum.*

This formal similarity between the collective goals and criteria in a social economy and the final and modal goals of an isolated man is enhanced by the wide diversity of the macro-goals actually prevailing in different economic societies and even in one and the same society at different stages of its evolution. Ultimately the product of particular political organizations and cultural traditions, these goals vary with the disparity and change in these institutional constituents. But there is an important time factor which bestows on ruling macro-goals and, especially, on optimization criteria a degree of homogeneity and stability which need not prevail in Crusoe's dispositions. In principle, he can change his goals from one to the next act of provision, and nothing prevents him from squandering all his resources in a brief spell of plenty. In contrast, self-perpetuation is an essential trait of society, and its provisioning processes extend over generations.

This time dimension of social provisioning is one reason why socioeconomic behavior must be more strictly patterned. Another and even more important reason is a fundamental change in the nature of his basic resources as experienced by each member of an economic society. For the aggregate the ultimate means consist of course, as for Crusoe, of the total stock of material and immaterial resources. But each individual's potential resources include more than his own material possessions and his own energy and time. Normally he is occupied with merely a small segment of the technical manipulations on which his provision depends. Though, as a rule, everyone is busy with transforming some inputs into outputs, he expects to receive the bulk of his provision from the combined production activities of many others. The resources on which he depends thus extend to resources, material and immaterial, of which those others dispose. Therefore, with the progress of division and cooperation of labor, every member's task of provisioning shifts more and more from "molding matter" to "molding men," namely, to inducing fellow members to engage in such technical manipulations as serve his own ends as well as theirs.

We can now define the function of the *social patterns* of economic activity as distinguished from the merely technological patterns to which also a Crusoe must adhere. These social patterns are to make it possible for each economic actor to dispose of the resources of others as if these resources were his own. One can maintain that the ultimate purpose of these social patterns, be they obedience to command or performance of the task traditionally assigned to one's cast or adjustment of supply to changes in price, is technological after all, in that all social patterns invoke the physical manipulation of basic resources in accord with a given set of goals. But in adopting such a behavioral pattern my proximate intent is the *psychological manipulation* of others, by bending their actions to my desires as my action is bent to theirs.

If thus the function of social patterns of behavior differs radically from that of technological patterns, so do the rules they must obey. In searching for a source of such rules we can no longer take recourse to engineering principles and the underlying laws of nature. Even in an economy of servitude—the lowest level of social organization—physical mechanisms alone do not suffice to bring the activities of the slaves in agreement with the will of the masters. Obedience to command is ultimately a spontaneous response, and social as distinguished from technological rules are required to prompt spontaneous responses which conform to the intentions of the prompter.

These rules bear a "significative," or "symbolic," meaning, understandable only in a universe of human discourse and capable of being evaluated only in the context of human strivings. Such understanding and evaluation is achieved with the help of two kinds of institutions without which no economic society can survive. One is a *system of communication*. Such a system serves to express intentions and to evoke compliant reactions. Take as an example the decrees issued by a planning board to its functionaries or the increase of a price offer on the part of a prospective buyer. Provided that planners and executants, buyers and sellers, understand the "language" of the respective "signals," such decrees or price offers contain definite messages inviting the recipient to an equally definite response.

However, to assure compliance the system of communication must be supplemented by a *system of sanctions*. Institutional arrangements must exist through which adequate responses are rewarded and inadequate ones are punished. Such sanctions may take the form of specific penalties attached to the violation of a tabu, of legal and administrative requitals in a collectivist order, or of profit and loss in a free market.

So far we have confined our attention to the *macro-economic* function of social patterns of behavior and to the institutions which are to mold individual responses accordingly. This is to say that we have stressed the need for homogeneous and stable action patterns in the interest of continuous provision for all. But the question is still open as to the state of mind which makes the individual member actually conform to the macro-economically required pattern.

This leads us to the *micro-economic* linkage of the patterns of economic behavior with those factors which make a marketer or a functionary in a planned economy behave the way he does. Again our study of the forces which determine Crusoe's behavior proves a useful starting point. We found there two such forces—his final and modal goals (henceforth specified as *micro-goals*) and his common-sense knowledge culminating in more or less certain expectations. It is the same compound of motivational factors, even if considerably modified, which shapes individual behavior in a social economy.[17]

Beginning with the *cognitive* factors, we find the range of required common-sense knowledge vastly extended beyond what is sufficient for Crusoe's successful provisioning. All he needs to know bears a technological character: the quantity and quality of his resources relative to his final goals, and the pertinent laws of nature and engineering rules. Knowledge of the same facts and the technological expectations derived from them are indispensable also for an actor in society. But to this must now be added what can be called his "social" expectations. Again drawing on past experience and information, but above all on present "messages," he must form expectations about the intentions of his fellow members and, in particular, about their responses to stimuli emitted by himself. Crusoe's economic success depends exclusively on the extent to which his common-sense knowledge agrees with technological truth. Once he rejoins society his actions must also conform to "social" truth, and his own provision as well as that of all others will now be contingent on the accuracy of mutual expectations.

---

[17] Purposive and cognitive motives—action directives and expectations—are going to play a significant role as our argument progresses. Therefore it may be appropriate to dispose from the outset of the well-known behaviorist objections to such an approach.

Certainly attempts at ascertaining motivations are beset with considerable difficulties. Therefore confining one's data to overt actions seems, at first sight, a preferable short cut. Alas, such a procedure raises more problems than it solves.

First, it excludes from the program of research all explanations of behavior itself. Second, and perhaps more important, it bases all explanations and predictions of aggregate states and processes on the dubious hypothesis that the behavior ruling at the time of observation will persist over the time span necessary for the predicted event to materialize. Such a presumption seems to be quite safe in some fields of the natural sciences. In the social sciences it is made unsafe by the element of spontaneity which is inseparable from human decision-making, an element whose behavioral consequences cannot be understood without reference to underlying motivations. To exclude them reduces social inquiry to the mere registration of spot observations, from which no generalizing conclusions can be drawn.

For an individual member to arrive at correct social expectations is not difficult in a society in which all relevant knowledge is either fixed by tradition or is made public, e.g., by the controllers of a collectivist Plan. The situation is quite different if the prospective actor can draw only on his private and necessarily fragmentary experience as acquired by trial and error in an unplanned economic process. It will then not surprise us when we subsequently discover that, in economic regimes with predominantly decentralized decision-making, major obstacles to the adequate patterning of behavior arise from just this difficulty in forming correct expectations.

However, the micro-economic crux of social behavior patterns is the *purposive* factor—the underlying micro-goals and, in particular, the modal micro-goals or action directives. Only if these micro-goals are compatible with the prevailing macro-goals and optimization criteria is continuous aggregate provision assured. For instance, to make maximization of *individual* provision acceptable as action directive, maximum *aggregate* output must be established as criterion of optimization.

At first sight it looks as if we had already disposed of this problem. Is it not the function of the prevailing communication and, especially, sanction systems to bring about individual compliance with collective criteria? Alas, the spontaneous nature of decision-making emphasized earlier stands in the way of such a simple solution. Suppose a sanction system rewards one type of behavior by promoting the actor to a higher post, whereas he is punished for the opposite behavior by demotion. This combination of carrot and stick will prove effective only if the actor in question is sensitive to the rank he holds in the bureaucratic hierarchy. The same is true of the profit-and-loss chances that are to sanction specific kinds of market behavior. Once he finds himself above the threshold of a certain standard of living, no entrepreneur can be relied upon to respond in the required manner unless pecuniary benefits as such attract him. In sum, to be effective the prevailing sanctions must be in line with *pre-existing* action directives of the individuals concerned.

In searching for forces which *create* suitable action directives we cannot fall back on instinctual drives. Powerful as the latter appear to be in the organization of provisioning of certain animal societies, on the human level they do not produce a unique behavioral pattern even when survival is at stake. This shows in the variety of such patterns in primitive societies stagnating on the subsistence level—competitive maximization of output being at best a marginal case.

The answer lies in the highly complex processes of interaction through which social consensus in general is established. It is in this context that Man-Man relations encroach most strongly on the technological processes of aggregate provisioning. They are the medium through which belief is inculcated in the sanctity of rites and the value of tradition, loyalty is inspired to the commands of legitimate authority, and as we shall investigate with special attention, particular modes of bargaining are induced. But in contrast with their physical counterparts these social processes are not subject to laws of nature. For this reason their success depends on the extent to which the large majority of members in a given society identify, consciously or unconsciously, with the requirements of an ongoing process of provisioning—a condition which brings to light its inherent contingency.

5. *Economics—Taxonomy or Theory?*

The time has come to draw some conclusions for the manner in which the phenomena described can be comprehended in scientific terms. In what concepts can we describe the conditions under which economic events occur, and how are we to proceed in order to ascertain repeatable patterns of interdependence that would permit us to speak of an economic science?

Our earlier distinction between technological and social patterns of economic behavior suggests two different though complementary answers. There is a *technological core* in all economic activity, be it performed in isolation or in social interaction. To that extent Economics is simply a part of Material Technology. If we wish intellectually to grasp and practically to handle the relevant processes we are referred to rules of engineering and to laws of nature as the ultimate sources from which explanations and predictions can be derived. A body of more or less exact knowledge will thus be obtained, but it hardly deserves a special label as a science of Economics.

It is different with the *social patterns of provisioning* and the states and processes of the human aggregates to which they give rise. These patterns too are ultimately in the service of the complex technological processes which the division of labor creates. But their immediate function is the achievement of provision with material means through the manipulation of men rather than of matter. They fulfill this function to the extent to which each member of an economic society succeeds in making the other members behave as if they were matter-like means for his socially approved ends, while each one recognizes the human, namely, spontaneous quality of the other's actions. The formal problem of Economics is thus a variant of the time-honored part-aggregate issue. But it presents itself in a peculiar means-ends configuration in which it occurs neither in the natural sciences nor in any other of the social sciences. The former have no way of allowing for the "personal" attributes of means; the latter do not deal with the "means" attributes of persons.

To acknowledge a problem as germane to the realm of socio-economic inquiry leaves still undecided the scientific level on which it is to be studied. Is it mainly taxonomy—observation, description, and classification of a particular set of facts? Or is it mainly theory —deduction of confirmable general propositions from some not immediately given explanatory principles?[18]

---

[18] The qualifying "mainly" is to indicate that the above distinction emphasizes the focus of interest of the respective procedures, but does not set forth incompatible opposites. Not only have all sciences passed through the taxonomic or "natural history" stage of the Baconian type (see F. S. C. Northrop, *The Logic of the Sciences and the Humanities* [New York, 1947], chap. III), but even the most advanced one—theoretical Physics—has retained taxonomic elements.

Perhaps it is more important to stress that a predominantly taxonomic approach need not altogether dispense with explanations or even predictions. What matters is that the general propositions on which such explanations and predictions rest are not themselves elaborated in the course of the taxonomic inquiry, but are "borrowed" either from theoretical sciences or, more often than

What we have learned about the historical diversity of social behavior patterns speaks for the first alternative. So do the many deviations of actual behavior from the macro-economically required patterns in most economic societies. Indeed from the age of classical antiquity to the era of the Enlightenment students of economic events aimed at taxonomic surveys, unless they were fully absorbed by the normative—religious, moral, and political—aspects of economic behavior. And as has already been mentioned, similar considerations have since provoked periodic taxonomic reactions against the scientific trend on which Western Economics embarked two hundred years ago. Yet this trend itself has been moving ever more markedly in the direction of theory, and the question with which we started out must now be faced in all seriousness: why this change in approach, and why then and there?

A clue to an answer can be found in a strange bias which is indicative of all economic theorizing from its classical beginnings to the most elaborate treatises of today. It concerns the historical type of economic organization on which analytical work has concentrated. The researchers of the Historical, Institutionalist, and Functionalist schools pay, at least in principle, equal attention to the ritualistic forms of production and distribution in primitive civilizations or to the traditionalist maxims prevailing in ancient and medieval townships or to the bureaucratic rules governing the planned economies of the past, as they do to modern Western experience. In contrast, economic theory, as it is laid down in textbooks or is explored at the frontiers of research, concerns itself almost exclusively with market economies.[19] Such narrow preoccupation suggests a more than accidental coincidence of the rise of analytical Economics with the rise of capitalism.

This coincidence has been recognized quite frequently, but it needs precise interpretation if any conclusions about scientific pro-

---

not, reflect common-sense speculations about cause and effect. How this applies to historical inquiry has been well described in E. Nagel, *op. cit.*, chap. 15.

[19] This is even true of major parts of the economic theory of socialism, with the exception of the more or less fictitious case of a completely centralized system which is customarily treated in analogy with the Crusoe model.

cedure are to be drawn from it.[20] Markets in the sense of localized institutions of exchange or in the wider meaning of a network of commercial relations have of course a much longer history. But not only were most ancient and medieval markets of limited expanse and duration, they were subject to the traditional or bureaucratic rules which governed the political and social order at large. Only within and between the modern national states of the Western world did market relations assume the dominant role in mass provisioning, culminating in the so-called free markets of the nineteenth century, free, namely, from governmental interference, from privileges of status, and from institutional restraints other than those laid down in the civil and criminal codes of law.

The structural difference of this type of economic organization from all traditional or bureaucratic types is obvious. But this need not, and in fact did not, eliminate market systems from the catalogue of economic societies open to taxonomic investigation. If in addition it has been felt necessary to expose market behavior and the ensuing macro-states and macro-processes to deductive analysis, these phenomena must exhibit singular features which a merely descriptive-classifying technique of research cannot grasp.

The founders of modern theoretical Economics were fully aware of such a singular and even paradoxical aspect of their subject of study. This shows as much in the physiocratic belief in an "ordre naturel" which is to operate under the maxim of "laissez-faire et laissez-passer," because "le monde va de lui-même," as it does in Adam Smith's appeal to an "invisible hand" that leads any marketer who "intends only his own gain . . . to promote an end which was no part of his intention," namely, the interest of society. Similar statements abound in classical and modern literature. But for our purposes it will be more illuminating if we try to define the unique characteristics of a market order and the problem they pose in the terms in which we described the organization of economic societies in general.

[20] For an interpretation which in all essentials agrees with that in the text, see Eduard Heimann, *History of Economic Doctrines* (New York, 1945), chap. I.

The first characteristic is, as the statements quoted make clear, the absence of any explicitly postulated or implicitly acknowledged macro-goal, final or modal, on which the decisions of the micro-units could orient themselves. The more closely reality approximates the ideal type of the market the more radically decision-making is decentralized with micro-goals as the only focus of behavior. Secondly, the specific institutions—communication and sanction systems—which help to interlock individual actions and to promote stimulus-adequate responses have lost the transparency which marks them in all non-market societies. There signals as well as sanctions are "personalized," that is, directly transmitted from one individual to another. At the same time, the functions of communication and sanction are normally separated and entrusted to different agents. Thus the medieval artisan received his mandate to produce—his signal—from the explicit request of a customer, as the manager of a communist plant is signaled by local and central planning agencies. But it was the semipolitical organization of the guild that policed the responses of its members, just as it is the political and administrative arm of the Soviet state which administers the requitals for the fulfillment or nonfulfillment of the Plan.

Contrariwise, in a free market system signals and sanctions are combined and are carried out in a completely depersonalized fashion. Interaction among marketers and the integration of their actions into a macro-process of provision are not achieved by spreading articulate information from one person to the next, nor by meting out particularized rewards and penalties. The only medium is the aggregate of individual decisions to buy or not to buy, to sell or not to sell, made overt by higher or lower prices and by increases or decreases in the quantities demanded or supplied.

At the same time, there cannot be any doubt that continuous aggregate provision through the market depends as much on homogeneous and stable patterning of individual behavior as does such provision in the Trobriand Islands or in Communist China. But, as we have seen, in such traditional and bureaucratic societies the forces which mold individual behavior in accord with the requirements of the aggregate—rites, customs, command—are public knowledge and can thus serve as data for the explanation and forecasting of particular events. In a market economy the corresponding forces and their mode of operation are not even known to the actors themselves and are still less accessible to outside observation. Knowledge of the prevailing macro-goals, the stock of resources, the methods of indoctrination, the language of command, and the rewards and penalties which sustain the socially conditioned micro-goals makes the operation of a collectivist system fully transparent. In the absence of any publicly acknowledged macro-goal, with communications and sanctions depersonalized, and without overt social conditioning of action directives, aggregate provision through the market remains a mystery.

It was to solve this mystery that "a new science was developed; its task: to discover and analyze the hidden *law of coordination and integration* in a free economy."[21] And it is by no means surprising that the pioneers of this economic science—Cantillon and Quesnay, Hume and Smith—chose as their methodological paradigm the model dominant in the contemporary natural sciences. Not only did their efforts coincide with the explanatory triumphs of this model in its indigenous field, but there seems to be a striking affinity between the central problem of a theory of the market and the Newtonian theory of Mechanics. Both try to derive the state and motion of aggregates from the state and motion of their components.

We shall see that this analogy has deeply affected the development of economic theory to this very day. Hence it may not be premature to conclude this first sparring with the problems of a scientific Economics with a word of caution. Intuitively it is by no means obvious how such a theoretical construct can come to terms with the one property of social phenomena which has no counterpart in the world of Nature: the spontaneity of human decision-making. This unsettled question will accompany us when we now proceed to exploring more closely achievements and failures of the traditional theory of the market.

---

[21] *Ibid.,* p. 9 (italics added).

2

The Economics of a Market Society

1. *Freedom in the Market*

We have found preliminary solutions for two of our original puzzles: the late development of systematic Economics and the kinship of its methods with those prevailing in the exact sciences.[1] It has proved possible to relate both to the narrow preoccupation of economic theory with the structure and function of free market economies. We now turn to the third puzzle to which we pointed in our introductory remarks—the widely acknowledged discrepancy between the growing refinement of research techniques and the diminishing empirical relevance of the results.

At first sight one might wonder whether an answer to the third problem is not already implied in what has so far been stated. If it is true that traditional economic theory is concerned with the study of "free" markets governed by the politically and socially unrestrained decision-making of individual marketers, the empirical counterpart of such an economic organization hardly exists today, and has hardly ever existed full-blown. A brief epoch of near *laissez-faire* during the nineteenth century has long since been superseded by "mixed" systems combining decentralized with centralized decision-making, where it has not given way to even stricter bureaucratic forms of provisioning. What practical relevance can then attach to theorems which are derived from such unrealistic premises?

As our argument unfolds we shall have to question the realism

[1] See chap. 1, sec. 1.

and empirical relevance of much theorizing along traditional lines. All the more is it necessary to emphasize from the outset that the historical changes indicated in no way eliminate the study of even the "purest" of market relations from the list of legitimate problems of economic theory. This is so because the image of a free market has acquired *normative* significance in the political and cultural value system of the West, quite independent of the extent to which actual markets are really free.

The notion of a system of aggregate provisioning which is exclusively steered by the "free" decisions of its members perfectly agrees with the ideal of a "masterless man," which underlies the secular doctrines of Natural Law and has inspired all the struggles of political and social emancipation since the beginning of the modern age. Thus the treatises of classical and modern Economics can be said to offer on their part guide lines for a theory of Politics which reconciles the interest of each with the interests of all. This finds expression in the traditional claim that no other form of economic organization has ever succeeded, for a given distribution of purchasing power, in adjusting quantity and quality of the aggregate basket of output to the goals of its members as perfectly as does a free market system. This claim is raised not only by partisans of a capitalist mode of production. It received indirect support even from opponents, when leading socialist theorists tried to demonstrate that a central planning board could, in principle, not do better than promote that state of the aggregate which a perfectly competitive market would bring about automatically.

In trying to assess this claim of the inherent superiority of the market system, we shall penetrate to the core of our problem. But to do so we must, first of all, define more precisely what is to be meant by freedom of decision-making. So long as the concept refers to such phenomena as freedom of movement, freedom of occupational choice, and above all, to the free selection of the final micro-goals, it certainly helps us to interpret observations common to all genuine market societies. And a good case can be made for such unrestrained decisions as promoting speedy and accurate adjustment of inputs and outputs to the structure and changes in consumer wants. However, as we have had to stress again and again, individual decision-making goes beyond the choice of final goals; it includes the choice of modal goals or action directives. Can this latter choice also be left to "free," namely, discretionary decisions considering the need for the patterning of the actions which issue from these action directives?

This question alerts us to a dangerous ambiguity that beclouds the concept of "freedom of individual decision-making." So long as it concerns the choice of final goals—the purchase or manu-facture of hats rather than shoes—such freedom is fully compatible with the regime of the market. But since aggregate provisioning through the market is conditional on the prevalence of definite be-havioral patterns, the individual marketer must not claim the same unlimited freedom for the choice of his modal goals. That is, when buying a hat he must not aim *ad libitum* at minimum expenditure on one occasion, at minimum physical effort at the next, or at ostentation or whatever else the following time. True, even his "patterned" choices are *autonomous* in the sense of being inde-pendent of authoritarian constraints. But if they are to fulfill their macro-economic function of furthering the provisioning of all, they must conform to definite rules.

2. *Behavior and Motivations in the Traditional Theory of the Market*

That this is so in spite of popular protestations to the contrary has been implicitly acknowledged in the theory of the market from its earliest beginnings. It comes to light when we scrutinize the cen-tral proposition of that theory: the so-called Law of Supply and Demand. According to this law prices tend to vary directly with changes in the quantities demanded, and inversely with changes in the quantities supplied. If the initiating stimulus is a change in price, supply quantities are supposed to move in the direction of the price change, whereas demand quantities move in the inverse direction.

These propositions "are the cornerstone of economic theory.

They are the framework into which all analysis of special, detailed problems must be fitted"[2] and, as a matter of fact, has always been fitted. All other deductive inferences in traditional Economics as discussed in the analysis of households and firms or of interregional trade, or even in the modern theory of output and employment, are either applications of this general law to special problems or rest on the same basic premises.

No doubt the stimulus-response relations as described in the Law of Supply and Demand represent an effective communication system. Considering the manner in which the law connects price and quantity changes, a rise in a buyer's offer for a given good is an unambiguous signal for the seller that more units of this good are desired, enabling him to adjust his supply accordingly. Conversely, a reduction of the price on the part of a seller tells the prospective buyer of increased opportunities for purchase. Still, one may wonder whether these particular signals are the only ones which can transmit the relevant information. Suppose a price fall were conventionally used to express a rise in demand and a fall in supply, would such a usage not provide an equally effective system of communication?

At this point the sanction function of price changes comes into play. If a price rise serves as signal for a rise in demand, not only does it inform the supplier of new openings for sales but it holds out to him rising receipts per unit of sale and, in case he expands supply, an increase in his aggregate receipts. Conversely, by maintaining the quantity supplied in the face of a fall in the quantity demanded a seller will provoke a fall in price which will not only inform him of the discrepancy between demand and supply but bring upon him the penalty of pecuniary loss.

[2] See H. D. Henderson, *Supply and Demand* (London and Cambridge, 1932), p. 19. It seems hardly necessary to document Henderson's statement. Though the explicit formulation of the Law of Supply and Demand is due to J. S. Mill, it is presupposed in all classical discussions about the relation between "natural" and "market" prices. For its status in neo-classical theory, see, e.g., Walras, *Elements of Pure Economics,* Lessons 13 and 21; or Alfred Marshall, *Principles of Economics* (London, 1926), Book V, chap. III. What a contemporary author has to say about the "immutable" nature of the law, violation of which must lead to "disorder," can be read in P. A. Samuelson, *Economics* (New York, 1955), pp. 384–388.

Still, we know from our earlier considerations that a sanction system influences behavior only to the extent to which its rewards and penalties reinforce pre-existing modal micro-goals. Assume a buyer motivated by ostentation, not an infrequent case in a modern market if we can trust Thorstein Veblen's findings. Then the requitals associated with the conventional Law of Supply and Demand will leave him unaffected, and he will respond to a price rise in the "perverse" manner of raising his demand. In the same category falls a worker who, in the face of a rise in his hourly wage, reduces his supply of labor because with a rising payroll he begins to prefer more leisure to more earnings. Of even greater practical significance is the reverse case of a rise of labor supply under the impact of falling wages in the interest of maintaining a given family income.

These examples make clear that there is only one set of modal micro-goals or *action directives* which is compatible with the action patterns formulated by the Law of Supply and Demand and is reinforced by the price movements which this law describes. When acting as sellers marketers must be inspired by the goal of maximizing money receipts, whereas as buyers their action directive must be minimization of money expenditures. No concern with any final goals, be they prestige based on conspicuous consumption or preference for the *status quo* of provisioning, or with any other source of "satisfaction," may modify these modal goals.[3]

In emphasizing this restriction we only restate the consensus of classical and modern market theory. Whether we study Adam Smith's *Wealth of Nations* or Walras' *Elements* or glance into any modern textbook, maximization of receipts and minimization of expenditures are explicitly postulated or implicitly assumed whenever behavioral responses to changes in the market data are to be explained or predicted.[4] The label under which these modal micro-

[3] In the interest of logical consistency it must be admitted that the reverse action directives—minimization of receipts and maximization of expenditures—would serve equally well. The practical relevance of such "charity" incentives appears negligible.

[4] An apparent exception is the "utility" principle—an ostensible derivative of arbitrary final micro-goals—which is supposed to rule consumers' behavior.

goals appear has undergone many changes—from the classical "desire to better one's conditions" to "profit motive," "maximum principle," etc. We shall henceforth subsume this two-pronged action directive—maximization and minimization—under the concept of "extremum principle," pointing thereby to the logical affinity of this premise of the law of market motion with certain principles which ground the laws of Physics.

However, as we have had occasion to stress repeatedly,[5] the purposive strand of economic motivations as specified in a determinate action directive does not by itself suffice to create determinate behavior. To do so it must be supplemented by appropriate knowledge on the part of the actors, culminating in specific *expectations*. We know that such expectations refer to relevant future events in the actor's economic field of action. The anonymous character and, above all, the quantitative structure of all market relations greatly simplify the definition of the economic field. It presents itself to the individual buyer and seller as the order of those prices and quantities of goods and services which enter into his potential disposition. And his expectations are concerned with the levels and directions of change of these prices and quantities, as they establish themselves over the time span for which he plans his purchases or sales.

What, then, are the price and quantity expectations which, given the extremum principle as action directive, will make marketers behave in accord with the Law of Supply and Demand? Assume a retailer selling from inventory who is confronted with a rise of the price for his product. If he expects the price to rise further he will not expand his offerings as the law enjoins but will even cut down on his sales in the present. In other words, he will maximize his receipts by responding to the price rise by a reduction of supply. If we deal with a producer who fears that a present increase in demand will not outlast the time span required for an increase in output, he too is likely to violate the behavioral rules of the law by desisting from additional production. Only if the retailer expects

---

We shall have occasion (see chap. 8) to elaborate the true meaning of this principle.

[5] See chap. 1, *passim*.

the present price rise to be merely temporary and if the producer expects the rise in demand to be permanent can we rest assured that either of them will obey the law.

The same considerations apply to the expectations of a buyer. He will respond to a price fall in due fashion, namely, by at once buying more, only if he expects the price soon to move again toward the initial level. If he interprets the price fall as the beginning of a "trend" he will minimize expenditures by postponing his purchase.

These various alternatives have been systematized by Professor Hicks with the help of the concept of "elasticity of expectations."[6] Such elasticity defines the ratio of the proportional change in expected prices to the proportional change in present prices. Thus if both present and expected prices rise by the same percentage, say 10 per cent, we speak of "unit elasticity" of expectations. If in response to a present rise by 10 per cent future prices are expected to rise by less than 10 per cent, expectations are denoted as "inelastic," whereas the expectation of a rise by more than 10 per cent is defined as "elastic." Another important distinction, which applies to quantities demanded or supplied as well as to prices, refers to the "positive" or "negative" character of the elasticity of expectations. The former prevails if a change in present quantities or prices arouses the expectations of a future change in the same direction. We have negative elasticity if marketers interpret the present change "as the culminating point of fluctuation" (Hicks), to be followed by an inverse movement.

With these definitions in mind, we can now easily formulate the expectational premises which are implied in the conventional statement of the Law of Supply and Demand. Given the extremum principle as action directive, marketers will act in accord with the law if their quantity expectations have positive elasticity and if their price expectations have less than unit elasticity—a combination which will henceforth be defined as *stabilizing*[7] expectations.

[6] See J. R. Hicks, *Value and Capital* (Oxford, 1939), chap. IX, XVI, XX–XXIII. For a lucid exposition, see C. R. Daugherty and M. R. Daugherty, *Principles of Political Economy* (Boston, 1950), pp. 445–451.

[7] The concept as here applied is more inclusive than the conventional stability concept. A precise definition will be given in chap. 4, sec. 4.

This means that, given a present rise in price, stabilizing expectations will induce buyers, in the interest of minimizing expenditures, to shift purchases from the present to the future, that is, to reduce demand. Sellers on their part will be induced, in the interest of maximizing receipts, to shift sales from the future to the present, that is, to increase supply. Obviously a fall in present price must induce the opposite behavior.

3. *Macro-Equilibrium and the Micro-Forces*

We have arrived at a precise formulation of the motivational setup, purposive as well as cognitive, which creates the behavior pattern postulated by traditional theory.[8] But this does not do away with the fact that different action directives and expectations and, as a consequence, different behavior patterns are conceivable. Moreover, as our various examples have shown, some of them appear to have practical relevance. Why, then, has the "cornerstone of economic theory" been cut so narrow that there is no room left for any deviations?

There is no satisfactory answer to this question so long as the Law of Supply and Demand is interpreted merely as a micro-economic proposition, describing individual responses to individual stimuli. But as a matter of fact the law proclaims much more. It offers a very important prediction about the *macro-state* toward which the successive micro-responses steer the system.

Assume that the prevailing state of the aggregate is disturbed

[8] The professional reader may wonder how it is possible to discuss market behavior without explicit reference to the "state of competition." But in postulating the extremum principle and stabilizing expectations as conditions for behavior in accord with the Law of Supply and Demand, we have implicitly postulated perfect competition. In particular price expectations with less than unit elasticity—e.g., sellers expecting the rise, and buyers expecting the fall, in future prices to remain behind the rise or fall in present prices—are likely to prevail only in competitive markets. There a marketer has every reason to anticipate such immediate quantity responses—rise in the quantities supplied or demanded—on the part of other marketers as will counteract the present change in price. Therefore the state of competition, rather than being an independent determinant of market behavior, appears to influence it indirectly through the effect it exerts on the formation of specific economic motivations. More about this in chap. 3.

by an increase of demand for some particular good. Then the law not only describes a sequence of adjustments in that particular sector of the market—rising prices, rising supply quantities, falling prices—but also the properties of the macro-state in which these adjustments terminate. In this terminal state of the system, for which the term "equilibrium" has become customary, all quantities supplied are supposed to be equal to all quantities demanded, this equality occurring at the lowest level of prices that is compatible with the technical conditions of production.

Nor is this all. The law is supposed to apply also to the markets of the factors of production. As a consequence an increase in the supply of labor or of any other resource will evoke a fall in its respective price, to be followed by an increase in demand for the resource in question and by its eventual absorption into the productive process. Therefore one of the properties of the macro-equilibrium of the market as accomplished by the lawful motion of the micro-unit is the *full utilization of resources*.

At long last we understand the full significance of the movements which the Law of Supply and Demand describes, and as a consequence the central position which the law holds in the theory of the market. It formulates the general law of motion of the system or, more precisely, the law of intra-systemic adjustment to changes in the initial conditions. And the theory of the market itself appears as a deductive argument, in which the extremum principle and stabilizing expectations form the original higher-level hypotheses. From these premises is derived the law of motion, knowledge of which, jointly with the knowledge of the initial state of the system, enables us to deduce successive movements of adjustment to any change and also the system's terminal state.

We have arrived at a rather remarkable conclusion. Were we to discuss here behavior in a traditional or bureaucratic economic order, we should not be surprised to see the system tend toward a uniquely determined macro-state. We could easily explain this by referring to some collectively acknowledged macro-goal which is attained through the actions of micro-units that identify, under the influence of whatever social pressures, with the content of that macro-goal. But we know that no macro-goal exists in a free market which could serve as point of orientation for its members. Moreover, even if macro-equilibrium were publicly postulated as such a goal, no marketer could be expected to affirm that state as his own "goal." All the advantages in terms of temporary gains, which satisfy his modal goal as defined by the extremum principle, accrue to him from intermediate states of "disequilibrium," so that equilibrium will by no means appear to him as a desirable end. Nor is there any decision-maker outside the ranks of the marketers or any institutionalized tradition which could invest a macro-state with the quality of a goal.

And yet traditional theory has from its very beginnings treated macro-equilibrium as just such a goal. As it emerges from the interplay of actors (each one of whom is pursuing a micro-goal—pecuniary surpluses—which is quite incompatible with such equilibrium), this state has been singled out in classical as well as in modern Economics as the optimum state of aggregate provision.

The reason for such evaluation is not far to seek. In this state the final micro-goals of all marketers, as embodied in their consumption baskets, are realized to the largest extent possible within the existing constraints. To spell it out in the language of modern Welfare Economics: within the limits of the resources and the technical knowledge available, macro-equilibrium is a state compared with which there is no other state in which a consumer can obtain higher satisfaction without at the same time lowering the satisfaction of some other consumer. In fact, we arrive at a state of *maximum* provision with *taste-adequate* goods—the maximum being achieved through the full and technically most efficient utilization of available resources, whereas taste-adequacy is implied in the equality of quantities demanded and supplied in every sector of the market. Of course, this can be accepted as an *optimum* state of aggregate provision only if the initial distribution of means is to be the yardstick for individual provision, if the present tastes or final goals of the individual consumers are the only legitimate goals, and if the optimum is identified with the maximum.[9] But there is

[9] For the proposition that the optimum of aggregate provision—the so-called "Pareto optimum"—coincides with macro-equilibrium as defined above, see the writings on Welfare Economics. Compare, e.g., the summary in Kenneth Boulding, "Welfare Economics," in *A Survey of Contemporary Economics,* vol. II,

little sense in worrying about the welfare implications of macro-equilibrium before we are sure that such equilibrium is a fact of experience. Admittedly the traditional theory of the market presents a logically consistent construct. But is it a valid one for empirical research, namely, a tool for the explanation and prediction of actual behavior and the ensuing macro-states?

Some doubts about such validity arose earlier when we discussed the wide spectrum of conceivable motivations and behavior patterns. Action directives other than those which are conceptualized in the extremum principle, destabilizing expectations, and as a consequence, price-quantity responses different from those described in the Law of Supply and Demand appear, to say the least, empirically possible. These doubts are enhanced by a superficial glance at the records we possess of the typical macro-states through which industrial market economies have passed during the past century. It is no exaggeration to say that, in the majority of cases observed, these real states have deviated considerably from the theoretical prototype of equilibrium, especially in the degree of resource utilization.

All these and still other deviations from the simplistic propositions of traditional theory have of course been commented upon by numerous critical observers.[10] But in the present context it is decisive that no one has as yet succeeded in constructing an alternative deductive theory on divergent behavioral foundations. Even when the modern industrial market is *described* in quite different terms, generalizing *explanations* and *predictions* always fall back on the traditional hypotheses.[11] For this reason it is of great interest to

ed. by Bernard F. Haley (Homewood, Ill., 1952), pp. 1–34, and the literature quoted there. The original source is V. Pareto, *Cours d'Economie Politique* (Lausanne, 1897), vol. II, pp. 90 ff.

[10] For some representative specimens see the writings of Adolf A. Berle, in particular his well-known study, jointly undertaken with Gardiner C. Means, on *The Modern Corporation and Private Property* (New York, 1933), or his *Twentieth Century Capitalist Revolution* (New York, 1954). Also John K. Galbraith, *American Capitalism* (Boston, 1952).

[11] A striking example for this is Galbraith's concept of "countervailing power," allegedly a new "self-generating force" in the modern market (see

ascertain what the protagonists of traditional Economics themselves have to say about the truth value of their theory, and how they deal with empirical deviations.[12]

One foundation block of conventional theory, the extremum principle, received its most thoroughgoing vindication in classical Economics. There it was treated as avowing a universal propensity which "comes with us from the womb, and never leaves us till we go into the grave" (Adam Smith). This notion of an *anima natura maximans* has been perpetuated in much of neo-classical reasoning, at least when the action directives of sellers of commodities are discussed. But the critical attacks on the part of psychologists, anthropologists, and historians, no less than more careful observations of economists themselves, have compelled the apologists progressively to water down the original doctrine. As a result, what started out as a pronouncement on human nature is now sometimes reduced to a "methodological fiction" or a "heuristic principle," and the Economic Man stands then on the same epistemological level as do electrons in modern subatomic Physics.[13]

The consequences of such reinterpretation are far-reaching when the traditional theory of the market is to be submitted to empirical testing. So long as the extremum principle—and the same is, *mutatis mutandis,* true of any hypothesis concerning expectations—is

---

American Capitalism, chap. 10). Momentum and direction of this force "in the market of small numbers" are, however, imputed to the same action directives and expectations which in traditional theory are supposed to govern the fully competitive markets of large numbers. The case is different with certain notions in the works of Marx and Keynes, which will be extensively discussed in chaps. 7 and 9.

[12] Such a survey must confine itself to the conventional arguments in favor of the relevancy of the extremum principle and of macro-equilibrium. The essential role of the other highest-level hypothesis—stabilizing expectations—has been recognized only recently. The pioneering work of Keynes and Professor Hicks needs still to be incorporated into the general framework of market theory, in which expectations have so far been disregarded altogether or have been implicitly treated as stabilizing.

[13] See George J. Stigler, *The Theory of Price* (New York, 1952), pp. 148–149. For the most extreme position, see Milton Friedman, "The Methodology of Positive Economics," in *Essays in Positive Economics* (Chicago, 1953), pp. 1–43. See also Fritz Machlup, "Operational Concepts and Mental Constructs in Model and Theory Formation," *Giornali degli Economisti* (Settembre-Ottobre, 1960), pp. 3–32.

considered as an abstraction from experience, it can be confirmed, and certainly disconfirmed, by direct confrontation with observable data. If it is no more than a "hypothetical construct," it can be tested only indirectly by a confirmation or disconfirmation of the inferences which are drawn from it.

We have seen that the major inference thus drawn is the convergence of all sectorial market movements toward some state of macro-equilibrium. Hence it is the empirical presence or absence of such equilibria on which the truth value of traditional theory ultimately hinges, namely, the agreement of its predictions with the facts as well as the usefulness of its highest-level hypotheses. But the appeal to such an empirical test is usually hedged by a reservation which jeopardizes all such attempts at indirect verification. It was Marshall who most explicitly made the point when he wrote that all equilibria were to be regarded as states "which economic forces would bring about if the general conditions of life were stationary for a run of time long enough to enable them to work out their full effect."[14]

There is obvious sense in this definition, but at the same time it seems to exclude any disconfirmation of the equilibrium proposition. All empirical disequilibria can now be imputed to the absence of stationariness of the "general conditions of life," a proviso which is fulfilled in the vast majority of observations. One cannot help sympathizing with Professor von Mises' conclusion that the science of the market must be treated as a product of pure reason, since its "theorems are not open to verification or falsification on the ground of experience."[15]

And yet it is hardly surprising that such an attempt at raising Economics to epistemological parity with Mathematics has found little acclaim. If there is to be a science of market phenomena, aiming at explaining and predicting observable states and movements, its premises and (or) conclusions must somehow be amenable to confirmation or disconfirmation. But in accepting this methodological postulate we need not commit ourselves to any

[14] See Alfred Marshall, *op. cit.,* p. 347.
[15] See Ludwig von Mises, *Human Action: A Treatise on Economics,* p. 858.

special epistemology. Rather we shall try to test the premises both directly, and indirectly through the testing of their inferences. Considering the inconclusiveness which we have just seen to be inherent in indirect testing, one can hardly afford to miss any insights which direct testing may have to offer.[16]

4. *Direct Testing of Behavior and Motivations*

Our first impression, in turning to the empirical sources for direct information about motivational and behavioral facts, is one of shock at how little we know about this matter. Even within the framework of capitalism—much less for pre-capitalist economies—systematic inquiries into economic behavior and motivations are hardly older than the present generation and have been the concern of psychologists and sociologists rather than of economists.

What is especially regrettable is the absence of systematic research for the era of more or less unbridled free enterprise, that is, for most of the nineteenth century when autonomous micro-actions indeed predominated in the Western economies. To form at least a general notion of that period one must fall back on little-explored primary sources of a rather spotty nature: business reports, autobiographies, correspondences, and governmental bluebooks.

Many of these records disclose a widespread tendency toward the systematic extremum incentive—receipt maximization and expenditure minimization. So does the economic folklore of the age, e.g. when America is fancied as a land of unlimited opportunities, to be exploited by rugged individualists of the Horatio Alger type, who emulate the virtues extolled in Benjamin Frankin's *Autobiography*. In this respect it is also significant that the behavioral responses as postulated in the Law of Supply and Demand became part, to use Professor Galbraith's happy phrase, of the "conventional wisdom" of the average man of affairs, and as such the axioms of a businessman's Economics.

[16] In a careful examination of the claims of "positive Economics" Tjalling C. Koopmans arrives at the same conclusion. See his *Three Essays on the State of Economic Science*, pp. 137–140.

For obvious reasons there is no direct experience of past expectational patterns. We shall, however, subsequently[17] provide some circumstantial evidence in favor of predominantly stabilizing expectations, based on the mobility of the factors of production during the era under discussion.

In sum, one is probably not too far off the mark in considering the basic postulates of traditional theory as reflecting in the main the motivational and behavioral conditions which actually prevailed during the early epoch of Western capitalism. But what about the subsequent development and, above all, the contemporary situation?

Beginning with *action directives,* what modern psychological and sociological research has impressed us with is a truly bewildering variety of incentives which in ever-varying combinations affect market behavior. No doubt the micro-goals of maximizing receipts and minimizing expenditures are still in evidence. But they are accompanied, modified, and often thwarted by a wide spectrum of alternative goals.[18]

Not that the motivational strands recently unearthed are quite novel. The symbolic meaning of money and its disposal for necessary or conspicuous consumption, for accumulation through carefully planned enterprise or through gambling, with the purpose of acquiring power or prestige, immediate or distant security or even heavenly salvation, those and still other micro-goals have for centuries inspired different groups of marketers, and have done so side by side with one another. But these contrasting springs of action were of little concern to the economic theorist so long as they *manifested* themselves in a more or less uniform pattern of market behavior.

The analytical problem changes drastically once the emergence of conflicting action directives modifies and diversifies the ensuing behavioral pattern itself. But this is precisely what we encounter in many sectors of the organized capitalism of recent decades. At-

---

[17] See chap. 3, sec. 3.
[18] For an interesting survey, see Albert Lauterbach, *Man, Motives, and Money* (Ithaca, N.Y., 1954).

titudes such as the striving for fixed rates of return or business policies directed toward maintaining rather than increasing the value of assets or the share of the market seem in many a large corporation to take precedence over, or to modify in significant ways, the traditional struggle for maximum profit. These "homeostatic"[19] tendencies are strengthened and at the same time transformed by the concern of modern business with public relations and also by its growing regard for wider social interests. No less striking as a symptom of new attitudes is a certain insensitivity on the part of major consumer strata to price fluctuations over time or to price differentials for physically homogeneous products at one and the same time. There the traditional incentive of minimizing expenditures seems to give way to a preference for routinized purchases of branded goods at favorably located sellers.

All these examples indicate that the extremum principle has lost much of its former reliability as a guide to predicting the responses to the stimuli emanating from variations of demand, supply, or price. And yet all these divergencies are of small account compared with the growing ambiguity which, with the growth of industrialism, more and more beclouds the orthodox meaning of the extremum principle itself.

In order to appreciate fully this difficulty we must realize that the principle has no definite consequences for behavior, unless the time span is defined over which pecuniary magnitudes are to be maximized or minimized. Without usually spelling it out, most classical and neo-classical writings take the short run, that is, the exploitation of immediately given opportunities for buying and selling, as the proper time span. Such an assumption was not unrealistic for the technical and organizational order of early capitalism with its mobility of resources and relatively short procurement periods. But it is no longer compatible with the modern industrial regime defined by large fixed costs, highly specific and indivisible capital stocks, and the ensuing lengthy periods of investment and production. Not only does such growing "viscosity" of the industrial

[19] See Kenneth E. Boulding, *A Reconstruction of Economics* (New York, 1950), and *The Skills of the Economist* (Cleveland, 1958).

market exclude the short run as the proper horizon for calculation, but the diversity in the technical and organizational setup of agriculture, industry, and trade precludes the selection of any one time span as basis for a general maximization rule. Indeed, practically any output decision can today be justified as satisfying some standard of pecuniary advantage duly interpreted. In other words, considering the state of uncertainty in the modern industrial market, opposite actions such as increasing or decreasing output, raising or lowering prices, can be defended in one and the same situation as the most promising step for profit maximization.

We can now understand why the whole complex of *expectations* received theoretical attention only after the industrial system had come of age. So long as it was possible to fit all relevant economic actions into the framework of the short run it was permissible, not only for the scientific observer but for the acting marketer himself, to treat the major features of this framework as "remaining equal" over the relevant time span. Expectations as a separate component of the motivation compound could safely be disregarded or, what amounts to the same thing, their stabilizing nature could be taken for granted. With the progressive extension of the time horizon of the marketers into an indefinite future with uncertain content, this is no longer possible. And even if profit maximization were still the only modal micro-goal, market *behavior* in one and the same situation would differ radically according to the direction in which future demand, supply, or price is expected to vary.

Such volatility of expectations not only disconfirms the Law of Supply and Demand as a generally valid rule of empirical behavior but in conjunction with the growing variety of action directives it makes it extremely difficult to put any other determinate rule in its place. The newest methods of empirical psychology—sample interviews, questionnaires, etc.—are likely to founder on this rock. Even if one were to assume that the informants are willing and able correctly to articulate to the researcher their hunches about the future, this would still not permit us as observers to draw conclusions about their behavior beyond the very short run. For with every change in his "data" a marketer's expectations are likely to vary, and the more surely so the more rationally he evaluates his field of action. Thus to keep abreast of the actual forces at work, scientific observation could never stop and prediction of the future would have to turn into continuous re-examination of the present.

5. *The Ambiguity of Indirect Testing*

With these last remarks we have been forced to retreat from the direct testing of the premises of the theory of the market to their indirect testing, namely, to an attempt at *verifying the conclusions* derived from these premises. What, then, is the evidence for the alleged tendency toward self-equilibration with which the theory of the market invests those macro-processes?

This brings us back to the Marshallian warning that equilibrium is attainable in exceptional cases only, and that disequilibrium is the empirical rule whenever "extra-systemic" influences disturb an "intra-systemic" process which itself may well be equilibrating. In this interpretation the practical relevance of the laws of the market is put more or less on a par with the laws of Physics. Both types of laws are taken as unconditionally true only for a "vacuum" from which all extra-systemic "impurities" have been removed. They describe, in other words, the operation and the result of operations of real forces, but of forces which are never at work alone. Still, at least in principle even if not always in practice, physical as well as economic processes are regarded as open to complete explanation and correct prediction through a "summative" procedure by which the deflecting influences from the "outside" are added to, or subtracted from, the pure "theoretical" course.

Such superposition of extra-systemic factors upon intra-systemic ones may well be a cause of economic disequilibrium, but is it the only cause conceivable? Unfortunately disequilibrium may be due to another constellation of factors: irregular operation of the *intra-*systemic forces themselves, or, more precisely, to failure in the interlocking, and even to the partial absence, of regular behavior patterns. If this is the nature of economic reality, traditional theory breaks down completely, and it is difficult to see what could take its place as a tool of macro-economic prediction.

It is the methodological advantage of certain physical sciences that they can make use of a research technique that permits them to decide whether intra- or extra-systemic disturbances are at work in a given case. This is the case with the typical experiments in which the intra-systemic forces are artificially insulated from the disturbing influence of extra-systemic factors. It is a truism that only in rare cases can the social scientist apply an equivalent procedure. As a rule he must rely on the "impure" experiments which the historical process performs for him. Since such passive observations depict only the result of the total compound of factors at work, they cannot provide unambiguous answers for the tendencies of the intra-systemic forces acting in isolation.[20]

And yet, unless we abandon the attempt at verifying the theory of the market altogether, we must look for some approximative indicators of these tendencies, and of the supporting or distracting effect of extra-systemic factors. There are two possible approaches to this problem. One consists in examining some of those rare historical instances in which the influence of extra-systemic disturbances seems to have been reduced to a minimum. In these cases did the ensuing macro-processes fulfill the predictions derived from conventional theory? The other approach concerns the investigation of the extra-systemic factors themselves, and of the effect they have on the motivational and behavioral patterns characteristic for successive stages of the evolution of industrial markets. The remainder of this chapter will be occupied with the former approach; Chapter 3 will offer some reflections derived from the latter.

6. *Prediction of Macro-Phenomena*

In the search for historical examples which can be interpreted without reference to extra-systemic factors, Marshall's stress on long-

[20] Even the protagonists of "positive Economics" cannot help admitting this difficulty. See Milton Friedman, "The Methodology of Positive Economics," pp. 10–11.

run tendencies is of little help. For none of the successive phases of industrial evolution is it permissible to assume that the "general conditions of life" remained stationary for any considerable length of time. If the hypothesis of "other things remaining equal" is to have empirical and not only methodological significance, it can only be for the short run.

As in the case of direct testing of behavioral and motivational patterns, in the earlier stages of capitalist development the available evidence for the short-run tendencies of the motions of the market is very scanty. Still, considering what was said earlier about mobility of resources and the ensuing shortness of production and investment periods, equilibration may well have been the real tendency. Moreover, the popular acclaim which the classical theories of domestic and interregional exchange received at the time may be taken as an indirect confirmation of equilibrating movements, at least in the short-run adjustments between different sectors in national and international markets. On the other hand, no such tendencies could even then be noted in the long-run motion of the industrial market systems. Rather they exhibit fluctuations of varying length and amplitude, in which a macro-state of full resource utilization was at best a passing phase.

Turning to the modern age, for which much more accurate data are available, it seems quite difficult to discover equilibrating motion, and prediction of macro-states and macro-processes has proved a disappointing enterprise even in the short run. It is impossible to report here about the multitude of predictive experiments which, since the end of the First World War, have been undertaken all over the world. For a study of many different approaches and, above all, for their failures, the reader must consult the extensive literature on the subject.[21] Our interest centers on the question of whether these failures point to irregularities in the behavior of the intra-systemic factors themselves, irregularities that obstruct not only equilibration but *any persistent tendency* in the macro-motions of the market on which predictions could be based.

[21] For a general survey, see Sidney Schoeffler, *The Failures of Economics: A Diagnostic Study* (Cambridge, Mass., 1955).

To obtain a tentative answer, let us examine a few examples which, to the extent possible within the intricate network of social relations, satisfy the restrictive conditions for indirect testing. They all concern short-run processes, occurring within a framework the structure and tendencies of which were known at the time of prediction, and which varied very little during the prediction interval. In none of the instances considered did the nature and operation of extra-systemic factors undergo unforeseen changes. All examples refer to recent American experience, and are therefore well documented.

The first two instances are in a way complementary, since in one case a dangerous depression and in the other case a runaway inflation was predicted. The first is still widely remembered; it concerned the change-over to a peacetime economy after the end of the Second World War. Two extra-systemic forces were then recognized as strategic for the level of output and employment in the immediate postwar years: a sudden and dramatic cut in public expenditure and the latent demand for consumer and replacement goods backed up by many billions of savings accumulated during the war. In evaluating the relative strength of these opposite forces the overwhelming majority of experts, practical as well as scientific, came out for the preponderance of the deflationary tendencies, predicting a drastic shrinkage of economic activity possibly down to the level of the Great Depression.

Fortunately for the welfare of the country, the actual course of events refuted the pessimistic prognosis, as it did again five years later during the early phase of the Korean War. Then the extra-systemic force was, first, the superposition of a new defense budget on a productive apparatus which already operated close to full capacity, without any simultaneous restraint of consumption. To this was subsequently added the psychological shock of the entry of the Chinese into the war, with the prospect of a world-wide conflagration. As a consequence wholesale prices were driven up by 15 per cent during the second half of 1950 accompanied by a rise in the cost of living of half as much, both rises reflecting panic buying on the part of business and consumers. Desperate measures were debated, such as the issue of gold bonds for the protection of the real value of savings, and the mood of the Annual Meeting of the American Economic Association at Christmas 1950 was one of unmitigated gloom.

Finally after much prodding the federal government responded at the end of January, 1951, with a general freeze of wages and prices. Now, what was startling was the almost instantaneous success of the freeze, giving the lie to the general prognosis of a runaway inflation which the large volume of liquid assets still held by business and public was to set in motion. Within six weeks the wholesale price index was stabilized, a feat that more radical controls, such as consumer rationing, had failed to achieve in the much more favorable climate of the larger war.

Why, twice in short succession, did the predictions held by the large majority of competent observers go so far astray? The stillborn recession of 1946 is in some way the more striking case. An economy sustained over a number of years on the highest possible level of output and employment, through a volume of demand half of which was public, was to be reconverted to a peacetime structure mainly impelled by private consumption and investment. Assuming that aggregate purchasing power was not only maintained but even increased through the mobilization of wartime savings, believers in the traditional reasoning should have come out with the forecast of the very boom that actually occurred. Certainly the joint forces of the extremum principle and of stabilizing expectations should have appeared as ideally suited for accomplishing the necessary sectoral shifts of production, the increment in aggregate demand at the same time absorbing all the manpower released from war service.

It is somehow paradoxical that, by breaking away from one of the basic premises in the traditional economic syllogism, the experts should have been misled into a false prediction. The premise concerned the nature of both price and quantity expectations. More precisely, it was assumed that consumers and investors would interpret the unavoidable temporary dislocations in the major sectors of the war economy as the beginning of a general fall in prices and output. It was these pessimistic expectations which were supposed to initiate a deflationary downward spiral. Wrong as this supposition proved to be, it was by no means implausible. On the contrary, a number of common-sense arguments could be adduced in its favor, such as the technical difficulties of reconversion which were likely to reduce the employment capacity of the system below the critical threshold or, the other side of the medal, the precipitate inrush of the demobilized masses into the labor market, or the undercurrent of a general deflationary psychology left over from the preceding decade. With the large majority of observers, faith in the conventional wisdom was no longer strong enough to brush aside these portents of economic doom.[22]

The false prophets of the mid-forties must not be accused of faulty reasoning or disregard of ascertainable facts. They misjudged with plausible arguments the future behavior of one of the two basic intra-systemic forces. The reasons which led to a similar miscalculation in 1951 were even stronger. For six months elastic expectations on the part of buyers and sellers had sent the price level into an upward spiral. Freezing of prices and wages could not affect the objective state of scarcity. Rather as a formal acknowledgment of the existing dangers it might have stimulated further panic buying. And it is worth noting that in this case traditional theory had no explanation to offer for what did happen, namely, that the elasticity of both price and quantity expectations suddenly turned negative, from a vista of further price rise and supply shrinkage to an anticipation of price stability and rising provision.

Both in 1945 and in 1951 the deviation of actual from estimated expectations seems to be the reason for the failure of prediction. But even this proposition cannot claim more than plausibility on common-sense grounds. Observation could tell us only of unorthodox behavioral responses. These responses were the joint product of action directives and expectations. Therefore, considering the large variety of conflicting action directives characteristic for the

[22] At the time the pessimistic prognosis was given theoretical respectability by associating it with the teaching of Keynes. It has long since been realized that the actual course of events at the time fits equally well in the framework of Keynes's analysis.

contemporary scene, we cannot exclude the latter at least as a part-cause of deviating behavior.

The same considerations hold for our next example, with an outcome that is equally inconclusive in terms of a general theory. This example concerns the recession of 1957–1958 and the subsequent ups and downs in the activity of the American economy. But, whereas in the previous cases the experts largely agreed in their estimates, on this occasion diagnosis and prognosis varied from one extreme to the other. This became evident in the conflicting policy proposals which in the spring of 1958 ranged from demands for immediate and drastic governmental intervention to full confidence in the self-balancing power of conventional private incentives. And it is only fair to emphasize that the common-sense views held by the business community were as much at variance with one another as were the scientific analyses of the experts. Nor should the fact that in the end revival started without the drastic tax reductions and large-scale public works advocated by some be taken as proof of the better understanding of the relevant forces on the part of those who resisted such measures.

Changes in extra-systemic variables played hardly any role in the ensuing gradual improvement. True, certain stabilizers built into the modern fiscal system provided the opportunity for compensatory responses through the automatic creation of a budget deficit. But the forces that seized upon these opportunities, cushioning the downswing and stimulating the recovery, were intra-systemic. Once more it was the unorthodox behavior of consumers, this time joined by the promoters of fixed investment, who in the face of falling output and employment maintained a high level of aggregate expenditure.

The subsequent quinquennium, up to the early part of 1964, when these comments were drafted, showed only one persistent feature: refutation of expert forecasts by the actual course of events. Contrary to general anticipation, the recovery from the 1957–1958 recession proved weak and short-lived. The same was true of the business improvement which coincided with the inauguration of the Kennedy Administration. What was then hailed as a definite turn to the better soon lost its momentum, even if industrial production displayed some fitful gains. Unemployment remained frozen on a higher than 5 per cent level, provoking a still-unsettled debate about the ultimate cause of the economy's underperformance: income-induced lack of demand for goods or technologically induced lack of demand for labor.

In the course of 1962, supported by the slump in the stock market, the conviction became universal that drastic government action was required to prevent another and more serious recession. From this came the Administration's proposals for tax reduction, only to be confounded by a quite unforeseen autonomous spurt in economic activity beginning in the early months of 1963.

All this is not to deny that on some occasions economic predictions turned out right. But one cannot help wondering whether such success "is due to luck or to a genuine advance in quantitative knowledge."[23] This skeptical verdict refers, in fact, to a much broader scope of investigations and to a research procedure more sophisticated than traditional analysis. It summarizes the experience with econometric model-building, in so far as such models have been pressed into the service of forecasting. But in siding with this verdict one must lay the blame where it belongs.

Contrary to much facile criticism, the weak spot of Econometrics is not the statistical technique by which it is best known. What proves the source of embarrassment is the underlying theory, formalized in the so-called structural equations and, above all, in the behavior equations of the models. As a rule these equations formalize the same rigid patterns of behavior and oversimplified motivational hypotheses which characterize traditional theorizing generally, and in the nature of the case it cannot be different. How else than by postulating certain universal action directives and expectations can definite macro-states be inferred from micro-premises? Moreover, the computational work imposes severe limitations on the mathematical form of the critical propositions, and it should not surprise us that the basic hypotheses, which determine among other things the crucial "signs" of the strategic equations, differ

[23] See Koopmans, *Three Essays on the State of Economic Science,* p. 205.

little from the conventional wisdom embodied in the classical Law of Supply and Demand.

In summing up our observations of the recent past, there can be little doubt that, in the absence of any major extra-systemic disturbances, it must have been the intra-systemic variables and, in particular, the volatility of expectations which played the decisive role in counteracting equilibration, and at the same time in defying generalizations and predictions. But can we let the matter rest there? Should we impute this intra-systemic "disorder" to innate capriciousness of the economic actors? Or can the variety of action directives and the uncertainty of expectations themselves be traced back to more tangible factors? And if so, where else than in the natural, institutional, and technological environment of the industrial market could such explanatory principles be found? Not before at least a tentative answer has been given to these questions can the significance and limits of traditional theory be truly evaluated.

3

Economic Behavior and the Evolution of Capitalism

1. *Can Economic Processes Be Conceived as "Self-contained"?*

In the conclusion to his *Mathematical Principles of Natural Philosophy* Newton writes: "I have not been able to discover the cause of those properties of gravity . . . it is enough that gravity does really exist, and act according to the laws which we have explained."

Consciously or not, anyone who interprets the extremum principle along classical lines as a propensity of human nature—as the "economic force of gravity" (Wilhelm Hasbach)—or the positive economist of our day who sees in it only a hypothetical construct adopts Newton's methodological position. He treats the principle as an axiom for his theoretical constructions, an axiom which need not, and even cannot, be linked with more remote "causes." Still one wonders how Newton would have proceeded had the facts shown that, though the motions of the planets did obey the law of gravitation as he stated it, the paths of comets and the tides of the seas displayed different relations between mass and distance. Now, as we saw, this is precisely the situation which confronts the economist when he tries to subject the extremum principle to observational confirmation.

If he chooses the method of direct testing, a wide spectrum of action directives reveals itself. Within this spectrum the extremum principle plays an important role, but one that seems to diminish with the progress of industrial evolution. Nor has indirect testing, namely, the attempt to verify the conclusions drawn from the premise of the extremum principle, proved any more successful. There the attempt is made to establish the validity of the extremum principle through the empirical confirmation of predictions derived from it. The striking failure of many of these predictions cannot but throw doubt on the actual or the heuristic significance of the premise.

Whatever way we look at the problem, the traditional notion that the extremum principle and, for that matter, stabilizing expectations should be treated as axioms of the theory of the market cannot be maintained. The variety of motivational experience as well as the ambiguity of their behavioral consequences compels us to search for more remote "causes," which may still supply the unifying premises for a general theory of the market. At the same time this seems a grave decision to take. Does not such extension of the analytical framework eliminate the boundaries that separate intra- and extra-systemic processes, and thus entangle economic reasoning in a crisscross of hypotheses about the "general conditions of life"?

Such apprehensions compel us to look once more at the relationship between intra-systemic and extra-systemic forces in economic processes. How this relationship is conceived in traditional theory was indicated above, when a parallel was drawn between the so-called isolating method in Economics—the "ceteris paribus" reasoning—and the typical experiments in the natural sciences. In both cases the methodological aim is the same: insulation of those forces which are supposed to be necessary and sufficient for the explanation of "systematic" motion, from the distorting influence of coexisting but "accidental" forces. Though the latter may be an inseparable ingredient in the compound of factors that shape real economic or physical processes, economic and physical theory treats them as extraneous to the "pure" phenomena to which their respective laws refer.

Now, such a procedure rests on a very special hypothesis and only to the extent to which this hypothesis can itself be vindicated is the quest for a self-contained economic or physical system legitimate. Crucial experiments as well as "ceteris paribus" reasoning imply that, in the real world, intra- and extra-systemic forces associate without genuine interaction. To be specific, it is postulated that, though the force of the wind may deflect a falling body from its perpendicular course, it does not affect the relationship between time and distance as formulated in Galileo's law. Nor will the imposition of a tariff alter the Law of Supply and Demand, even if the ensuing prices and quantities differ from those prevailing under free trade. With this hypothesis in mind it was said above that the influence of extra-systemic forces can be treated as "additive" or "subtractive," relative to the result ascertained for the pure case.

Experience in the physical world seems to confirm this hypothesis of "non-interaction" rather well. One example among many is presented in Ballistics, when the actual motion of a projectile is calculated by "adding" to the impact of the forces operating on a freely falling body the retarding effect of the atmosphere, the deflections due to the movements of the air, the spin of the projectile, etc. And there seem as well to be plenty of examples for such simple superimposition of extraneous influences in the economic realm. An earthquake is bound to reduce productive capacity at least in proportion to physical destruction. And not only natural but also institutional factors can operate in this manner, when, e.g., the imposition of quotas curtails the flow of imports or an increase in reserve requirements cuts the supply of bank credit.

However, our brief survey of postwar events in the United States has already indicated that the effect of the institutional environment on the economic core process cannot always be calculated so easily. The respective forces at work may stand to each other in a relationship which is by no means simply summative. This can perhaps be demonstrated on an issue the practical outcome of which has been hotly debated.

The tax reductions recently enacted in the United States imply the prediction that the total flow of spending will increase if, to the current flow, a potential flow is added equal to the tax relief of business and the general public. Is this a prediction which can be regarded as valid under all circumstances?

It would be so if the American economy were a hydraulic system into which an additional source of water supply was opened. The motivational hypotheses underlying traditional theory postulate analogous consequences for the spending flow in a market economy. To that extent the general theory of economic motion on which the program rests is in perfect accord with orthodox analysis, even if deficit financing, the complementary item in the Administration's fiscal program, may be regarded as "unorthodox."

The lessons of the recent past retold above cannot but shake our confidence in such an unqualified prediction. Contrary to traditional assumptions, the determinants of the intra-systemic motions of the market are not constants, but are variables the values of which may be drastically altered under the impact of an extra-systemic change. Therefore if a tax cut had been interpreted by investors and consumers as a public confession of grave trouble ahead—a serious possibility in a less favorable business climate than prevailed in the spring of 1964—it might have actually reduced the total flow of spending below the level prevailing before the cut.

Examples of such interaction between extra-systemic and intra-systemic forces can easily be multiplied. They are, in fact, not the exception but the rule, and even the hypothetical instances of purely summative effects quoted above can be included here. While it is true that the *minimum* change brought about by an earthquake or an increase in reserve requirements must be in proportion to the extra-systemic impact, the secondary effect of this impact on action directives or expectations may raise the *actual* change far above that minimum.

We encounter here a most important difference between social and physical experience, namely the difference between insensitive particles responding blindly though lawfully to blind stimuli, and purposeful actors who "move" only after they have interpreted their field of action in terms of their goals and their common-sense knowledge. And there is, in principle, no extraneous event that is not capable of so affecting these forces from which action springs.[1]

Moreover, and this is really decisive, in any social economy these forces are themselves socially conditioned. As we remember, action directives are related to the prevailing political institutions and cultural value systems, as expectations were seen to vary, e.g., with the length of the procurement period, itself a function of technology. Thus it is not only a question of the impact which certain *changes* in extra-systemic variables make on the strength and direction of the intra-systemic forces. Even with no change in the environment, these intra-systemic forces acquire their determinate strength and direction only if they are constantly exposed to the regulatory influence of extra-systemic factors. For this reason economic processes even under the most ideal laboratory conditions can never be treated as "self-contained" in the way in which physical processes can indeed be so treated. The systematic forces of the former lack the universality, constancy, and above all the independence which the systematic forces of the latter evidently possess. Gravity manifesting itself as such a universal, constant, and independent force, Newton could well dispense with a study of its "causes." Nothing of this is true of the extremum principle or of stabilizing expectations, neither of which can claim an exclusive role in the compound of economic motivations. Therefore it is imperative to inquire into the possible causes of their diversity and mutability, even if this leads us beyond the confines of intra-systemic analysis.

2. *The Regulatory Function of Extra-Systemic Factors*

In pointing to the regulatory function which extra-systemic factors fulfill in the economic core process, we refer to the effect which certain environmental conditions exert on the formation of action directives and expectations. At first sight these conditions seem to include all the natural, social, and technical phenomena which traditional analysis treats as "data." But at second thought such a definition appears as too wide. Take, e.g., that indispensable

[1] See Alfred Schutz, "Common-Sense and Scientific Interpretation of Human Action," in *Collected Papers,* vol. I (The Hague, 1962), pp. 3–47.

set of data which form the initial conditions of any act of economizing: final micro-goals and a stock of resources. There is no reason to suspect that action directives will differ according to whether hats or shoes are in demand or that the mere size of the labor force or of the capital stock will influence expectations in a definite manner. Even *changes* in these initial conditions are unlikely to affect the prevailing behavioral and motivational patterns if they do not exceed certain limits. We shall, on the other hand, see that large and sudden changes in these basic data, due, e.g., to the caprice of fashion, to crop variations, or to technical innovations, may indeed alter marketers' patterns of response and thus qualify for inclusion among the regulatory factors.

However, what establishes and sustains such behavioral patterns in the first instance (even in an altogether stationary market process) are extra-systemic factors of a different kind. Their general character can best be seen in some concrete examples. In a market system in which the supply of resources and technical skills is so low that aggregate output barely comes up to the subsistence level, the aim of maximizing receipts and minimizing expenditures is a motivational condition for survival. Even in a highly productive market organization this may still be true if buyers and sellers are exposed to the rigor of unlimited competition. And even without the whip of competition the extremum principle may be in full force whenever the prevailing cultural value system gives pride of place to the accumulation of wealth.

Now contrast with these examples the state of affairs as typified by the medieval town economies. Their productivity was quite low when judged by our standards, and yet the unlimited pursuit of pecuniary gains was proscribed by law and custom. Bargaining in these markets must be interpreted in terms of "homeostatic" rather than extremum tendencies. We have already noted similar tendencies coming to the fore in the modern industrial market. And it is easy to imagine that the inculcation of this or some other action directive might become the object of a promotional campaign or a concerted educational effort—not to speak of more rigorous public controls of a legal or administrative nature.

What is common to these diverse environmental factors is the psychological constraint they impose on a marketer when he chooses his modal micro-goal, a constraint which is the more effective the heavier the penalties which resistance to it invites. Therefore the regulatory forces mentioned can be subsumed under the general category of *pressures,* with the subcategories of *automatic* pressures (the stinginess of nature or a low level of productivity), of *contrived* pressures (legal and administrative acts of public policy), and a hybrid subcategory that combines automatic and contrived elements in the form of *institutional* pressures, such as emanate from the state of competition, from the prevailing educational order, or from the ruling cultural value system.

These regulatory pressures can be defined as the *dynamic* factors of the environment, because they operate in the manner of forces, and as such act, first of all, upon action directives. To these dynamic factors we must now add *structural* factors which play the role of barriers to economic motion—barriers the absence or presence of which is mainly reflected in the content of expectations.

Thus consider an industry which changes over from pure competition to pure monopoly. Assume that demand and cost schedules remain unaffected by the change and that in both states the extremum principle is the sole action directive. Can we predict the resulting changes in output and price?

We can certainly do so if expectations also remain unaffected by this transformation of market structure. We remember from our earlier discussion[2] that a competitive structure (by evoking speedy compensatory responses to any stimuli) proves especially favorable for inducing stabilizing expectations. But it is the very purpose of monopolization to block such compensatory responses. As a consequence, price expectations are likely to change to unity with quantity expectations becoming negative. In fact, even this prognosis may well prove faulty. It fits the extreme case in which the monopoly and thus the barrier to compensatory responses can be regarded as permanent. In the majority of empirical cases such a

[2] See chap. 2, note 8.

surmise would be quite unrealistic, and the only safe generalization seems to be that expectations under monopoly just differ from expectations under competition in unspecifiable ways.

We found the common characteristic of the dynamic factors in the direct constraints they impose on the formation of action directives. The influence of the structural factors on expectations is less direct. It is mediated through the primary effect which these factors exert on the objective state of *resource mobility,* and thus on the relative ease with which quantities can be adjusted to changes in the initial conditions. In this connection it will be convenient to distinguish between factors bearing on *social mobility*—the institutional forms of exchange as manifested in the degree of competition; public controls of the terms of bargaining, such as price and wage controls; tariffs, banking policy, etc.—and factors bearing on *technical mobility:* the state of the arts and, in particular, certain features of the industrial forms of production, such as specificity and indivisibility of real capital. And the specific channel through which the structure of the market influences expectations is then the evaluation of the prevailing state of social and technical mobility in terms of the final and modal goals to be achieved.

Growing technical and social immobility has been an outstanding feature of the evolution of capitalism. But we must be careful in basing any generalizations about the nature of typical expectations during this era on this fact alone. Though an essential factor, the state of the system's mobility is not the only extra-systemic determinant of expectations. There are other structural conditions capable of offsetting any destabilizing effect which immobility by itself may evoke.

Again an example should clarify what is at stake. Assume a market in which social as well as technical immobility completely blocks adjustment of supply to changes in demand, practically eliminating any intersectoral shifts. But assume that at the same time aggregate demand for the output of all sectors is steadily increasing, owing to the growth of population, to a rising rate of investment in successive innovations, or to continuous expansion of exports. The presence of such structural *escapements* may then arouse price and quantity expectations that fully outweigh any pessimistic antici- pations due to immobility.

Thus *pressures* as above defined, *the state of social and technical mobility,* and *compensating escapements* offer themselves as the *major extra-systemic factors* which establish and sustain the mo- tivational patterns in a given market economy. In relating these different factors to specific motivational strands, namely, in linking pressures with action directives and mobility and escapements with expectations we have, as a first approximation, made their operation appear as more exclusive than it is in fact. Even the few examples cited for such linkage disprove a simple dichotomy. For instance, the state of competition is to be found among the pressures as well as among the factors influencing mobility. A similar double role is played by technology; in determining the level of productivity it influences action directives, whereas in determining the degree of technical mobility it is likely to affect expectations. Nor should the relationship between extra-systemic and intra-systemic factors be seen as only one-sided. Monopolistic organization, which tends to modify the motivational patterns, may itself be the outgrowth of extremum tendencies. And even the two motivational strands them- selves are not entirely unrelated. Single-mindedness in the pursuit of extremum goals may well sharpen the cognitive faculties, as an excessive degree of uncertainty about the future may blunt the aim of receipt maximization.

We shall presently see that all these relationships have played a role at some stage of capitalist evolution. But before we can apply our conceptual scheme to the explanation of certain historical facts we should form a somewhat more precise notion of the nature of these relationships themselves.

In describing them we have hitherto used such general terms as "influence," "inducement," "impact," or "interaction." Even when speaking of "determinants" having a specific "effect" we have care- fully refrained from claiming for the connection between extra- and intra-systemic factors the stringency of causal laws. In other words, the former must not be interpreted as necessary, and certainly not as sufficient, conditions for the existence and mode of operation of the latter. Thus the constraints which extreme poverty imposes in a subsistence economy may not suffice to induce extremum tendencies in every one of its members. Nor can the presence of such tendencies in each instance be traced back to extra-systemic pressures. Still looser appears the link between expectations and the structure of the system, because it is forged by an act of evaluation for which no strict rules are known.

It is worth noting that no such vagueness weakens our earlier propositions about the manner in which micro-behavior creates states of provision or motivations engender action. Once it has been understood that the former relationship is basically technical and subject to the laws of nature, it appears quite legitimate to interpret it in causal terms. And the connection beween motives and overt behavior—in our context, between particular action directives and expectations, on the one hand, and, on the other, the acts of buying or selling at a certain price—seems equally strict and exclusive. Only when it comes to the explanation of the *content* of these motives themselves do we enter a realm of less determinate relations.

The realm in question is the theory of motivation, and especially the manner in which specific motives are referred to the structure of the personality and to the natural and social environment respectively. The immense complexity of this problem and the difficulties which stand in the way of a satisfactory solution were aptly described more than a century ago by J. S. Mill. Though inclining toward a conception which imputes the dominant role to the environment, Mill had to admit that "the impressions and actions of human beings are not solely the result of present circumstances, but the joint result of these circumstances and of the character of the individual: and the agencies which determine human character are so numerous and diversified, (nothing which has happened to the person throughout life being without its portion of influence) that in the aggregate they are never in any two cases exactly similar." As a consequence, no strict causal relationship can ever prevail between a given external impulse and a specific motive. The impulse will always be channeled, as it were, through the sluices formed by the respondent's biopsychological endowment and past experience.

At the same time Mill regarded a satisfactory theory of motivation as so crucial for the understanding of social processes that he postulated a new branch of science specially devoted to its study. This "Ethology or Science of Character" was to determine, in conformity with the general laws of Psychology, "the kind of character produced . . . by any set of circumstances, physical and moral . . ." though "it would indeed be vain to expect (however completely the laws of the formation of character might be ascertained) that we could know so accurately the circumstances of any given case as to be able positively to predict the character that would be produced in that case. . . . It is enough that we know that certain means have a *tendency* to produce a given effect."[3]

Alas, Mill's program is still unfulfilled, and we do not at this time possess a theory of motivations from which, by deductive reasoning, generally valid predictions can be derived. On the other hand, so long as we do not claim for them the status of "laws," the conceptual scheme devised above will permit us to frame some working hypotheses for the "tendencies"—to use Mill's cautious phrase—which the regulatory factors of the environment induce in the determinants of the economic core process.[4] In testing these hypotheses against the facts of the relevant period of economic history we shall gain some deeper insight into the reasons for the failures of traditional theory.

3. The "Classical" Stage: Industrial Revolution

We are now going to discuss three successive stages in the evolution of Western capitalism, by relating the market movements characteristic for each stage to certain regulatory factors of the environment. At the same time we shall examine the manner in which

[3] See J. S. Mill, *A System of Logic* (London, 1943), Book VI, chaps. II and V (italics added).

[4] We shall continue the discussion of the relationship between motivations and environment in chap. 5. For a systematic exposition of the problem, see Robert M. MacIver, *Social Causation* (Boston, 1942), esp. Part Three.

traditional theory has interpreted this historical experience, by contrasting the psychosociological facts as recorded for each stage with the premises of the contemporaneous stage of economic analysis.

We begin with the primary stage of capitalism, as it was ushered in by the Industrial Revolution. The period in question extends roughly from the middle of the eighteenth to the middle of the nineteenth century, though the initial as well as the terminal dates differ from country to country. We can call it the classical stage, because it is the era during which the blueprint was designed and elaborated for that "engine of theoretical analysis whose basic features were the same everywhere."[5] This engine was supposed to be driven by the openly postulated extremum principle and steered by implicitly assumed stabilizing expectations.

The scattered data available for behavior and motivations of a typical marketer during the classical era have already been shown as largely in accord with the theoretical premises.[6] Is it possible to support these observations by our explanatory hypothesis based on the pressures and the state of mobility prevailing during these decades?

There are few historical periods on record which show such a perfect convergence of natural, social and cultural forces in molding the dominant economic *action directive* as does this critical century. The combined pressures of mass poverty, of social isolation of the individual in a competitively organized civil order, and of a cultural climate in which economic success had become the prime source of power and prestige make it easy to understand that the extremum principle became the supreme maxim of market behavior.

This is not to say that all these pressures are historically bound

---

[5] See J. A. Schumpeter, *History of Economic Analysis* (New York, 1954), p. 952. The passage quoted actually refers to the subsequent "neo-classical" stage. But in an earlier section (*ibid.*, pp. 536–540) Schumpeter rightly insists that classical methodology did not differ from that formulated and practiced during the neo-classical stage. "All the leaders of that time, such as Jevons, Walras, Menger, Marshall, Wicksell, Clark, and so on, visualized the economic process much as had J. S. Mill or even A. Smith; that is to say, they added nothing to the ideas of the preceding period concerning what it is that happens in the economic process and how, in a general way, this process works out" (*ibid.*, p. 892).

[6] See chap. 2, sec. 4.

up with the rise of modern capitalism, nor that each one of them bore with equal force on all the major social strata. As far as the masses of the urban population were concerned, it was the new technology that exposed them to the triple coercion of a subsistence standard, of employment insecurity, and of the mechanical control of their working lives in the factory system. It was true that the transformation of the serf into the free laborer was a radical step toward human emancipation. But it was no less true that during the classical stage his new freedom, symbolized in his right to sell his services to the highest bidder, was practically eclipsed by his compulsion to do so.

Material privation did not exert pressure on the leading groups in capitalist enterprise. In them the extremum motivation was engendered by the pull of wealth creation—a new source of social power and also a new measure of self-esteem, secular and transcendental. Finally, there was the all-around pressure of competition—a "peaceful struggle" to which rich and poor, agrarian and urban classes, buyers and sellers of commodities and productive factors, were indiscriminately exposed.

Thus there are strong reasons to impute to the combined operation of these several pressures that striking conformity of attitude among all groups of capitalist marketers which has found its theoretical formulation in the concept of "Economic Man." Far from being a figment of deluded doctrinaires, this concept can be regarded as a genuine abstraction from the experience of the classical stage. The simultaneous presence, even in the heyday of this phase of capitalism, of action directives other than the extremum principle or the existence of profit-maximizers in Ancient Society or in the large commercial cities of the Middle Ages do not refute this conclusion. In the former case we deal with certain margins of tolerance intrinsic to all social organizations, margins which were kept well within the critical range by the pressures described. The latter phenomena were no more than incidental deviations from very different motivational patterns and were confined to the fringes of the societies concerned.

Turning now to the type of *expectations* which prevailed during the classical phase, we meet with a more difficult problem. First of all, as was pointed out before, direct evidence of the nature of these expectations can hardly be obtained, and an element of speculation enters not only into any explanation but already into the account of that which is to be explained.

Analytical considerations have taught us that the traditional theory of the market is valid only for such micro-behavior as is steered by stabilizing expectations. To this insight we have now added the hypothesis that the elasticity of expectations is largely a function of the prevailing state of the system's mobility. If it can be shown that, in the classical stage, impediments to both social and technical mobility were largely absent, and that the factors of production were able to adjust themselves speedily to any shifts in demand for them, a strong case can be made for the applicability of traditional theory.

Now these are precisely the sociological and technological characteristics of the period under examination. Even where the factory system had fully replaced earlier forms of business organization, the small-scale technology of a predominantly commercial capitalism gave way only gradually to the new industrial methods of production with their ever-growing demand for highly specialized lumpy equipment. Concerning the mobility of labor, the practical disregard and final abolition of the Statute of Apprenticeship, by which Elizabeth I had made the medieval guild regulations the law of the land, acknowledged with Adam Smith that "the free circulation of labor from one employment to another" was of equal benefit to workers and employers.

There is agreement among economic historians about these facts. But it is no less interesting that they have entered as unquestioned presuppositions into the basic theorems of classical Economics. "If at any time it [to wit: the quantity of a commodity supplied] exceeds the effectual demand . . . the interest of the laborers . . . and of their employers . . . will prompt them to withdraw a part of the labor or stock from this employment. . . . If, on the contrary, the quantity brought to market should at any time fall short of the effectual demand . . . the interest of all other laborers and dealers will soon prompt them to employ more labor and stock in preparing and bringing it [to wit: the commodity in short supply] to market."[7] What is significant in this quotation, besides the assumptions of the extremum principle and of perfect mobility of labor, is the nature of the "stock" which is supposed to be withdrawn and re-employed at short notice. It is composed of easily adjustable working capital as "dealers" supply it.

None of the classical writers mentions expectations explicitly. But in the passage cited and in practically every other statement concerning adjustment processes stabilizing expectations are an implicit assumption. If, nevertheless, the actual macro-processes deviated considerably from the image of a market in steady equilibration, such distortions were imputed to the impact of erratic stimuli, and belittled as passing "frictions" incapable of diverting the core process from its long-run equilibrium.[8] And indeed the regulatory factors at work seem to have brought about an approximation between reality and conceptual scheme, close enough to establish classical Economics as a plausible theory of economic motion.[9]

4. The "Neo-Classical" Stage: Industrial Capitalism under Laissez-Faire

There is no sharp break separating the classical from the neoclassical stage. This is as true of the historical sequence of events as it is of the doctrinal development reflected in Mill, the early Marginalists, Marshall, and the school of Lausanne. Extending roughly to the beginning of the First World War, the period includes, on the one hand, the maturation of the leading Western economies into full-grown industrial systems and, on the other hand, the purification of economic theory of many incidental misconstructions of its early beginnings. However, to the basic features of the theory of the market which it received from its classical pre-

[7] Adam Smith, *The Wealth of Nations* (Modern Library Edition, New York, 1937), pp. 57–58.

[8] A characteristic argument along such lines is offered in chap. XIX of Ricardo's *Principles of Political Economy* (Cambridge, England, 1951).

[9] For a more detailed exposition, see chap. 6.

cursors, neo-classical Economics added practically nothing. The standard patterns of behavior and motivation—with the extremum principle ostensibly generalized into the concept of utility maximization—continued to serve as major hypotheses from which an unswerving long-run tendency of macro-equilibration was deduced.

This clinging to scientific tradition was in striking contrast with the profound transformation of the institutional and technological environment of which progressive industrialization was both cause and effect. This is not the place to list all the significant changes and to give an account of the complex interplay of political, social, and economic forces from which these changes resulted. What we are interested in is the growing discrepancies between the structure and process of a fully developed industrial market and the contemporaneous theoretical constructs which were supposed to explain it.

The most striking difference concerns the shape which economic macro-processes assumed ever more distinctly as the nineteenth century advanced. Contrary to the theoretical image of a steady path only occasionally interrupted by some short-run deviations, industrial capitalism progressed in more or less periodic waves of prosperity and depression. And the amplitudes of these fluctuations were wide enough to cast increasing doubts on the dominance of equilibrating tendencies.

Of course, with interest in empirical-statistical work rising since the middle of the century, economists could not help taking note of "business cycles." What matters is that the mainstream of the scientific profession took up the challenge by offering any number of *ad hoc* explanations for the recalcitrant facts rather than by revising the fundamentals of received theory; ". . . they treated cycles as a phenomenon that is superimposed upon the normal course of capitalist life and mostly a pathological one; it never occurred to the majority to look to business cycles for material with which to build the fundamental theory of capitalist reality."[10]

When the problem is examined in the context of the regulatory forces at work, there is no reason to suspect that the pressures which

[10] See Schumpeter, *op. cit.*, p. 1135.

originally combined in creating the universal extremum incentive had relented by the middle of the nineteenth century. It is true that the mass standard of living was gradually rising. But competition in the commodity as well as in the labor market remained as fierce as ever, and was even quickened by the shock effect of successive innovations. Nor had accumulation as a way of life lost its lure; rather it steadily gained new converts in an ever-widening bourgeois society.

However, the state of mobility presents an entirely different picture. By then industrial technology had been adopted in most sectors of production. As a consequence, the key-sectors—especially those represented by the so-called heavy industries—found themselves burdened with vast stocks of highly specialized equipment, involving large and long-lasting financial commitments. The result was a progressive reduction of the elasticity of supply, which placed two obstacles in the path of equilibration. One can be defined as oversaturation of the market owing to the "longue durée" (Aftalion) of the construction of large-scale plant and equipment. In other words, an increasing lag between a rise in demand and the compensating rise in supply tempted in the interval an excessive number of investors into expansion creating periodically a ruinous oversupply of final output. The reverse danger concerns an indefinite delay of the contraction of output in the face of a falling demand. Once an investment with its inescapable fixed costs was undertaken, even receipts which no longer covered average total costs might be preferable to the losses bound up with a complete shutdown.

The over-all effect on the elasticity of expectations could only be destabilizing. In particular as the producers' field of action extended more and more into an unknown and unknowable future, it became ever more difficult to form precise notions about the prospective movement of prices and quantities. Such mounting uncertainty of expectations made it necessary to add to normal calculations, especially of the long-term profitability of new investment, a growing allowance for risk, a discount which might well depress the level of gain expected from future output below the level which would induce a positive investment decision. In a word, as it stimulated a tendency toward negative elasticities of expectations, industrial technology slowed down and even blocked altogether those compensatory actions on which the equilibration of the market depended.[11]

The only systematic treatment in the writings of the time of the new industrial (as contrasted with a pre-industrial) organization of the market was Marx's *Kapital*. We shall have occasion to evaluate his contribution to the development of economic science in greater detail.[12] With due acknowledgment of his aim of building a fundamental theory on the phenomenon of industrial fluctuations, what matters in the present context is his total failure in predicting the long-term evolution of industrial capitalism.

The adherents of orthodox reasoning, on the other hand, confined themselves to dealing with the unorthodox facts in "epicyclical" terms. The result was a vast catalogue of rivaling hypotheses trying to explain the special causes which were thought to superimpose cyclical fluctuations on an inherently equilibrating "trend." To the extent to which these causes were found in the singular features of industrial technology and its consequences for "over- and underinvestment" (Robertson, Spiethoff, Schumpeter), the *locus* of the critical factor was correctly diagnosed. But since no one succeeded in integrating this factor with the "normal" operation of the economic core process, Economics was for almost a century divided into two separate compartments without any channels of intercommunication: one concerned with the "Essence and Main Content of Theoretical Economics," namely, equilibrium analysis, and the other with a "Theory of Economic Development."[13]

Still the puzzle remains how such a dichotomy of analytical thinking could be maintained throughout the entire neo-classical period, and how it was possible that the standard treatises of the

[11] For an exposition of the problem in technical terms, see J. R. Hicks, *Value and Capital*, (Oxford, 1946), and O. Lange, *Price Flexibility and Employment* (Bloomington, Ind., 1944), chap. VI.

[12] See chap. 7.

[13] These are the titles of two of Schumpeter's standard works.

era, such as the works of Jevons, Walras, Marshall, Pareto, J. B. Clark, and Taussig, either entirely omitted any serious discussion of the real motion of the aggregate market process or dismissed it with meaningless metaphors.[14]

One answer suggests itself immediately. It points to the "ideological" function of academic theorizing which made it cling to an obsolete frame of reference long after the deviations of the real state of affairs had become a matter of daily experience. Though not to be rejected offhand, such an appeal to the sociology of knowledge had better remain a last resort. We might rather focus on a crucial property of the industrial market of the neo-classical stage, which linked it not only to the classical stage but also to a central proposition of traditional theory. This was the capacity of the market for self-regulation.

True, in the new turn of historical events, long-term fluctuations of aggregate output and employment took the place of the short-term shifts between expanding and contracting sectors as postulated by classical and neo-classical theory. But even if their periodicity was not strict, the swings between prosperity and depression followed each other in regular intervals and in apparently self-generating fashion. In the large industrial countries cyclical downswings lasted, on an average, no longer than three years. With a superior technical equipment and a sound financial basis an industrial producer was quite capable of weathering such storms, and those who did not could be denounced as lacking the proper motivation and therefore meeting a deserved fate. This polarization between the victors and the vanquished in the competitive struggle found its theoretical reflection in Marx's prediction of a growing concentration and centralization of capital, and perhaps even more pointedly in Schumpeter's distinction between "static" and "dynamic" entrepreneurs. The former might well be unfit to survive

---

[14] See, as a striking example, Walras, *Elements of Pure Economics*, p. 381: ". . . just as a lake is, at times, stirred to its very depth by a storm, so also the market is sometimes thrown into violent confusion by *crises,* which are sudden and general disturbances of equilibrium." This is the book's only reference to a phenomenon which, a year before its publication in 1874, had thrown the whole Western world into a state of extreme panic.

and, through panicky actions during their death struggle, periodically distort the equilibrating tendencies. But the latter seemed to restore order on a steadily rising level of provision.

The periodicity of business cycles has been the subject of much theoretical speculation. From the aspect of business planning the crucial issue was the regular recurrence of upturns which justified, even if with some delay, the long-term commitments of the investors. But most students of the problem have come to the conclusion that there was nothing automatic about these upturns. Rather they were due, and owed their strength, to another set of extra-systemic factors which we defined above as *escapements*.[15]

Rapid increases in population, a steady stream of innovations, the opening up of new markets both within and, above all, outside the nucleus of Western industrialization provided a steadily widening scope for investment and rising aggregate demand. Absence of large wars and of threats to monetary stability created an international climate of confidence conducive to the full exploitation of these opportunities. In a word, an almost uninterrupted process of *growth* brought all downswings to an early stop and gave the secular movement of output and employment the appearance of a continuous boom. It is true, all spheres of production and all regions did not equally participate in this steady expansion. But the majority of recessions resulted in a slackening of the rate of growth rather than in an actual fall of output. Certainly no important industry during this stage was compelled to contract permanently, as happened, e.g., to the British cotton industry in the subsequent period between the two world wars.

Thus it was ultimately an automatic escape mechanism which successfully counteracted the effects of the mounting technological immobility and at the same time mitigated the impact of innovations on routine modes of production. Emphasis on long-term tendencies to the disregard of short-run oscillations had already been a mark of classical Economics. Then, one can admit, the actually prevailing social and technical mobility vindicated such

---

[15] For a representative example, see Alvin H. Hansen, *Business Cycles and National Income* (New York, 1951), chap. 24.

bias. But the industrial organization of the later nineteenth century
gave little justification to the identical bias of neo-classical theory.
It was extra-systemic forces making for continuous growth that reduced the risks of investment and created an expectational climate
conducive to maintaining self-balancing tendencies, at least over
the long run. In focusing attention on these tendencies, neo-classical
Economics maintained a hold, even if a tenuous one, on the real
world.

5. *The Modern Stage: Organized Capitalism*

It is difficult to find a simple designation for the epoch following the First World War, which includes the incertitudes of the
interwar period and also covers the contemporary scene. This is
so because the economic trend of the past fifty years of Western
history appears ambiguous, whether we study the medley of historic
facts or the conflicts of economic doctrines. In particular what com-
plicates the search for a proper label is the sudden extension of the
sociopolitical horizon which, while drastically limiting the scope of
capitalist forms of economic organization in one part of the world,
is putting it to a new test in another where "economic development" is at stake.

Different observers have stressed different aspects of this third
stage of capitalist development, but it is worth noting that, for the
first time, the protagonists of the system, such as Keynes and
Schumpeter, and not only its political enemies have turned critics.
Our own interest centers again in the influence which new environment factors exert on the motion of the economic core process.
From this aspect it is essential not only that obstacles to mobility
are multiplying but that the automatic escapements as well as the
institutional pressures are progressively losing momentum. As a consequence the fully developed industrial systems find themselves subjected to rapidly spreading public and private controls.

Again, transition from the second to the third stage was gradual.
Even if the international conflagrations of the twentieth century
offer the annalist a convenient caesura, the roots of the major

changes lie far back in the nineteenth century. This is especially true of the rise of social, as distinguished from technical, impediments to the system's mobility. Certainly social legislation, monetary and banking policy, protectionism, and even direct participation of governments in production were not intended as blocks to the mobility of resources. Rather these and other measures of public policy were meant to serve as instruments of stabilization, and thus as supports of the self-balancing tendencies of the market. Still, by blunting the sensitivity of buyers and sellers to changes in demand and supply conditions, they were bound to reduce the pressure of competition.

Similarly ambivalent were the simultaneous attempts on the part of the marketers themselves at mitigating unbridled competition. In spite of legal restrictions and a hostile public opinion, monopolistic forms of organization spread in the commodity as well as in the factor markets. Neo-classical theorists, in line with their classical predecessors, denounced these manipulations as economic aggression committed in the interest of sectional privileges. The parties concerned pleaded self-defense against the growing uncertainty and risks in an ever more complex industrial structure.

On the theoretical face of it the opponents to interventionism seemed to have the better argument. Such planned obstacles to mobility, even if reducing risk and encouraging equilibrating expectations in the short run, were bound to slow down adjustment and thus to increase uncertainty in the long run. Moreover, was not the high level of prosperity during the two decades preceding the First World War convincing evidence that, irrespective of short-term reversals, capitalism as steered by decentralized decision-making would always in the long run find its balance?

Such blithe disregard of recurrent vicissitudes, coupled with the theorist's advice to the ruined investor to let bygones be bygones, did not sit lightly with the trustees of heavy investment outlays nor with the governments that had to defray the rising social costs of the "transitory frictions." Their mood is well illustrated in Keynes's famous slogan that "in the long run we are all dead." In a Europe suffering from the aftermath of the First World War, the broadening of interventionism could still be construed as a temporary expedient and even as a means to the end of restoring the conditions necessary for a return to market autonomy, domestic and international. The real blow to the confidence in the "conventional wisdom" was administered by the Great Depression, followed by a decade of stagnation, which befell the one large industrial nation that had escaped the physical and political ravages of the war.

It was these interwar experiences which finally prompted some neo-classical theorists to re-examine the foundations of their reasoning. Quite different currents of self-critique, as represented by the neo-Wicksellians in Sweden, by American Institutionalism, and by a permeation of neo-classical orthodoxy with Marxist elements in Germany, found their systematic synthesis in Britain. J. M. Keynes's *General Theory of Employment, Interest and Money* marks a turning point for the science of Economics in more than one respect, and we shall have occasion to discuss his contribution at greater length.[16] What matters in the present context is his endeavor to show that the traditional framework of economic analysis is unconditionally applicable only to poor societies. To make it at least look applicable also to the wealthy societies of the twentieth century, the latter must be sustained by external forces making for steady or even accelerating growth.

Keynes's exposition is couched in terms very different from those used here. But it is easy to see that the pressures characteristic for the early phase of "poor" capitalism and also the escape mechanisms indicated above play a basic role in his analysis. As will be demonstrated below in greater detail, these two extra-systemic factors govern what for him is the strategic relationship: the interplay of saving and investment. If decentralized decision-making is to maintain equilibrium in the sense of full resource utilization, investment must be large enough to balance that part of aggregate income which marketers intend to save. Such balance and thus the maintenance of effective demand on the full utilization level is easily achieved if either the propensity to save on the part of the community is low or investment opportunities are high. The first is

---

[16] See chap. 9.

true for relatively poor societies, the second for wealthy societies so long as they have a high growth potential. But in Keynes's view it is the inexorable fate of advancing capitalism that, because of increasing wealth, the propensity to save is bound to rise, whereas spontaneous investment opportunities, owing to historical checks on the major growth stimuli, tend to rise at a much slower rate. As a consequence the equilibrium level of full utilization will prove unattainable unless it is supported by compensatory public policy.

We shall discover[17] that the singular constellation of forces from which Keynes derives his conclusions has, in fact, never materialized, and that the particular disequilibrium motion of the autonomous core process, which the General Theory describes, reproduces possible but not the actual tendencies which prevailed in the recent past. Therefore the true significance of the Keynesian Revolution lies not so much in the propositions underlying his "special" theory as in his emphasis on the motivational changes which industrial maturity and rising national wealth are likely to evoke in both consumers and investors. By relating the propensity to save to the level of real income, and by stressing the crucial role of long-term expectations for the inducement to invest, he has drawn attention to the variability of economic motivations and behavior under the influence of changes in the social and technical environment.

As a matter of fact, Keynes has not gone far enough in this respect, nor has his follower Galbraith elaborated all the repercussions of an "affluent society" on the behavior of its members.[18] It is not only the conquest of mass poverty but also the progressive limitation of competition and the rise of new cultural attitudes which together have weakened those pressures that in the past sustained a uniform extremum incentive.

Again this mutation of the environment has come about very gradually, and is still in progress. Rather than an independent development confined to the realm of meta-economic forces, this transformation is a product of reciprocal influences interacting between the economic core process and the institutional factors which

[17] See chap. 9, sec. 7.
[18] See J. K. Galbraith, *The Affluent Society* (Boston, 1958).

created the original pressures. Thus what lifted the burden of mass penury was the consummation of the Industrial Revolution through the continuous rise in productivity. And though expanding governmental intervention and self-organization of producers had been initiated as devices for the promotion of general welfare or as defenses against excessive risk, they weakened, as was already pointed out, one pressure toward extremum motivation that had hitherto acted on all strata of marketers: the edge of competition. Finally new practical philosophies, which stress security and the enjoyment of a rising standard of living, are corroding the earlier virtues of acquisitive daring and parsimony.

Less gradual was the transformation which, with the beginning of the First and with increasing momentum after the Second World War, narrowed if not closed the paths of escapement. Again it is doubtful whether the changes which Keynes holds mainly responsible for this development—a falling rate in the increase of population and the slowing down of technical progress—are the true reasons for the slackening of autonomous increases in aggregate demand. Moreover, the requirements of the newly industrializing regions of the globe seem to offer a more than adequate substitute for earlier forms of commodity and capital exports. What has changed and largely prevents these vast potentialities from materializing is the climate of confidence. Persistent international tensions and world-wide monetary instability turn investors' expectations negative even in the face of great objective opportunities, keeping the long-term rate of interest above the level which is compatible with prospective returns.

However, separate examination of the changes in action directives and expectations does not yet tell the whole story. For the sake of theoretical clarity we have found it so far advisable to distinguish between the effects which arise from the purposive and the cognitive strand of motivations, respectively. In practice the two components are subtly interrelated. Thus it stands to reason that the more vigorously the prevailing pressures turn action directives toward the extremum goal the more imperative it is for the actor to form a precise notion of the factual context in which he must act. For the modern stage of capitalism a reverse effect of expectations on incentives is more important. It makes itself felt once uncertainty about the future deepens to the point where maximization of receipts becomes a utopian micro-goal or, in other words, where a lower level of profits which can be expected with greater certainty becomes preferable to a higher but much less certain level.[19]

In the light of the changes described it would be idle to speculate what the consequences might have been for average market behavior, and thus for the survival of the market as a system of provision, had the motion of the macro-process been left solely to the free play of micro-actions. The early course of the Great Depression gives an idea what such laissez-faire would do to a mature industrial society. The fact is that varying combinations of public and private controls have created an organized type of capitalism, by transforming the economic order of every Western country into a "mixed economy," with a core process left to decentralized decision-making, and with expanding key-positions for central and sectoral control.

The over-all function of these controls can be defined as an attempt to substitute contrived sources of expanding demand for the earlier automatic escapements. The most significant instruments used for this purpose are today two: the steady rise of public demand (which by now claims everywhere one-fifth and more of total output) and fiscal and monetary policies advocated by the "New Economics" along Keynesian lines. The influence of these public policies on market organization is paralleled, though often counteracted, by private controls on the part of the large economic pressure groups. Taking the American economy as a paradigm, we find concentration of industry progressing to the point where less than a thousandth of all nonfinancial corporations hold fifty per

[19] Such influence of uncertain expectations on action directives is probably more relevant for the decisions of producers than of consumers, though the spread of installment buying also involves the latter. Quite possibly the rise of homeostatic tendencies noted above is due more to such changes in expectations than to the weakening of competitive pressures or of the traditional philosophy of accumulation.

cent of all the assets of such corporations, coupled with well-nigh
universal unionization in the industrial sector and a publicly supported farm block. Together these organized groups substitute for
the traditional "competition among the many" the "three-or-four-
person game" of countervailing powers.

In the sphere of private market control perhaps the most striking innovation is the new technique of demand manipulation, a
defense on the part of producers against the caprice of consumer
buying which reflects the new affluence of all social strata. Though
repellent to traditional standards of business ethics and taste, the
modern stratagems of sales pressure, by re-creating an illusion of
scarcity, serve to restore some sort of extremum motivation among
consumers, and thus to safeguard the traditional medium for the
interlocking of buying and selling decisions.

6. The Prospects of Organized Capitalism

A wide chasm separates the mixed systems of organized capitalism from the image of a free market kept to a path of steady
equilibration through the spontaneous interaction of innumerable
small units. An array of planning centers, public and private, is
engaged in counteracting destabilizing tendencies which the uncontrolled forces of decentralized decision-making evoke in an
environment of mature industrialism. This new environment has
itself evolved through the gradual transformation of the institutional and technological factors which had sustained the early
stage of unfettered capitalism. Steadily interacting with the economic core process, this transformation of the environment deprived,
first, expectations and, next, also action directives of their classical
determinateness. As a consequence, a veritable spectrum of behavior patterns is emerging, each line of which may well be traceable
ex post to specific conditions, but can no longer be deduced ex ante
from generally valid principles. It is the task of the new planning
centers to set limits to these varieties of spontaneous micro-behavior or even to take over their role in shaping macro-economic motion. In this manner an attempt is made to restore to the system

that minimum of stability which is necessary for the market to continue as an instrument of aggregate provision.

In fact, none of these changes has so far violated the basic integrity of the market system. Most expert observers admit that the prevailing techniques of public control—fiscal and monetary policies and public demand—do not seriously interfere with the allocation and productive transformation of resources or with the order of distribution as inherited from the past. Though setting definite limits to decentralized decision-making, the so-called indirect controls of the modern mixed economies have left their operation practically unimpaired. And yet there are ominous voices warning us that the present balance between decentralized and centralized decision-making is inherently unstable and that organized capitalism is only a passing stage on the "road to serfdom," namely, to the direct and total controls which define a collectivist order. What weight should be given to these forebodings?

At first sight, experience of the recent past seems to pronounce a verdict which contradicts these fears. In varying combinations the planning techniques applied in the Western countries since the Second World War have been largely associated with an equilibrating trend, moreover a trend which everywhere shows a sustained rise in aggregate per capita output. Thus the available evidence seems to suggest that organized capitalism, as we know it today, is in principle capable of reconciling technological dynamics and growing abundance with relative stability of employment and output, though perhaps not of prices.

However, we must be careful not to interpret concurrence as a causal relationship, but to give due weight to the exceptional circumstances which have marked the postwar period. Reconstruction and modernization of the war-torn European economies and the satisfaction of pent-up demand in the New World induced a worldwide investment boom during the first decade of peace. These spurs were reinforced by rising military expenditures and other types of public demand. Nor can it be disregarded that, since the mid-fifties, there have been signs of a gradual exhaustion of this extraordinary momentum. Though no serious depression has so far shaken the countries of the Atlantic Community, its most powerful member finds it increasingly difficult to assure steady utilization of capacity and full employment.

But so far we have spoken of symptoms only, without considering the underlying forces on whose operation equilibrating or disequilibrating motion depends. Here the crux of the problem is the effect which the indirect controls of organized capitalism have on the formation of motivational and behavioral patterns in the rigidified environment of mature industrialism, more and more deprived of automatic escapements. In this respect our earlier review of postwar experiences does not inspire much confidence.[20] Neither the built-in stabilizers of the modern fiscal systems nor all the other stand-by measures of anti-cyclical policy have proved very effective, least so as stimulants of investment. As a matter of fact, the major counteracting force was already at work thirty years ago when the New Deal Administration tried to combat the Great Depression by a policy of compensatory spending, anticipating that such a spur to aggregate demand would encourage resumption of private investment. The attempt proved abortive, largely because profound distrust in the long-term consequences of deficit spending raised rather than reduced the uncertainty of investors' expectations.

In a future emergency a public spending program is likely to find a more positive response, since the role of an unbalanced budget under conditions of all-around idleness of resources is now better understood by investors. But would we for this reason be prepared to make a definite prediction of the consequences which the foreseeable large increase in the labor force during the 1960's is going to have for employment and output?

Certainly a large labor supply offers to the private sector of the economy ample opportunities for spontaneous expansion—but will investors make use of them? This will depend on their expectations concerning the level of future demand. However, such demand will itself be largely a function of the very same investment decisions —a vicious circle which only a widening of controls or a vast expansion of public demand seems to be able to break.

[20] See chap. 2, sec. 6.

Even if its content is speculative, this example has paradigmatic significance. It points to a problem which, though always present in a growing industrial market, acquires critical dimensions once the risks of technical immobility are no longer compensated by the opportunities which automatic escapements offered in the past.

It is a truism that investment in any one line of production is profitable only if, simultaneously with the addition to aggregate output, an equivalent addition is made to effective demand. J. B. Say, a hundred fifty years ago, tried to argue in his famous Law of Markets that such symmetry between changes in supply and in demand is always assured, because the remuneration of the additional resources employed in producing the additional output must necessarily equal the additional costs and thus provide an adequate minimum revenue for the producer. In this sense supply was held always to create its own demand. Marx and after him Keynes objected that such necessary equality between *income* and outlays need not necessarily equate *expenditures* with outlays, since part of the additional income may be saved. Well-founded as this criticism is, it does not by any means go far enough. Even if the total increment of income arising from additional investment is always and immediately spent, *prima facie* such investment seems profitable only if the additional demand directs itself toward the additional output issuing from this very investment.

Now, whether this first impression is correct depends on the state of resource mobility. In the market structure of classical capitalism largely free of inescapable fixed costs, with which Say was concerned, the *qualitative distribution* of demand among the sectors of production was of little concern. Even if, an extreme case, none of the additional purchasing power was spent on the output of the particular sector in which it was created, resources could always shift toward the sectors favored by the additional demand without involving the disfavored sector in any but short-run losses.

The technical immobilities of mature industrialism present a radically different situation. To the extent to which resources are technologically prevented from moving out of a given employment —a condition which prevails for most specialized equipment and for large strata of the labor force—investment, namely, the application of these resources, is a serious risk. It will be undertaken only if the investor has reason to expect a rise in aggregate demand, much larger and quite independent of the addition to aggregate purchasing power which he himself can provide. The problem is the reverse of the danger of oversaturation discussed earlier,[21] when simultaneity of *identical* investment decisions in one and the same sector of production threatens oversupply. And its solution lies in the simultaneous launching of a number of *complementary* investments, creating an entire new circuit of buying and selling in which the additional income receivers in each firm become additional customers for all the others.[22]

Such mutuality or solidarity of decisions is crucial for all so-called autonomous investments undertaken in anticipation of a future rise in demand rather than in response to a present rise. In the latter case price rises serve as guides to profitable expansion. But there are no signals that could direct the autonomous investor to the satisfaction of a demand which will only arise as a consequence of his or someone else's investment.

A major task of such antonomous investment has always been the steady absorption of productive factors into income and demand creating activity. But the magnitude of the problem to be faced in the future will exceed anything experienced in the past, owing to the rapidly swelling numbers of seekers of employment. Reference was already made to the rising rate of the natural influx into the labor market. But the main challenge will come from the laborsaving effect of the "cybernetic revolution" and from the growing shift of mass demand from goods to services. So far the initial result of the former has been the denial of employment opportunities to newcomers rather than the displacement of old-timers. But there is little reason for complacency once the pace of

---

[21] See sec. 4 of this chap.

[22] Oddly enough the problem and its solution have received much attention in connection with the "take-off" and "balanced growth" of underdeveloped regions. (For a survey of this discussion, see, e.g., Benjamin Higgins, *Economic Development* [New York, 1959], chap. 16.) But it is rarely seen that the problem confronts sizable private investments also on the level of industrial maturity, once the automatic forces making for sustained growth slacken.

automation accelerates. The structural change in demand, on the other hand, is bound to check the expansion, if not actually to curtail the employment capacity of the staple industries, enforcing large sectoral and regional migrations and also degrading traditional skills. Suppose finally that these intra-economic upheavals coincide with a political *détente* followed by partial disarmament and a drastic reduction of public expenditures—can we really be confident that the present arsenal of indirect controls will measure up to the task of absorbing such violent shocks and of maintaining the system's long-term economic and social stability?

7. *Economic Science and the Future of Organized Capitalism*

For a second time we have been trying to improve our understanding of traditional theory by an appeal to facts. Originally we did so by subjecting its motivational and behavioral hypotheses to an empirical test. When this test failed, the question arose whether perhaps the frame of reference within which orthodox theory argues was too narrow. In this frame the intra-systemic processes were insulated conceptually from all extra-systemic influences—a faithful imitation of the standard procedure in the physical sciences. As a consequence the motivational hypotheses acquired the status of immutable constants, a position which is clearly denied to them in everyday observation. But these very observations suggested an alternative procedure. Instead of isolating the economic core process by methodological fiat, its relationship to the social and technical environment has now been explicitly included in the analytical setup. This has enabled us not only to conceive the motivational forces as variables but also to gauge their strength and direction under varying conditions.

Our survey of capitalist evolution has shown that such extension of the analytical frame of reference is useful. Keeping in mind our earlier reservations to imputing strict causality to the nexus between environment and motivations, we do not claim more than plausibility for our findings. But in relating the observed variety of action directives and expectations to different pressures and different states of mobility generated by different social institutions and technologies, a working hypothesis has been put forth that appears to be well confirmed by historical experience.

It is tempting to rest content with this modification of the traditional procedure and to rebuild the theory of the market on such an integration of the environment with the core process. However, two serious objections stand in the way of this solution. The first refers to the role which the extra-systemic factors assume in such a theoretical construct. They now stand in the place which was formerly held by motivational hypotheses, namely, as axioms in the deductive syllogism. But there are no better reasons for assuming constancy for the factors of the environment than for the constancy of action directives and expectations. Quite to the contrary, our historical review has pointed up the continual transformation of the environment and, accordingly, of its impact on economic motivations.

But perhaps one should not give up so easily. Could one not widen the framework of theory still further by including yet more remote factors which on their part are responsible for the transformation of the environment? In order to realize that such a program is quite impracticable, we need only remember that the *explanandum* is now the sum total of natural, social, and cultural phenomena which at any time may have affected the economic core process. It implies regress to ever more distant "causes," a regress which, though not necessarily infinite, amounts to an attempt at explaining the entire course of human history.

The second objection is even more fundamental. Suppose it were possible to establish the "ultimate" factors which, through however many chains of interactions, in every instance shape action directives and expectations and also all conceivable combinations of the two. Even in this case a universally valid theory of market processes would elude us. For perhaps the most important result of our critical survey was the insight that regular patterns of motivation and behavior and, as a consequence, the regularity of macro-motion on which such a theory is to build are conditional on the operation of a set of quite singular extra-systemic factors. Only if *specific* pressures are at work in a *particular* state of mobility are the typical actions of buyers and sellers uniquely patterned, and with them the market processes themselves. Once automatic pressures relax and mobility is impaired without compensating escapements, uniform patterning dissolves in a multitude of discordant motivational elements, with the consequence of growing "disorder" in the system at large. But order of state and regularity of motion are prime conditions for any scientific explanation and certainly for theory.

In emphasizing disorder as a possible mode of the states and processes of a market system we do not yield to flights of fantasy. Our discussion of the third stage of capitalist evolution has shown that, under modern industrial conditions, the autonomous market forces progressively subvert the orderly motion of the system. But one may ask whether there is still need for explanations and predictions of the autonomous tendencies of the market. Are not these tendencies progressively subjected to planned control, namely, to centralized decision-making, the content of which need not be inferred by scientific reasoning because it is publicly known? And, at the same time, are not the chances of successful theorizing steadily improving, as public controls render the motion of the economic system more and more immune to the motivational and behavioral vagaries of the micro-units?

Indeed the role of theory is in the process of a drastic change. Economics as a medium of passive contemplation, observing and systematizing autonomous processes, is gradually being converted into *Political Economics,* namely, into an instrument of active interference with the course of these processes. But it would be a major fallacy to conclude that, short of full collectivization, the autonomous tendencies of the processes to be controlled can be disregarded.

Precisely at this point the New Economics along Keynesian lines falls short. It has inspired practically all the measures of indirect control put into practice during the postwar era. But these measures have proved incapable of coping with the heart of the matter: the volatility of the micro-units' motivations. To overcome this impasse a theory is needed that can inform the controllers of what the responses are with which their actions are likely to meet. But not before these public actions effectively control the macro-processes does it seem possible to construct such a theory. How can this Gordian knot be cut?

PART TWO

THE LOGIC OF
ECONOMIC SCIENCE

4

A Model for the Traditional Theory
of the Market

1. *Restatement of the Problem*

Our inquiry into the present state of economic science has cul-
minated in a grave challenge. Let us retrace the major steps of the
argument so that the crucial problem appears in clear focus.

Confrontation of traditional economic doctrine with the actual
course of events in the modern industrial societies of the West has
forced us to acknowledge a widening rift between theory and observations. In itself such a discrepancy is no cause for alarm.
Similar difficulties have been encountered in practically all fields
of empirical science at some stages of their development. They
were overcome by recurrent changes of the conceptual framework,
which readjusted theory to experience.

For a strange reason this way out seems to be blocked to traditional Economics. Its underlying presuppositions, especially its behavioral and motivational axioms, have so far proved the only ones
on which a theory of economic motion could be built. This is so
because the theorems derived from these premises—summed up
in the Law of Supply and Demand—seem to describe the only
process which exhibits sufficient regularity to be accessible to scientific generalizations.

True, we also have met some unorthodox doctrines which, in
contrast with classical and neo-classical theory, have tried to account for certain "irregularities" of motion. However, our quite

cursory references to some of these tenets have already indicated what closer study of the major heretics, Marx and Keynes, will amply confirm: the greater realism in some of their assumptions has been purchased by a loss in deductive stringency that has precluded any gain in predictive accuracy. Therefore it is only fair to state that all attempts to supplement, not to say replace, traditional theory by a more realisic logical equivalent have so far failed.

While studying the historical record we began to wonder whether this failure may not be due to the nature of our object of inquiry rather than to the lack of imagination and analytical prowess of generations of researchers. But this conjecture can only heighten our discomfort. It leads to the conclusion that, once the facts disagree with the theorems of traditional Economics, it is the facts rather than the theory that are at fault. What this discrepancy points to is a measure of irregularity of motion in the modern industrial market, so large that it defies interpretation in scientific terms.[1] Whatever may have been true for an earlier era, the student of contemporary capitalism seems to be forced to join the ranks of the Historical and Institutionalist schools, which have reduced Economics to taxonomic and historical description.

All these qualms concern the realm of methodology. But behind them is hidden a most serious practical problem. It comes to light when we relate the apparent eclipse of economic theory to the levels of experience on which economic events are met with. We saw that the "facts," which traditional theory tries to systematize, are the actions of buyers and sellers and their aggregation in the macro-processes of the market. But these manifestations of reality are themselves the result of the strivings and expectations which shape marketers' behavior. It is this primary experience of the participants in economic activity that is the basic material from which the theorist abstracts his secondary knowledge.

Now, this seemingly inescapable dependence of economic science

[1] The reasons why a probabilistic approach cannot do better will be discussed in sec. 5 of this chap.

on the notions dominating economic practice creates, under the conditions of contemporary capitalism, a veritable paradox. It comes to light in the strategic role which prediction plays on either level of economic experience.

We saw that, in our concerns with the world of Man, prediction has a function as legitimate as and, in fact, much more comprehensive than it has in our dealings with the world of Nature. There prediction is confined to the reasoning process of the observer without playing any part in the world of molecules and planets, of cells and organisms that he observes. Contrariwise, on the stage of human performances the common-sense predictions of the actors enter, together with their action directives, as a major force into the social drama itself, quite independently of the ruminations of the spectators. Moreover, the scientific spectators' capacity to predict is conditional on the behavioral consequences of these primary purposive and cognitive forces. Only to the extent to which the latter achieve patterns of interlocking behavior will the ensuing macroprocesses display a degree of orderliness sufficient to permit verifiable scientific inferences.

So long as the autonomous motion of the market exhibits such regularity the economist's predictions play more or less the same role as those of the physicist: they anticipate conceptually a course of events the progress of which is independent of the observer's cogitations. But this role changes drastically once, owing to the spread of incompatible action directives and of uncertainty of expectations, marketers' behavior ceases to interlock. Then not only will the resulting macro-processes prove refractory to analysis, but they will fail in their practical function of group provisioning. And the task arises of, first of all, restoring adequate operation of the market with the help of public policy.

The major aim of such policy must be either to re-establish consistent patterns of marketers' behavior or to guide, if not to supplant, decentralized decision-making by central control. Both types of policy are conditional on the policy-maker's possessing knowledge of the prospective course of events, more accurate and more certain than the prevailing common-sense predictions of the marketers themselves. Such knowledge, however, only scientific analysis can provide.

Now, the contemporary dilemma—a dilemma no less frustrating for practice than it is for theory—can be precisely stated. If it is true that economic theory can be built only on observations of or speculations about actual behavior, and if it is also true that, to be amenable to theoretical generalizations, the patterns of actual behavior must be regular and stabilizing, the prevailing variety of conflicting action directives and the climate of expectational uncertainty are incompatible with any theory, and there can then be no scientific knowledge capable of guiding public policy in overcoming disorder on the primary level. The dilemma can also be stated in another way. We do have an economic theory, but it refers to situations in which there is no practical need for theoretical guidance, since the automatism of the system assures that all goes well. However, once this automatism begins to fail, scientific prediction turns into an indispensable condition for restoring the viability of the market process. But with the failure of the automatism the empirical basis for such prediction—the regularity of micro- and macro-movements—seems lost.

Can this vicious circle be broken? We have come to understand that on the answer to this question depends more than the scientific status of Economics. What on the surface looks like a problem in methodology really concerns the future of decentralized decision-making in the framework of modern industrialism.

This at any rate is the conclusion which the state of organized capitalism forces on the critical observer. Since causes as well as effects of the present impasse are located in the realm of practical experience, any attempt to break the circle on that level seems to be frustrated from the outset. Rather we must try to lift ourselves off the other horn of the dilemma, in searching for scientific knowledge that can be used for remodeling the field of practice. But such scientific knowledge can only be derived from a theoretical frame of reference which is less closely tied to the experience of the actors than is traditional analysis. What this frame of reference is, in what manner it deviates from the conventional procedure, and above all, what new insights it can provide will be the topic of this part of our investigation.

For this purpose we must, first of all, subject traditional theory to closer scrutiny. What interests us in this connection is not the variety of substantive propositions contained in a body of doctrine, which by now looks back over a history of two hundred years. Nor shall we pay attention to some of the critical turning points in that history, an issue which is to occupy us in Part Three. Here we are searching for certain formal principles which have ruled the logic of economic reasoning from its early beginnings. We shall try to construct a model which depicts these common features of traditional theory, stripped of all individual peculiarities that are of no importance in the present context. This will be our task in the present chapter.

However, such a model, though abstracted from past and present procedures, will prove of more than historical importance. The reason is that we shall find it open to important realistic modifications and, above all, to a basic reinterpretation of its meaning. What follows from this for the construction of a model of Political Economics, capable of reshaping the primary experience of the actors and thus of rebuilding the foundations of genuine theory, will be the concern of Chapter 5.

2. *Mechanical Interpretations of Traditional Theory*

It is not really surprising that, in spite of considerable substantive differences, the logical structure of all the versions of traditional theory can be presented in one and the same model. Ultimately all of them deal with the same formal problem: how to relate the macro-phenomena of the market process—aggregate output and employment, consumption and investment, levels of prices and wages, etc.—to the motions of their constituent elements: behavior of households, firms, and productive factors. Even where interest centers exclusively on the macro-process itself, as is, e.g., the case in the theory of economic growth, the movements of that process can be regarded as fully explained only if the mode of operation of the impelling micro-forces and, especially, the manner of their integration has been demonstrated. In a word, all formal problems of market theory concern the *interaction between an aggregate and its parts.*

In speaking of a "model" for this interaction we make use of a methodological device which is widely employed in both the physical and the social sciences. It helps us to express the relations between the essential variables of a theory, rather than through an abstract calculus, concretely in terms of familiar notions with empirical content. A good example can be found in the kinetic theory of gases. There a gas is conceived as the aggregate of a large number of perfectly elastic particles, subject only to the forces of impact which they exert on one another and on the walls of the container. As this example shows, the advantages of model formation are twofold. First of all, it helps us to visualize, by way of a representable analogy, a process which itself cannot be observed. Second, and more important, when properly chosen such an analogy in terms of the familiar may offer a clue to the explanation of an unknown phenomenon: in the case of the behavior of gas molecules by reference to the known laws of Mechanics.

Few of the social phenomena which are relevant for the formation of an economic theory, such as incentives, expectations, or even the "meaning" of overt action, are accessible to observation. Therefore it is only natural that from its earliest beginnings Economics should have availed itself of model formation as an analytical technique. But at closer inspection one is struck by the nature of the analogies which have become typical in economic reasoning.

Obviously the device of model formation is not without pitfalls.[2] Hardly ever do two phenomena coincide in all respects, and there is always the danger that some incongruous features of a model are imputed to the theory it tries to represent. For this reason, in the

---

[2] For a careful evaluation of the procedure, see Ernest Nagel, *The Structure of Science,* pp. 90–97, 107–117.

study of nature the analogical use of concepts and larger systems is generally confined to one and the same domain of inquiry, such as Physics, Chemistry, or, at most, to the physical sciences as a whole. In the same vein one would expect that economists would use for their market models notions which are either universal in social experience or have served successfully as explanatory hypotheses in some other realm of social inquiry, such as Sociology or Political Science. That this is not so, a cursory survey of some representative statements, old and new, will clearly demonstrate.

We start with two well-known quotations. In one of the first systematic descriptions of the market process which we possess Adam Smith speaks of the market price of any commodity as "continually *gravitating*, if one may say so, toward the natural price."[3] Seventy years later J. S. Mill discussed production, distribution, and exchange in terms of what "by a happy generalization of a mathematical phrase has been called the Statics of the subject," to be followed by "a theory of motion—the Dynamics of political economy."[4]

That more than a mere figure of speech is implied in these mechanical analogies is shown by Mill's insistence that the only proper analytical technique for handling economic problems is the "physical, or concrete deductive method," as applied in Astronomy.[5] More explicit reference to a particular mechanical model was made thirty years later when Jevons postulated that

the Theory of Economy . . . presents a close analogy to the science of Statical Mechanics, and the laws of Exchange are found to resemble the laws of Equilibrium of the lever as determined by the principle of virtual velocities.[6]

At about the same time Walras presented the first fully elaborated mathematical model of the market, proclaiming that the

---

[3] See *Wealth of Nations,* p. 59 (italics added).
[4] See J. S. Mill, *Principles of Political Economy* (London, 1848), Book IV, chap. I, par. 1.
[5] See J. S. Mill, *System of Logic,* Book VI, chap. IX.
[6] See H. S. Jevons, *The Theory of Political Economy* (London, 1871), Preface.

pure theory of economics is a science which resembles the physico-
mathematical sciences in every respect, [and is in fact] a physico-
mathematical science like mechanics or hydrodynamics.[7]

Still more instructive is Marshall's use of a mechanical analogy
in interpreting the specific manner in which the micro-forces of the
market integrate themselves into a macro-state of a stable equilibrium:

When demand and supply are in stable equilibrium, if any accident
should move the scale of production from its equilibrium position,
there will be instantly brought into play forces tending to push it back
to that position; just as if a stone hanging by a string is displaced
from its equilibrium, the force of gravity will at once tend to bring
it back to its equilibrium position.[8]

Perhaps the most ambitious enterprise in analogical reasoning
is a recent attempt to reproduce Walras' and Pareto's theory of
general equilibrium with the help of models of Thermodynamics
and Statistical Mechanics.[9] But there is no need for multiplying the
evidence, since the widespread use of mechanical analogies in economic model-building is not only generally acknowledged but has
for more than a century been the subject of a major controversy.
To quote a counsel for the defense, take the following plea for the
unity of science:

. . . the conceptual devices sketched (to wit: statics, dynamics, equilibrium) have nothing to do with any similar ones that may be in use
in the physical sciences . . . they embody nothing but habits of the
human mind that are as general as ordinary logic. . . . Since the
physical sciences and mechanics in particular were so much ahead of
economics in matters of technique, these conceptual devices were consciously defined by physicists before they were by economists so that
the average educated person knows them from mechanics before he

[7] See Leon Walras, *Elements of Pure Economics,* p. 71.
[8] See A. Marshall, *Principles of Economics,* pp. 345–346. See also Walras,
op. cit., pp. 109–110.
[9] See Jacques Dumontier, *Equilibre Physique, Equilibre Biologique, Equilibre
Economique* (Paris, 1949), Part II.

makes their acquaintance in economics, and hence is apt to suspect that they were illegitimately borrowed from mechanics.[10]

But there are dissenting voices asserting that

many of the current disputes with regard to both economic theory and economic policy have their common origin in a misconception about the nature of the economic problem of society. This misconception in turn is due to an erroneous transfer to social phenomena of the habits of thought we have developed in dealing with the phenomena of nature.[11]

Finally Marshall, who invented the pendulum analogy, really favored an alternative model but one which, no less than the mechanical model, draws its concepts from a subsocial domain:

The Mecca of the economist lies in economic biology rather than in economic dynamics. But biological conceptions are more complex than those of mechanics; a volume on Foundations must therefore give a relatively large place to mechanical analogies . . .[12]

We cannot avoid taking a stand in this controversy if we want to grasp the significance and limits of traditional theory in tackling the underlying part-aggregate problem. Is it true that the concepts and the mode of their linkage, both apparently borrowed from Mechanics, reflect only the universality of scientific logic? Would an organismic schema, as Marshall suggests, be a superior explanatory device? Or is it the lack of a genuinely *social* model that is responsible for the failure of the tradition to meet the challenge of contemporary experience?

3. *Valid Mechanical Analogies*

The first step toward an answer to these questions must be to examine whether there is a "zone of analytical validity" of mechanical models, that is, whether there are any features of traditional

---

[10] See Schumpeter, *History of Economic Analysis,* p. 965.

[11] See F. A. Hayek, "The Use of Knowledge in Society," *American Economic Review,* vol. 35 (September, 1945), p. 520.

[12] See *Principles of Economics,* pp. xiv and 764–769.

theory which can be properly described in mechanical terms. Let us state once more that, at this stage of our investigation, we are not concerned with the *empirical validity* of traditional theory but with its *logical structure*. It may turn out, as Schumpeter suggests, that mechanical analogies perfectly simulate traditional economic reasoning. This in itself would neither establish nor abrogate its claim of being able to explain the actual course of economic affairs. Only a separate inquiry into the relationship of the logic of economic reasoning—mechanical or otherwise—to the "logic of events" can decide this claim—a crucial inquiry but one which must be postponed until the traditional mode of thinking itself has been fully clarified.

For this purpose we must cut through the imagery of the specific statements cited above to certain fundamental hypotheses which underlie the theory of Mechanics as a whole, hypotheses which must be compared with basic explanatory principles of the theory of the market.

There are indeed three such hypotheses, all of them cornerstones of Classical Mechanics, which have a logical counterpart in traditional Economics. One concerns the structure of the elements—the ultimate "state of matter"—of which the universe to be studied is composed: *the atomic hypothesis*. Another one, the economic meaning of which we have already discussed at length, concerns the mode of behavior of the "atoms": *the extremum principle*. Finally, there is a *conservation hypothesis* and the related postulate of the "closure" of the system, from which follows the calculability of intra-systemic motions. What is the significance of these hypotheses for the theory of the market?

It has become a commonplace in economic analysis to speak of *"atomistic competition."* This concept refers to the "perfect" order of the market in which large numbers of small and independent units buy and sell homogeneous and divisible commodities and services. Smallness and independence of the units in particular are to exclude any noticeable influence on the part of individual buyers or sellers on price and aggregate output.

At the same time the units bought and sold—be they commodities or factors of production—can be interpreted as comparable quantities of "economic energy" measured in terms of relative prices. Since the prices of the outputs are, at least in the long run, governed by the prices of inputs, and the major price-bearing inputs—labor and capital—can within wide limits serve as substitutes for each other, the qualitative differences among commodities and factors vanish in the dimension of market relations—another property of an atomic structure. As in Mechanics we seem to deal with an order of pure quantities, for the analysis of which mathematics appears as the appropriate tool.

In now turning to the *extremum principle,* which traditional theory postulates as the universal action directive underlying market behavior, we can interpret it as the economic equivalent to the principle of least action and other extremum principles established for different branches of Physics.[13] But there is more to such a comparison than the applicability of the calculus of variations in both sciences. The principle illuminates another aspect of the atomic hypothesis, by pointing to a genuine affinity between physical mass points and market units as conventionally conceived. What is at stake has best been formulated by Professor Knight:

The "economic man" is not a "social animal," and economic individualism excludes society in the proper human sense. Economic relations are *impersonal.* The social organization dealt with in economic theory is best pictured as a number of Crusoes interacting through the markets exclusively. . . . The relation is theoretically like the "silent trade" of some barbarian peoples.[14]

In other words, in a free market system the partners in exchange are to regard one another as "data" inaccessible to mutual influence, though each partner is supposed to know about the others all he needs to know for his own behavior to interlock. As is the case in Newtonian Mechanics, each unit of economic matter is and remains independent of any other unit, meeting these other

[13] The label of "lex parsimoniae," which was attached to these physical extremum principles during the period of the Enlightenment, raises an interesting question of priority.

[14] See F. H. Knight, *The Ethics of Competition* (New York, 1951), p. 282 (author's italics).

units in purely external relations analogous with push and pull. Their inner constitution as revealed in action directives and expectations is not to be affected by such encounters.[15]

But even if the structure of the market is atomic and is exposed to the universal operation of the extremum principle, it forms a determinate system only if the aggregate of elements is finite and constant or if possible changes are themselves subject to calculation. Therefore the economic universe must either be closed or must expand and contract in a predictable manner.

Here a principle of *conservation* becomes crucial, and its validity has always been taken for granted. From the early beginnings when the ultimate economic matter was defined as "the sum total of the annual produce of the land" (Quesnay) or as the "fund" constituted by "the annual labor of every nation" (Smith), the market process was understood as the circulation and transformation of an indestructible aggregate of energy. Say's Law quoted earlier, according to which supply creates its own demand, is perhaps the most striking conclusion drawn from the postulate of conservation of economic energy. Considering further that economic matter in terms of the original factors of production—labor and natural resources—needs continuous replenishing, the system within which the energy total is conserved includes the sources of factor supply.[16]

[15] The underlying notion has been formalized in the concept of "parametric behavior." See T. C. Schelling, *The Strategy of Conflict* (Cambridge, Mass., 1960), pp. 86–87, note 3, and the writings quoted there.

[16] This account of a parallelism between certain principles underlying both Economics and Mechanics is at variance with the inferences which F. C. S. Northrop has drawn from his review of the same problem (see his *The Logic of the Sciences and the Humanities,* chap. XIII). He failed to discover in the contemporary theory of economic statics either an objectifiable "state of matter" or any "conservation law." Therefore he was forced to conclude that within this analytical framework no theory of dynamics, understood in the wider sense of a theory of motion, can be constructed.

The reason for this negative result lies in the fact that Northrop defined the economic universe in the terms of "classical Austrian Economic Theory." It is indeed true that the purely subjective valuations, on which this particular theory builds, do away with any "public postulated objects with *specific* [author's italics] . . . properties." This makes it impossible not only to define the state of the system for any given moment but also to predict any motivational or behavioral responses to change.

4. *The Explanatory Gap in Mechanical Analogies*

Our first step has yielded quite promising results. There is indeed a zone of analogical validity within which certain physical hypotheses are helpful in elucidating basic propositions of traditional economic theory. Still, we must ask, are these hypotheses sufficient to describe among themselves *all* the essential characteristics of this conceptual scheme?

Let us for this purpose examine more closely Marshall's comparison of the equilibrating tendencies in the market with the oscillations of a pendulum. At first sight the analogy seems perfect. In both cases we deal with conservative systems isolated by practical or mental experiment, moving under the impact of formally identical forces of "gravitation" and displaying the features of atomism described above. As a consequence, in Economics as in Mechanics, equilibrium proves stable: any "accidental" dislocation of the quantities demanded or supplied from their equilibrium position stimulates compensating forces which "push back" these quantities to their initial size.[17]

Marshall's emphasis on equilibration and stability is fully justified. Since the theorems of traditional Economics describe that particular order of the market in which spontaneous adjustments achieve aggregate maximum provision through time,[18] only such mechanical systems can be used as analogical models which display a similar order of equilibrating self-regulation. But can one for this reason say that return to the initial position—the essence of the pendulum motion—defines the essence of the market process?

The market could hardly serve as an instrument of provision if any distortion of an original equilibrium between demand and

By subsequently demonstrating the purely tautological character of the Austrian theory of value if taken literally, and by offering an alternative interpretation for it (see chap. 8), we shall be able to reconcile Northrop's position with the statements in the text.

[17] For a comprehensive study of the stability conditions of economic equilibrium, see P. A. Samuelson, *Foundations of Economic Analysis* (Cambridge, Mass., 1947), IX and X.

[18] See chap. 2, sec. 3.

supply were always followed by a restoration of the initial state.
Rather the fundamental law of market motion, the Law of Supply
and Demand, postulates adjustments of a much more complex nature. First of all, the initial disturbance—a change in the quantity
demanded or supplied—is not to be interpreted as an "accident,"
as stability analysis does, but as a systematic stimulus. Second, the
terminal state of equilibrium which the Law predicates is by no
means identical with the initial one: the "forces" stimulated by
the initial disturbance are supposed to respond to, say, an increase
in demand not by a countervailing decrease in demand but by an
increase in supply. As a consequence the micro-structure of the
terminal equilibrium differs characteristically from that of the initial
equilibrium, namely, by a change in the relative distribution of inputs and outputs over the sectors of production.

Obviously this notion of equilibration is more inclusive than the
notion current in Mechanics. Moreover, the mechanism which answers a change in demand by a change in supply or conversely is
radically different from the mechanism which assures "stability" in
the physical model. As Professor Nagel shows,[19] the physical
stability mechanism describes situations in which the restoring pull
is directly related to the disturbing push. Given, as in the pendulum
example, the strength of the latter, the former must be of equal
magnitude, because the gravitational pull is uniquely determined
by the impulsive force.

In contrast with this setup, the change of the forces making for
a change in supply which is supposed to compensate for the preceding change in demand is quite independent of the forces causing
the change in demand itself. Complete knowledge of all the forces
operating on the demand side—action directives and expectations
—tells us nothing of the strength and direction of the forces active
on the supply side. And this dissociation of the response from the
stimulus, the major difference between the motion of the pendulum
and the adjustment processes in the market, is so crucial that the
manner in which the compensating force does arise is the very

[19] See Ernest Nagel, *The Structure of Science,* pp. 411–421.

issue on which all explanations of the part-aggregate relationship in Economics center.

What holds for the pendulum is, in fact, true of all physical and chemical processes.[20] None of them offers a model in which the autonomous movements of the parts do more than maintain a preordained state of aggregate equilibrium. Nor does the structure of equilibrium itself change in accord with changes in the environmental stimuli. To find an analogy for such internal shifts in the equilibrium structure we must advance beyond the Physics of "non-organized entities," classical or statistical.[21]

5. *The Engineering Model*

The processes which naturally suggest themselves for this purpose fall in the realm of Physical Engineering.[22] Rather than studied in isolation, such engineering processes are investigated in an organized sequence, itself governed by an engineering *goal* which this particular arrangement of the parts is to achieve. In principle any pur-

[20] The exception is Field Physics. See note 22, p. ff.

[21] In this connection it is essential to realize that the model of Statistical Mechanics referred to earlier proves equally unsatisfactory. It is true that, other than the pendulum model, it poses the part-aggregate problem quite explicitly. And it has indeed proved possible to relate temperature and other properties of the macro-state of a gas to the mean kinetic energy of the molecules of which it is composed. However, such reduction of a macro-state to micro-motions succeeds only when some additional statistical assumptions concerning the positions and momenta of the molecules are added. In other words, in this theory certain stable probability distributions concerning the "independent" behavior of the molecules take the place of any logically and empirically prior principle of organization which would regulate their behavior systematically.

In order to apply this model to the theory of the market one would have to frame corresponding statistical assumptions for the behavior of the micro-units, assumptions which should subsequently be confirmed by agreement between the computed mean values referring to the micro-order and measurable quantities of the macro-order. The fundamental reason why so far no one has succeeded in doing this will presently come to light. See sec. 5 of this chapter.

[22] One might, first of all, think of Field Physics. Indeed an electromagnetic field is the purest, namely, entirely autonomous model of organization in the sciences dealing with inorganic matter. But it lacks the feedback characteristics which, as we shall presently see, are indispensable for depicting the part-aggregate relations as formalized in the theory of the market.

poseful action exhibits this general feature of "directive organization."[23] It takes on material form in the designing of a machine,
which harnesses an entire set of elementary natural forces and the
laws which they obey, for a "goal-adequate" performance.

At this point it is important to define once more our problem.
We are searching for a physical model of self-regulation, in which
a system spontaneously adjusts to varying stimuli in the environment, absorbing them by internal shifts in the structure of equilibrium. Now, by no means do all engineering devices fall in this
category. All those must be excluded which bear a "linear" character, such as a clock or a bicycle. In such contrivances directive
organization produces effects from which there is no spontaneous
redress. Take a bicycle. Once it deviates from the perpendicular
position in which alone it can operate, the mechanism itself does
not release any compensating forces which would restore balance.
To achieve such a feat of self-correction, a machine must be
equipped with a different type of mechanism, namely, the "circular" type which has recently come into prominence under the
label of "feedback" mechanism.

A feedback mechanism is a directive organization in which a
set of causes operating at time (1) produces an effect at time (2)
which in turn reacts back on the original set of causes at time (3).
Expressed in physical terms, the initial transfer of energy from some
input is followed by a re-transfer to the system of some or all of the
output in the form of a new input. Of special interest for our concerns is the application which this model has received in the modern
theory and technology of communication.[24] Emphasis is there, not
on the backflow of energy in general but on the signal function of
such backflow in evoking impelling or impeding forces.

Several models depicting such processes of communication have
been offered in recent years as paradigms for market processes.[25]

[23] The term has been taken from E. Nagel, *op. cit.*, p. 417. See also E. S.
Russell, *The Directiveness of Organic Activities* (Cambridge, England, 1945).
[24] See Norbert Wiener, *Cybernetics* (New York, 1948), esp. chap. 4.
[25] See Arnold Tustin, *The Mechanism of Economic Systems* (Cambridge,
Mass., 1953). For an application to business cycle theory, see Richard M.
Goodwin, "Econometrics in Business Cycle Analysis," in Alvin H. Hansen,
Business Cycles and National Income, pp. 436–459.

Perhaps the most illuminating analogue is the thermostat, for the operation of which we quote the following description:

There is a setting for the desired room temperature; and if the actual temperature of the house is below this, an apparatus is actuated which opens the damper, or increases the flow of fuel oil, and brings the temperature of the house to the desired level. If on the other hand the temperature of the house exceeds the desired level, the dampers are turned off, or the flow of the fuel oil is slackened or interrupted. In this way the temperature of the house is kept approximately at a steady level.[26]

Is not indeed all we need, in order to transform the above account into a statement of the Law of Supply and Demand, the substitution of "quantity demanded" for temperature desired, of "price" for damper, and of "quantity supplied" for flow of oil? In either case we begin with an initial disequilibrium—in the one instance between the level of temperature established by a given flow of fuel and the desired level of temperature; in the other between the level of demand for goods as satisfied by a given flow of supply of goods and the desired level of demand. Such disequilibrium brings a mechanism into operation—opening or closing the damper; raising or reducing price. This mechanism then restores equilibrium by inducing a change in the flow of fuel or of supply of goods.

At the same time the analogy brings home the important fact that circularity of motion as such is not enough to assure the more comprehensive order of stability which is characteristic for successfully operating feedback systems, namely, equilibration in the sense of autonomous adjustment to changes in the environment. To achieve this, the critical signal which connects output with input must induce a distinct type of response, and must on its part vary in a specific manner whenever the objective conditions change. If in the above example the desired level of temperature or goods supply lies, to begin with, above the actual level, and such a gap were to induce the closing of the damper or a fall in price, and if in turn these responses were to cause a reduction in the flow of fuel

[26] See Norbert Wiener, *op. cit.*, p. 115.

or goods supply, the original gap would be widened rather than closed. On the other hand, in order to prevent overheating or a glut in the market, the gradual closing of the original gap must evoke such motion of damper or price as will prevent further increases in fuel or goods supply. In a word, to assure the stability of the feedback mechanism, the successive movements of the parts must be compensatory or "negative," that is, gap-reducing.

Trivial as these considerations may appear on the level of daily experience, they are by no means so in the context of a theory of Engineering or Economics. They teach us that the operation of neither the "heating machine" nor the "goods provisioning machine" can be explained on the basis of any laws which describe the behavior of its parts *considered in isolation*, be it the motion of the lever or possible relations between price and supply. In order to understand the principles which make such machines "work," we must know specific *rules of organization*. Only from such rules can we learn (1) why such and no other items are chosen from the universe of available elements; (2) the specific spatial and temporal order in which these items are to be arranged as "members" of a whole rather than as parts in a randomly assembled aggregate; and (3) the required direction of the movements of these members.

What such a rule of organization amounts to can easily be demonstrated on the thermostat. Among the "parts" necessary for its construction we can enumerate such items as the furnace, fuel and a receptacle for its storage, pipes, etc. and, in particular, those items which concern the servomechanism itself: a regulatory dial, a damper, and an "actuator" which, e.g., expands or contracts with changes in temperature. Before construction begins, these and other parts lie around most likely in random fashion. But it is the essence of construction, and even of the preceding stage of blueprinting, that they be arranged in a definite spatial order with a "closed sequence." It is in and through this sequence that the operational principles of the machine regulate the succession of the movements of the parts in such a manner that the negative responses of the feedback are assured.

Now, it is of the utmost importance to realize that such organizational rules cannot be reduced to more elementary principles. They are original determinants of the motion of the parts. In particular, to use Warren Weaver's formulation,[27] they cannot be inferred from the relations between the constituent variables and their derivatives—so powerful a tool in the analysis of non-organized physical processes—or from the "mathematics of averages" which masters the "disorganized complexity" of systems with large numbers of variables behaving randomly. Rather these organizational rules, which determine the configuration of the parts and their relative motion, must be established in their own right. Their function is to assure not configuration and motion as such but *adequate* or *suitable* configuration and motion or "good working order," in accord with a preordained *goal:* a "desired" level of temperature or of goods provision.

To trace the organizational rules which govern a market in good working order we must, first of all, specify the properties of the over-all goal the attainment of which the respective feedback mechanisms are supposed to serve. At this point the definition of the macro-goal implied in the Law of Supply and Demand, which was above elaborated in agreement with modern Welfare Economics,[28] proves useful. It describes a state of maximum provision with taste-adequate goods and services, to be achieved through the full and technically most efficient use of available resources, the resulting outputs to be distributed in proportion to the inputs.

This formulation of the goal guides us in *selecting,* from the universe of socioeconomic facts, those *"items"* which are *relevant to goal attainment*: the members of a social group, perceived not in their colorful individuality but reduced to the "roles" of consumers and producers, of buyers and sellers, with all the psychological and institutional preconditions for the performance of these

[27] See Warren Weaver, *The Scientists Speak* (New York, 1947), pp. 1–13; and Michael Polanyi, *Personal Knowledge* (Chicago, 1958), pp. 174–179, 328–332, and *The Study of Man* (Chicago, 1959), pp. 47–52. Also Kurt Goldstein, *The Organism* (Boston, 1963; German Edition, 1924), especially chaps. VI, VIII, and IX, and Wolfgang Koehler, *The Place of Value in a World of Facts* (New York, 1938), especially chaps. III and VIII.
[28] See chap. 2, sec. 3.

roles; the stock of material means available and its distribution among the members; a system of communication and of sanction; a medium of exchange; and so forth. Furthermore, the social and subsocial items must adopt the *configuration* of two circular flows: a money flow of incomes—expenditures—business receipts—business outlays, which again turn into incomes; and a technical flow, moving inversely with the money flow, transforming resources into outputs which as inputs, in the form of consumption and of capital replacement, sustain the steady supply of such resources.

Even so the attainment of the over-all goal is assured only if the system obeys at the same time definite *operational principles*. They are the condition for the basic configuration to be established and maintained. Conversely, only within the configuration of the two circular flows can autonomous behavior of atomically structured micro-units oriented on the extremum principle and isolated from extraneous distortions by conservation achieve the compensatory movements of a negative feedback.

At long last we seem to have come across a model which depicts the essential features of the part-aggregate nexus of the market, as conceived by traditional theory. And we begin to understand the bias of generations of economists in clinging to that theory even after its empirical validity has become more and more doubtful. If it were true what modern "positive" economists are wont to assert, namely, that they are concerned with describing and explaining the actual motions of the market, such bias would be indefensible. But wittingly or unwittingly economic theorists have always concentrated on the conditions which keep a free market in *good working order*. And they have done so not merely, and not even primarily, for the sake of promoting welfare. Without spelling it out in so many words, they have rightly taken it for granted that good working order is the only order amenable to theory.

And we can now finally understand why this should be so. The rules of organization, from which the theory of the market is abstracted, can only be "rules of rightness." They tell us what means are adequate for the attainment of a desired goal. There are many conceivable factors which may cause the breakdown of a machine or otherwise prevent it from achieving the purpose for which it has been built. It may well be possible in each case to discover the cause of failure, and knowledge of the laws governing the parts in isolation may be the key to such discovery. But there are no "rules of disorganization" on which a general theory of "bad working order" could be built. Even if—an absurd but not a logically contradictory idea—a particular state of disorder were chosen as engineering goal, the suitable state of "disconfiguration" of the parts and the fitting principles of "malfunctioning" would have only casuistic significance.[29]

This is the reason why the "irregularities" of the market order have proved refractory to genuine theorizing. There the problem is one of explaining states and processes which do indeed fall short of optimum provision and, in particular, of maximum resource utilization. The same is true of business cycle analysis, which has as its topic the explanation of fluctuations in general activity, in contrast with the bipolar oscillations which fit into the equilibrium model. It cannot surprise us that no general rule has so far been discovered according to which amplitude and duration of the successive phases of empirical cycles could be predicted. Whereas there is only one order of the market which satisfies the conditions for optimum provision as defined by traditional Economics, there are any number of processes leading to states of more or less imperfect provision. The very multitude of rivaling hypotheses in this field, most of them quite plausible, testifies to the fact that, in Economics as in Engineering, the relationship between parts and aggregates becomes indeterminable *ex ante* outside the good working order of goal-adequate organization.

These considerations make it finally possible to dispose of an issue which has been lurking in the background ever since we had to acknowledge the empirical defects of traditional theory. It concerns the role of *probabilistic explanations* of the motion of industrial markets.

Considering the immense complexity of the causal nexus in all

[29] See Michael Polanyi, *Personal Knowledge,* pp. 328–332.

social processes, one might be willing to adopt a procedure which is less strict than deductive analysis. More specifically, one might accept the varieties of action directives, expectations, and ensuing overt actions with which observations present us as material for a sampling process. If it should then prove possible to derive from such samples characteristic frequency distributions for our behavioral premises, explanations might ensue which, though logically inferior to deductive laws, could still be practically useful for prediction.

Admittedly this procedure has celebrated veritable triumphs in all fields of the natural sciences. Therefore it is not surprising that much recent work in Economics shows a similar trend in the direction of "stochastic" analysis.[30] But on the background of what we have learned about the market as a directively organized system, it is now easy to understand why stochastic procedures cannot be substitutes for deductive analysis.

First, it is doubtful that sampling of empirical patterns of motivations and behavior will yield a probability distribution, displaying constant characteristics with a residual error small enough to be practically meaningful. At least, this is unlikely for observations which refer to the industrial markets of organized capitalism. There, as we saw, the critical variables exhibit a peculiar combination of fickleness and intercorrelation, which is incompatible with analysis in terms of either stable relationships or randomness. In other words, the micro-data fall in that statistically inexpedient range which can be defined as "semi-disorganization."

However, and this second point is decisive, even if the obstacles to a satisfactory statistical micro-investigation could be overcome, the true problem would still remain unsolved: how to arrive at verifiable *generalizations about the macro-motions* of the system. The macro-states and -processes, into which the micro-patterns stochastically established will integrate themselves, may or may not possess the characteristics of good working order. Only if they do so

[30] For a survey, see, e.g., K. J. Arrow, "Alternative Approaches to the Theory of Choice in Risk-Taking Situations," *Econometrica*, vol. 19 (1951), pp. 404–437, and "Utilities, Attitudes, Choices: A Review Note," *Econometrica*, vol. 26 (1958), pp. 1–23.

can we derive from them "laws of the aggregate." But whether they do so cannot itself be decided by statistical techniques. Only systematic knowledge can tell us which patterns are *adequate,* the kind of knowledge that only theory can provide.[31]

6. *The Organismic Model*

All the same our search for a fully congruous analogue to the self-balancing market of traditional theory is not yet concluded. Organization and operating principles of a servomechanism offer essential clues to its understanding but are deficient in two important respects.

The first point refers to the special meaning which the concept of "organization" carries in Engineering. Organization of the parts of a thermostat is the task of the designing engineer. It is he who selects from the multitude of available physical elements those which he regards as suitable for the attainment of his "heating goal"; and it is he who determines the sequence and direction of their operation. In the traditional model of the market there is no room for such an extrinsic mastermind. The design of an equilibrating market is seen as "built into" the unwittingly performed actions of the individual marketers.

True, after having constructed his mechanical device the engineer too withdraws, leaving his creation to its autonomous motions. But he does so only until further notice, that is, until receiving notice that something has gone wrong and must be set right. In the market of traditional theory a repairman has no place. Even when an active role is assigned to public policy, such policy is supposed to

---

[31] In support of this position see also Warren Weaver, *op. cit.*, p. 13. At the same time these observations are by no means meant altogether to exclude stochastic procedures from economic theory. Should it prove possible to establish "adequate" patterns of market behavior by techniques other than aprioristic postulation or stochastics—our entire enterprise is directed to the discovery of such a possibility—probabilistic procedures may well acquire an important secondary function. Even a market in good working order is likely to exhibit a considerable range of tolerance for minor deviations from the rules which adequate patterning must obey. Determining the actual range of such deviations and predicting the most probable course of the macro-process within this tolerable range will then be a legitimate task for statistical techniques.

counteract undesirable *effects* of the operation of the intra-systemic forces rather than to deflect their *systematic course.*[32]

The other point of major discrepancy between economic and engineering processes concerns the issue of "growth." This does not show so long as market analysis is confined to the short-run *shifts* of a constant stock of resources between sectors of production in accord with shifts in demand. Yet even in this case, as was mentioned earlier, the closure of the narrowly economic circuit cannot be complete. In order to assure steady operation of the system the stock of basic resources currently used up requires steady replenishment from the natural and social environment of the market. In the same sense the "loop" system regulated by a thermostat must have an opening through which a steady flow of fuel can be fed into it.

Now, either system is capable of performing motions which can be defined as expansion or growth, involving *increases in the rate of aggregate input and output*. Again, a servomechanism displays such aggregate changes only in response to discontinuous and, above all, contrived interference from without, e.g., a turn of the pointer on the dial of a thermostat. Contrariwise, traditional economic theory has always interpreted increases in the aggregate rate of output as more or less continuous processes and, moreover, as autonomous responses of the individual marketers to autonomously arising stimuli.

For both these reasons it is not surprising that, as far back as the beginning of Classical Economics, allusions were made to another feedback model, in which equilibrating adjustment to changes in the environment was maintained without the action of an extraneous directional force. This was the organismic model, an explanatory scheme for biological systems.

It was already Adam Smith who, with due reference to the physician Quesnay, his illustrious rival for the title of Father of Economics, pointed to "some unknown principle of preservation" in the human body, the economic equivalent of which he saw in the

---

[32] This is certainly true of all pre-Keynesian economic policy. Keynes's innovations themselves spring, as will be shown, from a quite different theoretical frame of reference.

effort that everyone devotes to the betterment of his condition. And in analogy with that mysterious biological force he supposed such effort not only to preserve the political body but even to heal it from the bad effects of the folly and injustice of man.[33] A similar vision found expression in the elder Mirabeau's comparison of Quesnay's Tableau Economique with the bones and muscles of the human body, not to mention the much-overworked analogy of that Tableau with Harvey's notion of the circulation of the blood.

However, even more than some of the mechanical analogies, these comparisons of economic with biological processes are little more than figures of speech. In view of the mechanistic hypotheses dominant in pre-Buffonian Biology, one may even wonder whether they meant anything fundamentally different. Nor did such analogies gain precision when, half a century later, the Romantic and Historical schools of Continental Economics used them as weapons in their polemics against the "mechanistic" and "individualistic" doctrines of the classical writers. Even Marshall did not advance much beyond the methodological declaration of faith cited above.[34]

Thus economic literature does not contain any explicitly formulated model of the organismic type. But it is not difficult to state some axiomatic principles which underlie all biological constructs and which, like the mechanical principles discussed above, seem to have a counterpart in the traditional theory of the market. They come into relief if we focus on the particular rules of organization which define organismic processes and contrast them with the rules valid for engineering feedbacks.

It is at once clear that the operation of an organism cannot be interpreted by following up the sequence of its "construction," as we do in the case of a machine. Rather one might want to say that biological entities are given to us "fully constructed." We are neither in a position to "select" from a random assembly of items those which appear to us suitable for the achievement of a goal postulated by ourselves nor is it in our power to arrange the

---

[33] See Adam Smith, *Wealth of Nations*, p. 638.
[34] See his discussion of the "representative firm" in *Principles of Economics*, pp. 459–461.

chosen "members" in a suitable spatial and temporal configuration. Thus at first sight it looks as if the only source of our knowledge of the organizational rules which determine the "good working order" of an organism is passive observation rather than active participation.

This is, of course, a trivial statement if it is to stress no more than the fact that we cannot—at least, not yet—"make" an organism in the sense in which we put together a machine. But it would be far from trivial, in fact wrong, were we to conclude that we could establish by passive observation of empirical cases what good working order "is" in Biology.

What is at stake here becomes clear when we compare biological organization with the organization of a magnetic field. If we expose a number of iron filings to the forces emanating from a bar magnet, the filings distribute themselves in a definite structural order for which immutable laws have been discovered. Though the grouping of the filings may have a certain aesthetic appeal, it would be meaningless to speak of a "good" order. This is the only order which has ever been observed, and it is the task of physical theory to formalize what has been observed. Contrariwise, organisms just as machines, and even more so, operate on various levels of performance, and the decision which of these levels should be *defined* as "good" working order cannot itself be traced back to observation. To make such a decision the observer, who may himself be "embodied" in the organism under observation, must establish criteria, which in turn must be related to some "goal" chosen by him.

It cannot be emphasized too strongly that these considerations have nothing to do with the time-honored controversy about "teleological" explanations. What we are concerned with here is those particular states and processes of an organism which, though occurring in full autonomy, cannot be singled out as "good" unless they are *affirmed by an observer*—sentient, empathetic, or scientific. Such affirmation is quite independent of our views about efficient or final causes, or about the origin of biological organization in "creation" or the laws of chance. Even if all evidence were to speak for the former alternative, it would remain an incontestable fact that organisms have been observed in many different states, from the one extreme of "perfect health" to the other extreme of "death." To single out the former state as the over-all goal, by the approximation to which we decide to judge configuration of parts and motion, does imply an extraneous act of discrimination between different sets of observed facts though it need not imply more than that. Such an interpretation goes well together with the fundamental maxim of "biological engineering" or Medicine, which binds its adepts through a solemn oath to the support of one rather than any other of the observed tendencies.[35]

The affinity of this setup with the organization of the market of traditional theory is evident. As is true of biological organization, the "selection" of the socioeconomic elements and their arrange-

---

[35] The position taken in the text is, as experience has shown, exposed to two opposite misunderstandings. Therefore it should be made explicit that it neither sides with "reductionism" nor does it presuppose one inherent "telos" of the organism.

By emphasizing the presence of autonomous tendencies in the organism as an "organized" entity, any attempt at reducing the operational principles at work to more elementary factors of, say, a physical or chemical nature is implicitly disavowed. On the other hand, the observational fact of a plurality of such inherent tendencies—the most striking one being the simultaneous presence of a tendency toward "life" and a tendency toward "death"—makes it impossible to "observe" in the behavior of the organism what can indeed be observed in a physical field: one and only one state which must be accepted as "intrinsic." Rather a "decision" is indispensable when, from the plurality of possible and even actual states, one is to be singled out as "good" or "adequate." This is not to imply that such a decision may be taken "arbitrarily" or by throwing dice. It is a choice of a goal which involves a decision on the fundamental meaning of all life processes and, for this reason, needs be vindicated on the basis of ultimate principles. But it is a choice which cannot be supplanted by ever so intensive study of the biological object.

The alternative, and it is the one chosen by most anti-reductionist biologists, is to invest one of the plural tendencies observed with the character of "essentiality." (See, e.g., Kurt Goldstein, *op. cit.,* chap. X.) Thus the essential tendencies of the organism are said to be those which serve the realization of its potentialities for "life." But in the face of its "death tendencies," to impute essentiality to the life tendencies of the organism is not an act of observation but a metaphysical fiat.

Obviously the ultimate principles on the basis of which an observer makes his extrinsic choice also bear a metaphysical character. This reduces the controversy to one of choosing the *locus* where scientific inquiry should be transcended: when the foundations are laid for scientific thinking, or somewhere in the course of specific investigations. Since transcendence in the former sense is anyhow inevitable, in the latter sense it is, if nothing else, redundant. More about this in chap. 12.

ments in a real and a monetary circular flow has resulted from a highly complex "evolution" rather than from some demonstrable fiat of deliberate planning. At the same time the "field" thus established is not governed by any equivalent of Maxwell's laws. There is no one order of market relations the perpetual realization of which can be taken for granted. Like organisms, market societies function on very different planes of achievement, accomplishing widely divergent levels of more or less taste-adequate provision and resource utilization. In gearing his theory to the working order of the "perfect" market as defined above, the traditional economist like the biologist postulates a particular state of organization as the over-all goal, though—again like the biologist and in contrast with the engineer—he may only *register* facts without trying to *manipulate* them.

The organismic model proves useful in two other directions. On the one hand, there is not only an immanent evolution which has raised both the organism and the market from quite primitive and undifferentiated states to their present complexity, but also the processes through which the micro-units in either realm establish an equilibrating macro-state are independent of any external controller. One need only compare the processes which regulate the temperature level in the animal body with the contrived mechanism of a thermostat to realize the much closer affinity of biological "homeostasis"[36] to the self-balancing tendencies allegedly built into the strivings of the individual market units.[37]

On the other hand, in the organism an external controller is absent also from its exchange of matter and forces with its surroundings, thus offering a model of self-sustaining equilibrium growth. An autonomous metabolism not merely maintains but expands the system by steadily absorbing "resources" supplied by the environment, involving the species as well as the micro-units in an

[36] See W. B. Cannon, *The Wisdom of the Body* (London, 1932).
[37] It stands to reason that these differences between engineering and biological processes would not disappear if it should prove possible to "reduce" the explanation of all *elementary* biological phenomena to the level of Physics and Chemistry. We should still be confronted with the problem of contrived versus autonomous organization.

evolutionary process. We shall see that such integration of the long-term motion of growth with short-term adjustments to changes in the environment is the essence of the classical theory of economic growth.

7. *A Hybrid Model for the Core Process in Traditional Economics*

And yet, as was said before, the organismic analogue has never found a real home in the methodology of Economics. There are at least two reasons for this. One is the relative vagueness of most biological concepts, at least when compared with the mathematical strictness of mechanical and engineering models. But the major reason lies in the fact that the organismic model fails in one important respect. If the engineering pattern, by deliberately imposing an organizational design on macro- and micro-motion, is too restrictive as an economic analogue, the organismic pattern errs in the other direction.

Homeostasis of the organism is achieved by more than one set of operational principles. Many functions can be performed in several ways; there is the phenomenon of self-regeneration of mutilated organs; and there is the wide field of morphogenetic regulation which permits, e.g., the development of a normal embryo from artificially detached germ cells.[38] No such variety of operational principles is compatible with the traditional theory of the market. The "free" decisions of marketers are supposed to issue in a monistic behavioral vector, a hypothesis which is much closer to the mechanical motions of push and pull. To make the distinction quite clear one can say: *autonomy* of market behavior interpreted as independence from an external controller—this is the meaning we shall henceforth impute to the term—is well depicted in the organismic analogy; the *direction* which traditional theory ascribes to market behavior follows the fixed course of mechanical processes.

What, then, is the upshot of our lengthy investigation? When closely analyzed none of the paradigms offered by the natural sciences prove fully satisfactory. The processes studied in classical

[38] See for the variety of operational principles in Biology, Paul Weiss, *Principles of Development* (New York, 1939).

and statistical Mechanics are defective because they lack organization in the characteristic sense of self-equilibration under the impact of changes in the environment. But the complex artifacts dealt with in Mechanical Engineering and the natural organisms explored in Biology, though in closer affinity with the organization of a free market, also leave something to be desired. The critical factor is the measure of autonomy and *spontaneity*—the latter term referring to free choice among alternative action directives—which the parts possess in these analogical models. This measure proves to be either below or above the level which is compatible with economic micro-behavior in a classical or neo-classical market.

However, we need not let the matter rest there. Instead of simply adopting or rejecting these models one by one, we can use relevant components of each for a new synthetic construct. Though such a hybrid model has no precise counterpart in the world of nature, analogues to each one of its properties can be found in some sub-human realm.

This *hybrid model of the market* borrows from both Biology and Mechanical Engineering the feature of a directive organization of the bargaining units. In addition it takes from Biology the image of micro-units acting autonomously without any deliberately imposed design for the order of the whole. On the other hand, it limits the micro-motions to the pursuit of an extremum course—a property of mechanical systems from which the model also borrows its atomic structure. To assure determinacy of motion it introduces a conservation principle, to be interpreted in biological rather than in mechanical terms. This yields an understanding not only of the steady renewal of the system's basic resources but also of its equilibrating growth. The over-all result is then a configuration of the micro-units in *two circular flows,* subject to the operational principles of *atomism, conservation, micro-autonomy,* and *extremum action.*

In elaborating this hybrid model we have completed our first task. This task has consisted in translating the essentials of the abstract calculus of traditional theory into a concrete, representable schema. Moreover, the ultimate constituents of this schema as well as the relations between them have proved amenable to interpretation in terms of concepts current in the natural sciences. Thus Schumpeter's belief in one universal method of concept formation, cited above, seems largely confirmed by our findings. Even if his one-sided emphasis on Mechanics needs to be qualified by Marshall's stress on the role of Biology, the sciences dealing with the world of the subhuman taken in their entirety seem to offer an explanatory framework for economic experience—at least for that range of experience to which traditional theory is applicable.

8. *The Hybrid Model and the Regulatory Factors of the Environment*

The reservation stated in the last remark warns us that our task is still not completed. Clearly such a reservation conflicts with the universal validity which traditional doctrine claims for its theorems, and thus implicitly also for the properties of the hybrid model which underlie these theorems as premises. However, our discussion in Chapter 3 has left no doubt that intra-systemic configuration and motion can be understood only in the context of the environmental factors which govern the structure and the forces of the core process. Thus the question arises: what are the characteristics of an environment that induces and sustains a market process as depicted in the motions of the hybrid model? And are these characteristics compatible with the origin of the hybrid model as a natural science analogue?

We already anticipated part of the answer when we realized that regularity of the structure and motion of market processes is conditional on the presence of specific institutional and cultural pressures operating in a state of near perfect mobility. As a consequence, we cannot impute universal validity to the lessons of the hybrid model unless we impute the same validity to those particular pressures and that particular state of mobility. In other words, these environmental conditions will then have to be treated as *trans-historical*, and as *irresistible* in their effect on motivation and behavior, thus eliminating true spontaneity of decision-making.

From our earlier discussion we know that they are neither. Their empirical validity, if any, is confined to a brief period of early capitalism. And the nexus between environment and motivations is not strict enough to be conceived in terms of a causality that would quite generally deprive the individual marketer of the freedom to deviate.[39]

Still, one can conceive of an extreme case in which the environment is shaped in such a manner that social and even physical survival depends on marketers behaving in accord with the pattern formalized in the operational principles of the hybrid model. Though even then no actor is prevented from preferring death to survival under constraint, the average marketer is likely to yield to such pressure in a manner analogous with a strict cause-effect response. He still retains his *autonomy* in the sense defined above— impersonal forces rather than a "controller" govern his decisions. But he is deprived of the *spontaneity* of choosing between alternative action directives.

We remember that the specific pressures at work during the early capitalist era—mass poverty, unbridled competition, and an unquestioned belief in the virtues of limitless accumulation—placed practically all strata of marketers under just such duress. Thus the claim to universal validity of traditional theory and its hybrid model amounts to the hypothetical perpetuation of an economic society *in extremis*.

But is this an economic *society?* Rather than freely and deliberately choosing between alternatives, its members are forced to respond in a pseudo-mechanical manner to pseudo-mechanical stimuli. Or to use another metaphor, they are supposed to behave like hungry rats driven through the windings of their maze by conditioned reflexes—not as men aware of a field of interaction with other men, in which all pursue freely chosen goals. Thus incorporation of the pertinent environmental factors into the hybrid model, far from contradicting its natural science origin, only confirms its affinity with the world of the subhuman. At the same time it emphasizes once more the merely marginal significance of tra-

[39] See chap. 3, sec. 2.

ditional theory as an explanatory and predictive tool, and therefore the need for breaking through a logical framework in which human action and interaction are reduced to the play of blind natural forces.[40]

And yet, when all this is admitted, the hybrid model describes the good working order of an economic system in continuous equilibration, assuring maximum provision with taste-adequate goods and services. How are we to proceed in order to surmount its shortcomings as a replica of human spontaneity, while still satisfying the conditions necessary to preserve good working order? How, in other words, can we do justice to that synthesis of freedom and order which distinguishes social interrelations from the mere sequences of natural events?

[40] A different but no less critical verdict must be passed on the model of interaction which the Functionalist School of Sociology has proposed as a replica of social and, in particular, economic systems. (See Talcott Parsons, *The Social System* [Glencoe, Ill., 1951], and Talcott Parsons and Neil J. Smelzer, *Economy and Society* [Glencoe, Ill., 1956].)

Basically the construct is a version of the organismic model, though it claims to be derived from the totality of patterns of social behavior and motivations observed. In fact, only those patterns and ensuing processes are admitted into the model which have "functional relevance" for the system, a relevance to be judged "in terms of stability or production of change, of integration or disruption" (*The Social System,* pp. 20–22).

Now, like the hybrid model of traditional Economics, the functionalist model is to serve as a tool for the explanation and prediction of actual events. But it can do so only to the extent to which the tendencies of real actors are directed toward that which is "significant" for stability and orderly change. In claiming general validity for their model the Functionalists imply a universal propensity toward social integration, disparaging as "deviant" not only individual digressions from a given behavior pattern but any alternative patterns.

Such a hypothesis may be compatible with the order of certain animal societies, but it contradicts experience on the human level, and the more strongly the higher the stage of civilization. If the hybrid model is incompatible with the social nature of Man, the functionalist model fails because it "oversocializes" him. (See Denis H. Wrong, "The Oversocialized Conception of Man," *American Sociological Review,* vol. 26 [1961], pp. 183–193.)

It is only fair to add that Professor Parsons' model lends itself to quite a different interpretation from the one he gives himself. In this interpretation the motivational and behavioral patterns described are "relevant," not as actual determinants of social systems generally but as requirements for the establishment and maintenance of a very special social system: a group which perpetuates itself through nothing but the spontaneous conformity of its members. We shall presently see that the same transformation of an allegedly general cause-effect nexus into a particular ends-means nexus bestows a new meaning also on the hybrid model of economic relations.

5

Toward a Science of Political Economics

1. *Beyond the Hybrid Model*

In pointing to the "synthesis of freedom and order" that marks genuine social interrelations we return to familiar ground. When first inquiring into the "socialization" of the technical processes which form the core of all economic activity we discovered *interlocking behavior of the micro-units* as the prerequisite for successful provisioning and thus for the establishment and maintenance of the good working order of any socioeconomic system. What imparts to this prerequisite a distinctive social quality is its origin in the spontaneous decisions of the actors. There are, in other words, neither laws of nature nor rules of engineering which would make mutual compatibility of individual actions and of the underlying motivations a matter of course. Whether aggregate order rather than disorder arises from the interplay of micro-decisions depends on adequate patterning of behavior, which in turn is contingent on affirmation freely given or withheld by the ultimate decision-makers.

At least this is true of all societies that have risen above the threshold of extremity. For this reason the hybrid model, the ideal replica of extreme economic states, cannot offer a general explanation for the socialization of market relations. Still, even extreme states are not entirely devoid of social characteristics. And the hybrid model could not depict that singular stage in the evolution of capitalism which it does depict did it not contain some latent rudiments of social traits, its essence as a natural science analogue notwithstanding.

In our search for the rules which govern the construction of a *general model* of market relations it will be helpful to trace these social rudiments of the special hybrid model by asking three questions. First, are there features in that model which are of such broad validity that they must be preserved in any market model displaying good working order? Second, does it contain properties which are exclusively associated with its empirical counterpart— classical capitalism—and which for this reason are incompatible with the varieties of action directives and expectations typical for modern industrial markets? Third, what new principles must be introduced into the model so as to make it applicable to these changed conditions?

In search for an answer to the first question—*generally valid features of the hybrid model*—we find a clue in our original distinction between the basic configuration of the data and the operational principles which govern the motion of the system. It is at once obvious that the two circular flows in which the basic configuration takes shape must remain intact in any market model that is to depict good working order. Alteration or rupture of the circular sequence of incomes—expenditures—business receipts—business outlays is bound to destroy the steady process of provisioning. So does any tampering with the flow of goods from firms to households and other firms as these goods move through the technically fixed stages and sectors of production, or with the flow of productive factors to the firms. Therefore changes in the hybrid model must be confined to one or more of the operational principles: the postulates of atomism, conservation, micro-autonomy, and extremum action.

As a matter of fact—and this leads to our second question—we know from our historical survey that in an industrial system the empirical manifestations of *all four operational principles are open to change*. But in order to recognize the theoretical consequences of such changes we must remember that the role of these operational principles in shaping the system's motion is not the same for all. The strategic role is played by the action principle, because it determines the direction in which the constituent elements move. It represents the "forces" of the system, and can for this reason be defined as the *dynamic* principle of the model. Contrariwise, the other three principles which refer to the size of the micro-units, the constancy or manner of change of the aggregate, and the *locus* of decision-making do not as such affect the motion of the system. They are part of its *structure,* influencing working order only indirectly through the effect they exert on the dynamic principle of action.

Now, it is decisive for the operation of the hybrid model that there the influence of structure on action can be treated as neutral. To be specific, two of the structural factors assume a form—atomic size of the units; constancy or steady change of the aggregate—which gives full play to the original tendencies of the action principle as they take shape under the pressure of the environment. As a consequence the third structural principle—micro-autonomy—becomes feasible, and the *locus* of decision-making can be transferred to the micro-units.

All this must change once the system assumes an industrial structure. The effect of molar organization and unsteady change on action is no longer neutral. Rather the ensuing immobilities and technological shocks—mediated through growing uncertainty of expectations—are bound to divert the extremum tendencies from their equilibrating course or even to transform them altogether. Hence decentralized decision-making by itself can no longer assure negative feedback relations. And as a general answer to our third question we conclude that the *principle of unlimited micro-autonomy must yield* to a new operational principle of decision-making.

2. *Control as an Operational Principle*

Stated in the simplest terms the issue is now one of finding a substitute for the impersonal factors of the environment—pressures and resource mobility—a substitute capable of inducing motivational and behavioral patterns which assure good working order under the changed conditions. Such a substitute can only be a personified force, henceforth denoted as *Control.*

By capitalizing the word when used in the singular I wish to emphasize the difference in function which separates Control as an operational principle from the controls of conventional economic policy. It is the essence of the latter that they take the behavior of the micro-units for granted, confining themselves to modifying the natural and institutional framework within which micro-actions take their course. Making use of a physical analogy one can say that these controls operate like an outside force which compresses or releases a spring but leaves the elastic forces in the spring itself unchanged. In contrast, Control as here understood refers to a public policy that concerns itself with the shaping of the behavioral patterns themselves—by influencing the purposive and cognitive motivations of the actors immediately, or in a roundabout way through reorganization of the system's structure.

This distinction between Control as an operational principle and the controls of conventional economic policy cuts across the dichotomy of so-called direct and indirect controls or, as I prefer to say, of *controls by command* (price, wage, or investment control, with the limiting case of full collectivization), and *controls by manipulating marketers' spontaneous actions* (banking and fiscal policy, tariff regulations, etc.). Both techniques are, in principle, suitable for Control, the latter trying to alter the direction of decentralized behavior, the former supplanting such behavior partially or totally by centralized action.[1]

Since introduction of Control violates the principle of micro-autonomy, it runs counter to the basic tenets of classical and neoclassical theory.[2] Both identify the good working order of the market with unconstrained individual decision-making. We are now in a position to reduce the fallacy, which is implied in such an identification, to the essential point.

The illusion that the so-called "free" market is sustained by the

[1] More will be said about this distinction and its relevance for a model of the modern industrial market in section 5 of this chapter.

[2] Recognition of Control "as the only practicable means of avoiding the destruction of existing economic forms . . . and as the condition of the successful functioning of individual initiative" (*The General Theory* . . . , p. 380) is the true meaning of the "Keynesian Revolution." See chap. 9.

unconstrained decisions of its members rests on the assumption that the behavioral and motivational patterns of the micro-units can be traced back to spontaneous choices among alternative action directives. This, then, suggests the traditional dichotomy between well-functioning markets—the result of such spontaneous choices—and malfunctioning markets—the result of outside constraints deflecting micro-decisions from their spontaneous course.

Our historical survey and, even more cogently, our discussion of the extended hybrid model has shown that this dichotomy is false. Indeed the market as envisaged by traditional theory is in good working order, but it is far from "free" in the sense of resulting from spontaneously chosen modal micro-goals. Rather the choice of these goals is imposed on the individual marketer by a very peculiar state of his environment. Conversely, experience during the laissez-faire stage of industrial capitalism demonstrated only too clearly that increasing spontaneity of decision-making by no means guarantees the good working order of the market. Rather the need for securing the minimum of stability required for continuous provisioning has made it imperative to counteract such spontaneity by contrived pressures of economic policy.

The true dichotomy between the possible types of industrial market organization is a different one. It places on one side a system at the mercy of truly unconstrained decision-making, constantly threatened with disorder and kept afloat only through the operation of escape mechanisms—the era of uncontrolled industrial fluctuations. On the other side are the systems of good working order in all of which individual decision-making is constrained. There, and not in the former category, belongs the system described in traditional theory. But this does not preclude the possibility that forces quite different from impersonal pressures of the environment may accomplish conformity of behavior patterns equally well if not better, namely, personified forces of Control which deliberately pursue good working order.

In speaking of the deliberate pursuit of good working order we raise entirely new problems. Not only does Control introduce into the apparent automatism of market processes a new decision-maker.

But being concerned with the operation of the system at large this decision-maker must orient himself on criteria—purposive and cognitive—which hardly ever rule the motivations of the micro-units when left to their own devices. In other words, before Control can become effective as practice a number of theoretical problems must be solved.

To begin with, the controlling authority must select the particular state which in a given case is to represent good working order—the *purposive problem of establishing a macro-goal*. Next—a consequence of this primary decision—good working order must now be defined as goal-adequate working order, and its operational principles must be inferred from the content of the respective macrogoal. Such inference proceeds in three steps. First, there must be determined the course of those processes that will move the system toward the terminal state in which the postulated macro-goal takes shape. Second, there must be ascertained the behavioral and motivational patterns which will integrate the actions of the micro-units into such goal-adequate processes. Third, after these particular patterns are known, the measures of central regulation can be specified which are likely to induce goal-adequate motivations. These three steps together form the *cognitive problem of establishing suitable motions, micro-forces, and controls*.

Traditional Economics does not offer any answers to these problems. To find such answers we shall have to adopt a different mode of inquiry, henceforth defined as *Political Economics*. It is to its exploration that we now turn.

3. *The Variety of Macro-Goals in a Controlled System*

In speaking of macro-goals we remember the apparent paradox which this notion creates in the context of traditional theory. On the one hand, it is of the essence of the principle of micro-autonomy that no one acting in the market makes any decision about, or is even aware of the existence of, an over-all goal toward which the system is to move. On the other hand, there is that particular state of macro-equilibrium defined as Pareto optimum, which modern

Welfare Economics treats not only as the objective result but also as the "purpose" of the motions in a competitive market.[3]

In fact, there is no contradiction between these assertions, once one realizes that they refer to the bearers of different "roles." The first statement is concerned with the motivations which impel the *actors* in the market place; the second statement can only be enunciated by an *observer*. As was pointed out earlier, the former are interested in surplus-yielding disequilibria rather than in an ultimate well-balanced equilibrium. It is the latter who, in evaluating a multitude of macro-states, selects one particular state as an "optimum," taking into account the relative satisfaction levels of the micro-units attainable under the given constraints. He need not be a scientific observer but may even be an actor himself. Still, in affirming as optimum the unwilled result of quite differently oriented micro-actions including his own, he changes his role from that of an "insider" to that of an "outsider." The hand may be invisible which leads every marketer "to promote an end [the public good] which is no part of his intentions." But the mind which postulates what the public good is to be can in every instance be traced back to some arbiter who places himself outside the nexus of actions.

We encountered a similar situation when looking for criteria for the good working order of an organism. Again the judge was found in a human observer who, for reasons which lie outside the biological realm, is likely to affirm as over-all goal the result of the homeostatic processes subsumed under the notion of health. As is the case in a market moving toward a Pareto optimum, such affirmation of a biological optimum in no way implicates the tendencies of the micro-units. The separation is even stricter since, without introducing dubious teleological hypotheses, nothing can be made out about any micro-goals of the biological elements.

Now let us once more consider the organization of a machine. Even less than in Biology is it possible to speak of micro-goals of the parts of a mechanical device. But the major difference concerns the macro-goal. In contradistinction with both the market and the

[3] See Koopmans, *Three Essays* . . . , p. 42. Also chap. 2, sec. 3, above.

organism, the engineering goal is not selected on the basis of observing a multitude of autonomously forming macro-states, but is set from the outside by the only actor in the organization. It is he who then creates a macro-state in the image of his macro-goal, the actor absorbing as it were the observer as the macro-goal absorbs all autonomous tendencies of the parts.

An actor setting a macro-goal and contriving its realization in a macro-state—an observer affirming as macro-goal one of many autonomously arising macro-states—an observer affirming as macro-goal that particular macro-state which arises from the actions of autonomous micro-units when they orient themselves on extremum micro-goals: these are the distinctive characteristics by which the engineering model, the organismic model, and the hybrid model of traditional Economics can be recognized. How does a market subject to Control fit into this scheme?

One might feel tempted to answer that the introduction of Control into the motions of a market transforms the economic problem into an engineering problem. The thermostat and similar servomechanisms seem now to reappear as legitimate analogues of controlled market processes. But before we commit ourselves to this conclusion we must scrutinize more closely the content of the respective macro-goals in the two fields and, in particular, the criteria for the respective optima.

Whether an engineer designs a thermostat or builds a loom, his optimization criterion is one and the same. It may take the form of producing a maximum of heat output per unit of fuel input or of approximating the specifications of the cloth designer as closely as possible. He is always concerned with achieving *maximum technical efficiency.*

Now, it is essential to remember that the same criterion plays a strategic role for the determination of a Pareto optimum in the theory of the market. This follows from the constraint which the extremum principle places on the modal choices of the marketers: they are always to prefer the larger to the smaller quantity. As a consequence the *aggregate optimum* of provision must also turn into a *maximum.* Given taste-adequacy of provision, it is the maximum technical efficiency of production, namely, the procuring of the largest possible output which in traditional theory distinguishes the perfect order of utilizing a given stock of resources from all less perfect orders of utilization.

Thus we arrive at the important conclusion that it is the hybrid model of the *uncontrolled*—even if not unconstrained—market which shares its optimization criterion with the engineering model. One might even claim that technical efficiency is more germane to the setup of the former, because it is not imposed from the outside as in Engineering but results from the autonomous tendencies of the parts. What, if anything, changes in this respect if we now introduce Control into the motion of the market?

In examining any particular instance we may find that nothing essential has changed. True, an efficiency criterion for the macrostate must now be postulated explicitly before any measures of Control can be devised. But the controlling authority may well choose maximum technical efficiency as the point of orientation for such measures. What is decisive, and indeed introduces an entirely novel constellation, is the fact that the authority *need not do so*. Quite different criteria may be selected, such as, e.g., the attainment of a more or less fixed level of aggregate or of per capita output, or the protection of immobilized resources by restricting competition or by slowing down technical progress, or conversely the acceleration of growth by overutilization of resources.

Each one of these alternatives is realistically significant. The first is characteristic of all traditionalist markets; the last plays a role in the industrialization programs of developing regions; the other two are often advocated in the interest of stabilizing organized capitalism. All of them conflict with the criterion of maximum technical efficiency as interpreted in Engineering and in traditional Economics. But they need not for this reason conflict with the yardstick of "optimum" aggregate provision. What has happened is that the primacy of the technical criterion has been superseded by other criteria.[4]

4 For an interesting attempt at defending Pareto optimality against other notions of optimum states, see Francis M. Bator, "On Capital Productivity, In-

There is no contradiction between this result and our earlier stress on the technical core of all economic activity. It remains true that, so long as the Man-Matter problem must be solved in a world of scarcity, technical efficiency of production must not fall below the level which assures *minimum* aggregate provision through time. Above this threshold, however, the scope for social as distinguished from technical criteria widens progressively. It is not at all inconsistent to ascribe "optimum working order" to an economic system which affords its members no more than a traditional standard of living, provided that this state of provision meets both the efficiency minimum and the social criteria of the controlling authority.

There are other aspects of the traditional macro-goal which are greatly modified once Control is introduced. In the conventional formulation it is not merely resource utilization that is rigidly determined in quantitative and qualitative terms, but also the state of *taste-adequate provision*. Only that state of provision is accepted as taste-adequate which agrees with the present choices of the consumers—choices which of course include future provision as presently desired by them. This cannot be otherwise as long as the micro-units are the only decision-makers in the system.

With the establishment of Control a new "chooser" appears. He may simply adopt the micro-choices of consumers as his own criterion, but again he need not do so. Provided that his "macro-scale of preferences" does not conflict with the threshold minimum of the micro-units, he is free to direct the resources available above that threshold to the satisfaction of "tastes" which form no part of any micro-scale of preferences. A major part of the so-called "public needs"—defense, conservation of resources, even education—falls in this category. Another example concerns the determination of the level of aggregate savings and investment. In many developing countries it is set by the controlling authority above the level which individual time preferences and profit expectations would

---

put Allocation and Growth," *Quarterly Journal of Economics,* vol. LXXI (1957), pp. 86–106. Since his opponents implicitly acknowledge maximum technical efficiency as the optimization criterion, Professor Bator has the better of the argument. This changes of course with a change of the criterion.

bring about. In other words, a future level of provision is decreed as taste-adequate, though it is at variance with individual tastes as presently experienced.

The criteria for the optimum degree of utilization as well as for taste-adequate allocation of resources are inevitably monistic in orthodox welfare theory. The same is true when we turn to a third characteristic of the Pareto optimum, which is traditionally defined as *functional distribution*. It is only fair to stress the fact that modern Welfare Economics no longer presents the distributional claims on total output, as they arise from the competitive bargaining of the factors of production, as an optimum of *personal* distribution. Functional distribution, as the rewards for the contribution of each factor to total output bring it about, may conflict with criteria such as justice, political expediency, or even the universal attainment of a minimum standard. In order to conform to such criteria, it is admitted that the automatic result of functional distribution may have to be modified *ex post* with the help of taxes and subsidies.

Control as defined above, namely, as a deliberate influence on the patterns of market transactions, is not confined to such *ex post* corrections. It can intervene *ex ante* in the allocative process itself through regulation of factor prices and (or) commodity prices, even if such interference with functional distribution deflects output from the optimum of technical efficiency.

We have come up with important results. Introduction of Control radically changes the limitations of the hybrid model as far as its implicit macro-goal is concerned. It substitutes for the traditional monism a pluralism of possible optima of production and distribution. Whereas the traditional criterion is basically *technical*— exclusively so in determining the degree of resource utilization and the order of functional distribution; partly even in determining tastes, since "more" is always supposed to be preferred to "less"— Control opens the door to genuinely *social* criteria. These criteria are founded in a realm that is closed to all subhuman phenomena and to the natural sciences which describe and explain them. Their content and source will be further explored when in the last chapter the question of the "vindication of goals" will be raised. At this point the emphasis is on the fact that Control, rather than approximating the movements of the market to engineering processes, is a means of exposing their inherent social character.

4. The Logic of Goal-Seeking: Instrumental Inference[5]

Inferring the means suitable to attain a postulated goal was earlier defined as the cognitive problem which a theory of controlled economic systems must solve.[6] But trying to do so we must keep in mind that we are no longer concerned with the micro-economic relationship between ends and means which is in the center of traditional theory. Both ends and means now refer to the system at large, micro-behavior being itself one of the means.

We specified the sum-total of macro-economic means as consisting of suitable motions, suitable micro-forces, and suitable measures of Control. To relate these prerequisites of good working order to the goal they are to serve, and also to one another, we shall make use of a technique of analysis which significantly differs from orthodox procedures. The simplest way of expounding it is by contrast with the conventional mode of reasoning.

Like the other sciences whose concern is with general laws, traditional Economics avails itself of the hypothetico-deductive method. Its theorems are derived in a syllogistic demonstration from a set of highest-level hypotheses the content of which we have since formalized in the configuration and the operational principles of the hybrid model. These hypotheses are the premises from which observation statements—explanations and predictions—are deduced as conclusions.

What this amounts to in logical terms can be summarized in the

---

[5] The methodological position taken in this section was first set forth in a paper on "A Reconsideration of the Law of Supply and Demand," *Social Research*, vol. 9 (1942), pp. 431–457, subsequently elaborated in my study "On the Mechanistic Approach in Economics," *Social Research*, vol. 18 (1951), pp. 401–434. The present version is indebted to the "post-critical philosophy" expounded in Michael Polanyi's *Personal Knowledge*, especially chap. 11, and to extensive discussions with my colleague Professor Hans Jonas.

[6] See sect. 2 of this chapter.

proposition that whenever theory is *applied* the inferences are from antecedents to consequents or, if we prefer, from known causes to unknown effects. This procedure must be strictly distinguished from the one by which a theory and, in particular, its premises are *established*. As we discussed at length,[7] traditional Economics asserts that these premises are either abstractions from observations or heuristic principles. However, and here we encounter our methodological problem, this was not the manner in which we came by the configuration and the operational principles of the hybrid model. Neither did we start out by sampling random observations of the factors or "causes" which determine structure and motion of empirical markets, nor did we introduce the properties of the model as freely created fictions. They were the result of an inference.[8] How is this type of inference to be defined?

When we set out on our search for a fitting analogue to traditional theory we knew nothing about any "causes," the antecedents in the deductive syllogism. Rather these causes—configuration and operational principles—were among the unknowns to the discovery of which the inquiry was directed. On the other hand, the "effect" —a state of aggregate provision specified as a Pareto optimum— was a datum, though again it was not given as a fact observed but as a postulated goal.

Such transposition of knowns and unknowns—regressive inference—with the principal known given by *fiat* rather than by observation, is characteristic for the formation of theory in all directively organized systems.[9] To elucidate this procedure we had best examine it on the more elementary level of Engineering. So we return to our former example and ask: what are the knowns or data from which the designer of a thermostat derives his blueprint?

These data can be subdivided into three categories. There is, first, the heating *goal* itself, to be specified according to such items as temperature range, area to be covered, the kind of fuel to be used,

---

[7] See chap. 2, secs. 3–5.

[8] See chap 4, sec. 5.

[9] Regressive inference as such is, of course, the logical form of induction. Why nevertheless the "logic of goal-seeking" is here distinguished from inductive logic in general will become clear as the argument progresses.

the construction material and, last but not least, the type of actuator: a fluid, a metallic strip, or a thermoelectric current. Next come certain *optimization criteria* such as maximum thermal output, minimum oscillation, minimum costs of construction or operation, etc., all of them specifications of the over-all criterion of maximum technical efficiency. Should some of these criteria prove incompatible with one another, the designer must choose between them according to a pre-established hierarchy—a reason why these criteria are often included in a wider definition of the goal itself.[10] Third, the designer must be in full cognizance of the relevant *laws of nature and engineering rules* which govern the behavior of the parts of the device and their assemblage.

It is his knowledge of the heating goal and of the optimization criteria which enables the designer to select from the body of laws and rules those which govern the particular case. These laws then determine the specific form which the relevant mechanical, thermal, electrical, chemical, etc. processes assume, with the parts of the machine as their material substrata. The selection of these parts as well as their spatial and temporal arrangement is determined simultaneously with the selection of the proper laws and rules.

Can this logical schema be applied to the manner in which configuration and operational principles of an economic model are established? The answer is affirmative. In designing the hybrid model we started out from the postulation of a macro-goal defined as the maximum level of provision with taste-adequate goods and services obtainable from available resources. In this formulation the definition of the macro-goal already contained the optimization criteria. Thus two of the aforementioned conditions have been met. But what about the third condition: is there an equivalent to the laws of nature and engineering rules which govern the behavior of an engineering device?

First of all, as far as the attainment of production goals is concerned, the very same type of laws and rules—physical, chemical, biological laws and the rules of physical, chemical, biological engineering—must be applied. This is so because the selection of goal-

[10] This was our procedure in sec. 3 of this chapter.

adequate inputs, their productive combination, the spatial and temporal disposal of outputs, etc. are, in the first instance, technical problems.[11] One can imagine the limiting case of a monolithic collectivism in which the prescriptions of the central plan are carried out by functionaries who fully identify with the imposed macrogoals. In such a system the economically relevant processes reduce almost completely to technical manipulations. And, as we have stressed repeatedly, even the market of traditional theory offers little more than technical problems, notwithstanding the "symbolic" role of prices.[12]

However, the situation changes drastically when we investigate economic systems which lie between the extremes of full collectivism and the pure market of traditional theory. Then knowledge of macro-goal, optimization criteria and the ensemble of laws of nature and engineering rules, though still necessary, is no longer sufficient for the determination of the unknowns. Now the nexus between behavior and motivations and, above all, between motivations and environmental factors—automatic or contrived ones—can no longer be disregarded, and additional laws and rules must be taken into account. Whereas the former nexus obeys ascertainable psychological laws, our knowledge of the manner in which motivations respond to impersonal pressures and personalized Control is largely conjectural, as we have repeatedly had occasion to observe. Nevertheless, though a range of indeterminacy is thus introduced into the analysis, these tentative generalizations about the influence of extra-systemic factors on economic motivations must not be ex-

[11] As we saw in section 3 of this chapter, this technical nature of production does not compel us to judge the solution exclusively by the standard of maximum technical efficiency.

[12] ". . . something like a price system is inherent in any problem of maximisation against restraints. . . . The 'logic of choice,' now that it has been fully mathematised, appears as nothing but pure technics—the distilled essence of a general technology." (See J. R. Hicks, "Linear Theory," *Economic Journal* [December, 1960, pp. 671–709, esp. pp. 706–709).] Hick's suggestion in this context that the minimax theorem of the Theory of Games might help to restore to Economics the character of a social science is very doubtful indeed since "in the minimax strategy of zero-sum game—most strikingly so with randomized choice—one's whole objective is to avoid any meeting of minds, even an inadvertent one." (See T. C. Schelling, *The Strategy of Conflict,* p. 96.)

cluded from the data if the suitability of specific measures of Control is to be evaluated.

We can now summarize our results in the following proposition. Given the initial state of an economic system, regressive inference enables us to derive the set of unknown "means": (1) macro-motions, (2) micro-patterns of behavior and motivations, and if necessary (3) measures of Control, from the knowledge of (1) a macro-goal or terminal state specified by optimization criteria, (2) laws of nature and engineering rules, (3) laws and empirical generalizations concerning sociopsychological relations.

We propose to denote this particular mode of regressive inference as instrumental analysis.[13] Its role in the study of social and, in particular, of socioeconomic processes is fundamental. It is not only that instrumental analysis is logically prior to the progressive inferences or deductive syllogisms which demonstrate the systematic processes and terminal states as effects of specified causes. But in contrast with what is customary and legitimate in the natural sciences, *instrumental inference* of these causes or highest-level hypotheses *is an ongoing task of the social theorist,* in principle to be repeated every time a particular event is to be explained, not to say predicted.

In elucidating this decisive point we must, first of all, differentiate instrumental analysis from the more conventional type of regressive inference: induction. Let us define induction as the logical procedure in which empirical generalizations and, in particular, scientific hypotheses are derived from systematic observations and experiments. This type of regressive inference is obviously a prerequisite for the establishment of theory in any field of science, though in the everyday application of theory to explanation and

---

[13] It is hardly necessary to point to the difference between an instrumental mode of investigating particular ends-means relations and the instrumental interpretation of theory generally as propagated by Pragmatist philosophers. Nor does my present use of the term coincide with an earlier application (see my *Economics and Sociology* (London, 1935), pp. 78–80, 139–140), which equated it with what is usually defined as "partial equilibrium analysis." But it well accords with Professor Parsons' concept of "instrumental orientation" (see his *The Social System,* pp. 49 and *passim*).

prediction the inductive origin of the theory is usually taken for granted. There is good sense in this elliptic procedure so long as the hypotheses inductively inferred at some time past can be regarded as *invariant*. This presumption seems indeed justified in the natural sciences, and it would be a waste of time for the researcher to re-examine the ultimate foundations each time he wants to apply a theory—all the more so since successful predictions can be interpreted as an indirect confirmation of the underlying hypotheses.

The assumption of invariance of the highest-level hypotheses is valid even for the theory of those directively organized systems which deal with subhuman entities. To the extent to which the goals and optimization criteria of Engineering and Biology can be treated as single-valued, the singularity and constancy of these determinants of the final state from which regressive inference takes its bearings are transferred to the resulting generalizations. In other words, there is no need for the student of Biology constantly to re-examine the general principles which distinguish normal from pathological states.

This is no longer true of social systems which admit of a *plurality of macro-goals*. There any inductively established hypothesis, established with reference to a specific macro-goal, is valid only until further notice, notice, namely, that another macro-goal or a different optimization criterion has been chosen. Once this variability of the ultimate point of reference is recognized, social and in particular economic theories can no longer be formulated elliptically in terms of deductive syllogisms alone. Rather for any particular variant among the many possible terminal states, both the regressive and the progressive chains of inferences must be elaborated and explicitly presented. In other words, since every social theory of economic processes is goal-determined, it must contain an instrumental part.[14]

---

[14] In view of the goal-relatedness of its inferences, instrumental analysis might be described as a teleological method of inquiry. But this can be done only if such a label is not meant to imply incompatibility with causal analysis. The perennial question whether the operation of directively organized systems can be fully explained in a cause-effect nexus or requires a "holistic" hypothesis concerning the behavior of the micro-units poses a false antinomy. Once the

There would be little sense in trying to detail the procedure of instrumental analysis in abstract methodological terms. Only in applying it to the clarification of concrete topics can we usefully discuss the intricate problems which the procedure poses. The concluding part of this essay has been set aside for that task, in particular for presenting a few case studies. What remains to be done at this juncture goes in a different direction. On the one hand, the precise manner in which regressive and progressive—instrumental and deductive—inferences are linked up with one another is to be illustrated on an example. On the other hand, it must be made clear that such combination of regressive and progressive inferences, though indispensable, is still not sufficient for the establishment of confirmable laws and theories in Economics.

Both issues can be demonstrated in the case of the so-called Law of Supply and Demand. In its conventional formulation, as we discussed it in Chapter 2, it confines itself to stating a succession of progressive inferences. To repeat its gist: "If the quantity demanded exceeds the quantity supplied, price tends to rise; if price rises, the quantity supplied tends to increase; if the quantity supplied increases, price tends to fall toward the lowest possible level at which the quantity supplied equals the quantity demanded."

Now, we have shown earlier that, when taken at their face value, these propositions cannot be accepted as a confirmable general "law." Nevertheless, they are not practically meaningless, but contain some empirical truth. What this truth is can be gauged only if the "law" is, first of all, given an instrumental substructure. More specifically, in order to determine the empirical significance of the "law," the highest-level hypotheses from which its propositions issue must be made explicit by instrumental analysis. We then obtain the following sequence of regressive inferences: "If the quantity demanded exceeds the quantity supplied and a *terminal state is postulated* in which the quantities demanded are to equal the quantities

---

suitable causes are known, all states and processes of such systems can be derived as effects from these causes. But in order to select from the multitude of factors at work in any given situation those which are·to be regarded as suitable, we require criteria—criteria which can only be found in an acknowledged "telos" of the system at large.

supplied at the lowest possible price, particular *micro-actions will prove suitable* to bring about the postulated state—first raising the price, then raising the quantity supplied, finally reducing the price to the equilibrium level. Furthermore, to bring about these suitable micro-actions a particular *compound of motivations*—extremum incentives coupled with stabilizing expectations—*will prove suitable*. Ultimately these suitable motivations themselves will be brought about by *suitable environmental conditions,* for instance particular pressures operating in a state of perfect resource mobility."

Abridging these instrumental propositions and, at the same time, generalizing them for all cases of bipolar adjustment which the "law" is supposed to cover, we come up with a formulation such as this: "Given disequilibrium between the quantities demanded and supplied, and given the macro-goal of establishing equilibrium between these magnitudes, such and such micro-actions, motivations, and environmental conditions are suitable means for the attainment of the goal." The question now is: what empirical truth can be derived from these instrumental propositions if they are applied as the major premise in a deductive syllogism? In particular, can we derive from them the categorical propositions of the "law" that prices will *in fact* rise if demand rises, or that supply will *in fact* rise if price rises?

At this point the second characteristic comes into play which—besides the variability of its inferences—distinguishes instrumental analysis from induction in the natural sciences. It concerns the manner in which the "facts" are established from which regressive inference takes its bearings. In the natural sciences these facts are *observed terminal states,* that is, empirical effects the causes of which are to be discovered. And any valid induction transmits to the explanatory hypotheses or causes it infers the empirical truth that attaches to the effect observed.

In sharp contrast with this inductive procedure, instrumental analysis starts out *not from an observed but from a postulated terminal state.* Moreover, except when the preservation of an actually existing state is postulated as macro-goal—e.g., maintenance of "balanced growth"—the set of circumstances which enter as macro-goal into the data of instrumental analysis will differ more or less strongly from all states that are observable at the time the goal is postulated.

This does, of course, not impair the power of instrumental analysis to derive the means suitable for any chosen goal. Nor are the conclusions thus obtained devoid of empirical relevance. They participate in the truth of the natural and psychological laws, empirical generalizations, etc. from which they are derived, and describe to that extent the real means to the stated end. However, this is not the kind of empirical relevance from which laws of occurrence could be deduced. To be specific, the instrumental conclusion that certain actions, motivations, and environmental conditions are suitable means for the attainment of a certain goal cannot be used as major premise in a syllogism which is to predict that a rise in price causes a rise in supply. Such a prediction will come true only if the actions, motivations, and environmental conditions established by instrumental inference are not only suitable means to a rise in supply *but are the real actions, motivations, etc.* which the rise in price triggers. Otherwise a gulf separates what is real from what is goal-adequate, a gulf which even instrumental analysis cannot bridge.

Rather it now looks as if instrumental analysis were caught in the same predicament from which traditional theory suffers: that of advancing formally consistent propositions which, however, cannot be employed to the explanation and prediction of real events. Are we in a better position than the champions of the theoretical tradition to forge the missing link?[15]

5. *Instrumental Inference and the Function of Control*

The link between actual and goal-adequate states is Control. This sounds like a trivial statement if we focus on the task of making economic practice viable by deliberately establishing and maintaining real states that conform to a postulated macro-goal. But

[15] See chap. 4, sec. 1.

even to the solution of this task our inquiry into the logic of goal-seeking has made a contribution by clarifying the strategy of Control. It has circumscribed the kind of scientific knowledge which, to quote Mill, though "insufficient for prediction" is "most valuable for guidance." And it has familiarized us with an intellectual technique through which such knowledge can be acquired.

However, in defining Control as the link between actual and goal-adequate states more is implied than a one-way impact of scientific knowledge on economic practice. No less important and, for the construction of a workable theory, quite as essential is the reverse linkage from a reformed practice to more comprehensive scientific knowledge. What this amounts to can be summarized in the following terms: *only to the extent to which Control, while orienting itself on the findings of instrumental analysis, succeeds in making reality conform to the goal underlying that analysis will economic theory succeed in making confirmable predictions.*

Before we can substantiate this far from trivial thesis we must investigate the function of Control as an operational principle. To this effect we shall first define more precisely the techniques with the help of which Control is exercised, and then specify those properties of economic systems which are to be subjected to Control if a goal-adequate state is to be attained. This will be followed by a brief sketch of the measures of Control which promise to establish and maintain good working order in a mature industrial economy. Only then shall we have laid the foundations on which Political Economics—the theory of controlled economic systems—can be built.

Among the *techniques of Control* we distinguished above between command and the manipulation of the spontaneous actions of the micro-units.[16] In both instances the purpose of Control is to induce responses on the part of the controlled which conform with the intentions of the controller. Command tries to achieve such

[16] This distinction coincides with the difference between "command" and "manipulated field control," as emphasized in Robert A. Dahl and Charles E. Lindblohm, *Politics Economics and Welfare* (New York, 1953), chap. 4, esp. pp. 104–109.

conformity by prescribing the actions of the controlled and imposing a penalty for nonconformance, irrespective of the spontaneous action directives and expectations of the controlled themselves. Manipulative controls, on the other hand, attempt to mold those very action directives and expectations in such a manner that the ensuing behavior, though induced by the controller, is experienced by the actors as the result of spontaneous decision-making.

Of course, command too—in its legislative as well as in its administrative forms—plays on motivations of the controlled. But like the impersonal pressures of the environment of which it represents the contrived counterpart, it appeals, rather than to particular incentives, to the general need of the controlled for self-preservation or, in less extreme circumstances, for social status. It does so especially in collectivist systems where it is the prevailing technique of Control. As is true of the impersonal pressures in a laissez-faire market, command reduces the spontaneous choices between alternative behavioral patterns to a minimum. But since it also does away with the autonomy of the micro-units, the hybrid model is not applicable to such systems. They are the closest approximation of a social order to the engineering model.

Still, since even in such a system command to be effective must be acknowledged by the controlled, and since, as we shall presently realize, manipulative controls alone are unlikely to succeed, all effective controlled systems must make use of both techniques. Here we are especially interested in those combinations of command and manipulative controls which can assure the good working order of a mature industrial system with the characteristics of social and technical immobility, unsteady growth, a mixture of extremum and other incentives and, last but not least, uncertain expectations.

There are, in principle, two opposite combinations of the two Control types, both of which appear suitable for the purpose. One minimizes the role of manipulative controls by largely eliminating decentralized decision-making altogether, namely, by substituting for the actions of marketers oriented on private micro-goals public action directly geared to the attainment of the chosen macro-goal. In this solution the industrial market is transformed into a more or less collectivized order. On the other hand, a solution may be sought which tries to preserve the maximum possible range for decentralized decision-making, even if modified by certain manipulative controls and supplemented by the necessary minimum of command.

So long as the problem is posed as merely an analytical one, both these combinations and any intermediate ones are equally legitimate as subjects of study. This changes, however, if an independent value is ascribed to the mode of decision-making. Then centralization or decentralization becomes part of the optimization criteria which specify the macro-goals. We shall subsequently argue[17] in favor of adopting such a criterion and, more particularly, the criterion of preserving market relations to the largest possible extent compatible with goal attainment. Anticipating this dictum we shall henceforth conduct our investigation with this point of reference in mind.

Such narrowing down of the range of inquiry now makes it easy to define the *objects of Control.* They can only be those structural and dynamic properties of a market system on which its working order depends. In other words, what is to be subjected to Control is one or more of the elementary operational principles which the hybrid model depicts in the singular form of self-equilibration.

Beginning with *structural Control,* it appears at first sight that controlling the size of the micro-units and the rate of growth is a simple and effective manner in which legislative and administrative command can be employed in the service of market regulation. To the extent to which such controls succeed in reducing molar organization and in eliminating the forces making for unsteady change they promise, by restoring to the market its atomic and conservative structure, to recover unrestricted decision-making of the micro-units. This is the rationale which lies, e.g., behind such measures as the Sherman Antitrust Act and other policies directed against unreasonable restraints of trade.

However, the economic history of the past decades offers little justification for the claim that structural controls by themselves are

17 See chap. 12.

capable of restoring the viability of the free market.[18] One reason for their failure is that they concentrate on the social forces making for immobility and uncertainty, to the disregard of the underlying technological factors. At the same time this limitation seems unavoidable. If structure and changes of industrial technology too are subjected to Control, e.g., through the regulation of private investment, entrepreneurial autonomy—the aim pursued—is bound to be curtailed rather than strengthened. Furthermore, restoration of an atomic and conservative structure at the expense of large-scale organization and untrammeled innovation conflicts with the one macro-goal which goes unchallenged in all modern industrial economies: a high rate of per capita growth.

But even if structural controls were to prove effective, their effect would be mediated, as we know, through the motivations and actions of the marketers. And in view of the variety of incentives and expectations in an industrial system the true problem is always how to counterbalance "unsuitable" motivations, a problem which only dynamic controls, that is, Control of the motivational patterns themselves, can solve. Moreover, if successful, such dynamic Control makes structural Control redundant. It then insulates microbehavior from any distorting influences which molar organization and unsteady change might evoke, and bestows on the real structure of an industrial system the same dynamic neutrality which marks the ideal structure as depicted in the hybrid model.[19]

Turning now to *dynamic Control,* our first concern is with *action directives* and, in particular, with the function of the ex-

[18] The champions of such controls like to cite as evidence the so-called "economic miracle" of postwar Germany. They attribute it to a "social market economy" in which—in accord with the "neo-liberal" doctrine—government action is applied exclusively to the establishment and preservation of a sociopolitical framework that guarantees the operation of the free market. (See, e.g., Kurt L. Hanslowe, "Neo-Liberalism," in *Journal of Public Law,* vol. 9 (1960), pp. 96–113, and the sources quoted there.) In fact, the recovery and uninterrupted prosperity of postwar Germany seems to be due rather to the substitution of effective manipulative and command controls—among them what is probably the largest share of public demand in aggregate demand in any major country—for the faulty command controls of the preceding era.

[19] See sec. 1 of this chapter.

tremum principle in a controlled market. We have raised strong objections to the exclusive role which traditional theory assigns to extremum incentives. But this must not mislead us into denying these incentives their due place in the new context.

This place is easy to define. Whenever a market society adopts the goal of output maximization, the suitable action directives of the micro-units are maximization of receipts and minimization of expenditures, irrespective of the prevailing market structure. Hence the task of dynamic Control is either to transform non-extremum into extremum incentives or, failing this, to neutralize the effect of the former by public action.

In view of the low level of aggregate provision in most regions of the globe and the world-wide "revolution of expectations" of material improvement, the scope for such Control is likely to expand rather than to shrink, its task being to evoke extremum incentives where they are absent and to strengthen them where they are weak. Even the wealthy societies of the West, though in principle they can afford to adopt different output criteria compatible with different action directives, will be able to maintain adequate technical efficiency only if they retain some "extremum" tradition.

What this amounts to is that in all these cases dynamic Control is a substitute for the impersonal pressures of the past. In fact the discrepancy between the two is less sharp than may appear at first sight. We have only to realize that at least one of the anonymous pressures operating in early capitalism may well be classified as an instance of manipulative controls. This refers to the cultural climate in which the desire for unlimited accumulation evolved. To generate this desire—anything but an innate propensity—and to transmit it from generation to generation required an ongoing educational process, in which theological and moral doctrines combined with popular Economics to shape and to justify action in the market place.

The example is instructive in two respects. It shows that what on the surface appears as an automatic impact of the environment on human motivation may really be the result of manipulative forces however diffuse. And as a consequence extremum incentives may well be created and preserved in a social environment entirely relieved of all impersonal pressures. All that is necessary is the presence of manipulative controls—among them education in the widest sense of the word—powerful enough to arouse motivational substitutes for the wish to avoid moral or material ruin.

After that much has been conceded it must be emphasized that the suitability of any action directive can be judged only in the context of the modal macro-goal pursued. Extremum incentives may prove positively harmful in a market society oriented on criteria other than maximization of output. Suppose that a more or less fixed level of aggregate output is chosen instead. Then some pattern of homeostatic micro-behavior as discussed earlier, far from conflicting with good working order, appears as the only suitable means for the attainment of the new goal.[20]

Alas, our knowledge of alternatives to the extremum principle and, more specifically, of the correspondence between particular macro-goals and particular action directives is as yet very limited. For this reason the concept of "qualitative focal points," which Professor T. C. Schelling recently forged as a tool for the handling of these problems, deserves serious attention.[21] This concept is to supplement the purely quantitative focal point of the extremum principle, by emphasizing historical, legal, moral, and even aesthetic considerations in arriving at a bargaining agreement. As Schelling shows, adherence to precedent or to the *status quo,* striving for equality of advantage, preference for simple solutions such as settling on "round numbers," and many other constellations of a qualitative nature can serve as orientational maxims. What all of them have in common is their origin in *interdependent* decisions and mutuality, as opposed to "parametric" behavior.[22] One may even wonder whether what stability the empirical markets of historical capitalism have displayed is not to a large extent due to such "social aberrations" from the subsocial model of traditional theory.

[20] See chap. 1, sec. 4.
[21] See his *Strategy of Conflict,* esp. chaps. 2 and 3.
[22] See chap. 4, sec. 3.

However, even such an extension of the catalogue of possible incentive patterns leaves open the ever-recurring question of the nexus through which extra-systemic influences—impersonal or personal—affect marketers' motivations. In this twilight region of sociopsychological relations where we have only rules of thumb, speculative hunches, and other tentative hypotheses to guide us, general statements had better be limited to the following two. First, since the strategic role in transforming economic incentives falls to "education," the task is one for long-run controls. Second, over shorter periods the prevailing action directives of the micro-units must be treated as invariant, and any conflicts with the pursuit of the macro-goal thus provoked will have to be neutralized by command controls, in particular, by compensatory public action.[23]

There is one most important exception to this rather unpropitious rule. As was pointed out before,[24] deviations from extremum tendencies in contemporary capitalism may be due as much to uncertainty of expectations as to a weakening of environmental pressures. In such cases there is an indirect way of controlling action directives through the *Control of expectations*. As a matter of fact, it is in the reduction of expectational uncertainty below the critical threshold that manipulating Control and instrumental analysis from which such Control takes its bearings are likely to achieve their main triumph.

When we subsequently study some test cases we shall discover that, even more than is true of action directives, the content of suitable expectations varies with the macro-goal. We know that quantity expectations with positive elasticity and price expectations with less than unit elasticity are conditional for the equilibration of a stationary process.[25] But we shall see that quite different expectations defined by negative or more than unit elasticities are necessary

---

[23] A representative example is Keynes's notion of a "somewhat comprehensive socialization of investment" which is to assure full employment. See chap. 9, sec. 9, below.

[24] See chap. 3, sec. 5.

[25] See chap. 2, sec. 2.

in order to achieve full resource utilization or balanced growth. How, then, are manipulative controls to proceed in evoking the suitable cognitive responses?

To see the crucial point—it is also the point at which Control of expectations has a decisive advantage over Control of incentives—we must realize that every marketer is interested in improving his common-sense knowledge about his present and future field of action. Therefore, however strong his resistance may be to any obtrusion on his action directive, he can be supposed to accept gladly any public information capable of correcting the content of his expectations and of reducing the uncertainty of their coming true.

Now, this is precisely the service which manipulative controls can render the average marketer by publicizing the findings of instrumental analysis. Once it has established the macro-goal and the optimization criteria, the controlling authority can acquire by a process of instrumental inference precise knowledge of the adjustment processes through which the system is to move toward the postulated terminal state. Thus the successive market constellations—the future field of action of the marketers—are known at the moment when the decision about the goal is taken, and can be communicated to the prospective actors as the body of facts on which correct expectations can be built.

On one condition: that the findings thus communicated will be accepted by the micro-units as true. And they will be so accepted only if they do come true, that is, if the postulated adjustment path and terminal state turn out to be the real path and the real terminal state. How can this be guaranteed?

At this point manipulating controls by themselves prove insufficient. Only if the controlling authority is willing and able to supplement and, in extreme cases, to supplant private by public decision-making can the attainment of the macro-goal be assured and, as a consequence, the threshold minimum of expectational certainty be achieved. To be specific, the public sector of investment and consumption must be so organized that it can be expanded at short notice whenever the private sector fails to respond in conformity with goal requirements. Such stand-by measures of command control will then translate instrumental knowledge into direct public action.[26]

If it is true that anything that reduces the uncertainty of marketers' expectations is likely to stimulate goal-adequate behavior, it should, as a rule, be unnecessary ever to put such stand-by measures of command into operation. The more carefully such a program of Control is elaborated and publicized, and the more earnest the intent on the part of the controlling authority to act in case of emergency, the greater the effect on actual expectations and the smaller the danger that an emergency will in fact arise.[27]

6. *Political Economics: the Theory of Controlled Economic Systems*

Three different steps, all of them related to Control, are required to assure the good working order or goal-adequate motion of a market system no longer under the sway of anonymous environmental pressures operating in a state of perfect resource mobility. The first is *political:* postulation of a macro-goal and of the qualifying criteria to define the over-all purpose of economic activity. The second step is *scientific:* instrumental elaboration of the system's path, of the behavioral and motivational patterns, and of specific

[26] For an interesting discussion of some of the problems connected with manipulative Control, see Emile Grunberg and Franco Modigliani, "The Predictability of Social Events," *Journal of Political Economy,* vol. 62 (1954), pp. 465–478.

Altogether it is not the intention of this essay to enter the realm of policy-framing and to devise specific measures through which the operational principle of dynamic Control can be implemented. Among the recent experiments with capitalist planning the "French style" comes probably nearest to the ideas here expounded. (See, e.g., John Hackett and Anne-Marie Hackett, *Economic Planning in France* [Cambridge, Mass., 1963].) But it may well be that the most effective techniques combining manipulative Control with a minimum of command Control are still to be developed, varying with the political organization, business tradition, and cultural outlook of the industrial societies concerned.

[27] In all this the supposition is made that, though their conscious agreement is not required, the micro-units do not altogether reject the macro-goal or the means by which it is to be attained. There a different and much more complex problem of Control may arise, about which more will be said in chap. 12.

measures of Control, all of which are to be suitable to transform the initial state into a terminal state of goal-adequacy. The third step is *administrative:* application of the measures of Control as derived by instrumental analysis to the actual regulation of the structure and, above all, of the dynamic forces of the system.

To the extent to which especially the second and the third step prove successful, not only is the practical viability of the market established as an organization of aggregate provision but also are the preconditions fulfilled for a confirmable theory of economic motion. This means that the respective measures of Control and related motivational and behavioral patterns can now be treated as highest-level hypotheses or major premises from which verifiable paths and terminal states can be deduced in a conventional syllogism. Successful Control transforms the "means" which instrumental analysis infers from a postulated "end" into the real "causes" whence the terminal state originally introduced as an end can now be deduced as a real "effect." To put it differently, observable states and processes can now be explained and predicted on the basis of regular patterns of micro-behavior. Though these patterns represent, to begin with, no more than rules for suitable action, these hypothetical rules are transformed through the Control of action directives and expectations into categorical propositions about laws of behavior.

A theory built on these foundations is applicable to any market system whatever its structure, and whatever the dynamic forces initially at work. Neither molar organization nor extra-systemic shocks will deflect actual motion from the theoretically predicted one, so long as manipulative and—in the background—command controls keep the actual purposive and cognitive motivations of the marketers in line with those hypothetical motivations from which the laws of behavior have been derived. Since there is a good, namely, goal-adequate working order for all such systems, there is also a theory of their operation, even if they are burdened with social and technical immobilities, exposed to the vagaries of innovations, and peopled with members orienting themselves on qualitative rather than quantitative focal points.

We defined above the theory of controlled economic systems as
Political Economics. Considering the central role which the political
act of goal establishment and the administrative procedures of Control play in its design, the label is self-explanatory. What still needs
to be made explicit are certain features which distinguish Political
Economics as a scientific construct from more conventional forms
of theoretical reasoning, especially those prevalent in the natural
sciences.

One such characteristic has already been discussed at length.[28]
It concerns the *limited validity* of deductive inferences drawn from
instrumentally established premises. As was then emphasized, all
such inferences are empirically valid only until further notice, notice, namely, that some of the "data" have changed. This refers
particularly to those changes in macro-goal or optimization criteria
which require a change in the system's motion, or in the underlying
behavioral and motivational patterns, or in specific measures and
even the general technique of Control. Not before all the necessary
adjustments have been carried out, first on the level of instrumental
analysis and then on the level of practice, will the new premises be
obtained from which new confirmable conclusions can be drawn.
This was meant above when we spoke of instrumental analysis as
an ongoing task for the economist. In fact this task includes not
only the work of the theorist but also the political and administrative practice of the controlling authority.

From this there originates what is the most striking feature of
Political Economics: its *three-pronged structure* manifested in the
peculiar combination of theoretical and practical constituents.
There is, first, the dual procedure on the level of reasoning itself,
which in every case must elaborate not only the progressive but
also the regressive chain of the inference. To set it apart from the
conventional hypothetico-deductive method—which takes the empirical validity of the regressive conclusions for granted, once such
conclusions have been drawn from a properly chosen sample of
observations—we shall define this dual procedure as "instrumental-
deductive."

[28] See sec. 4 of this chapter.

Second, what introduces an entirely new element into Political Economics is its dependence on the practice of Control. Whereas the duality of reasoning is bound up with the *multiplicity* of terminal states which offer themselves as possible goals, the synthesis of knowledge with practice is rendered necessary because of the merely *potential* nature of the terminal state when understood as a *goal*. Rather than given as fact open to observation, the terminal state is set as a task for deliberate pursuit, requiring action which may radically transform the facts which initially present themselves to observation.

This complex structure of Political Economics is the reason why the topic of this essay has been denoted as economic *knowledge* rather than as economic *science* or economic *theory*. Certainly reconstruction of economic science is the ultimate aim of this inquiry, and such reconstruction is successful only to the extent to which it arrives at a confirmable theory. However, in the traditional view theory is the result of "contemplative" acts only, a conception which is too narrow when it comes to defining the procedure by which the theorems of Political Economics are obtained. Having a more comprehensive connotation, the term "knowledge," even if not specific enough for our purposes, at least is not bound by hallowed usage to exclude the introduction of an "action component" into the process of acquiring insight.[29]

The same three-pronged structure of Political Economics has far-reaching consequences for the *testing* of its theoretical propositions. The conclusions arrived at by the dual procedure of the instrumental-deductive method are empirically true — and not merely logically consistent—only to the extent to which Control, itself informed by instrumental analysis, succeeds in approximating

[29] In passing it should be stressed that the role which "practice" plays in Political Economics differs sharply from its role in the Baconian conception of knowledge or in the tenets of a sociology of knowledge. The former, by making usefulness the criterion of worthwhile knowledge, permits the choice of both subject and method of study to be governed by the practical consequences of the findings. The latter sees in participation in the social process by the seeker of knowledge the main source of his knowledge, even if such participation is likely to restrict the field of his intellectual vision. In neither case, however, does *reality-transforming action* enter as a precondition for scientific knowledge, as it does in Political Economics.

real states to the conditions of goal-adequacy. In other words, not before political and administrative action has gone into operation will the facts be available on which the theory can be tested.

It is finally worth noting that Political Economics satisfies the condition which, at the beginning of our methodological deliberations, was stated as a prerequisite for breaking through the vicious circle in which traditional theory seems to be caught.[30] This circle concerns the apparent dependence of theory on the common-sense knowledge of the actors, with the consequence that strivings and expectations of the marketers which are incompatible with the good working order of the system at large are bound to frustrate the theorist's search for confirmable regularities of motion. It was then suggested that the circle might be broken if scientific knowledge about the good working order of an industrial market could be gained independently of the common-sense knowledge of the marketers themselves. Instrumental analysis provides precisely such independent scientific knowledge. Moreover, through the medium of Control, the linkage is now reversed between primary experience and theoretical knowledge, the former being dominated by the latter.

That knowledge should be inseparable from action, because that which is to be known may first have to be created in the image of a rationally conceived design, is probably the one characteristic that, more than any other, separates the science of Society from the science of Nature. Though latently present in all historical societies, this essential feature comes into view only with Man's expanding power over his environment. There lies the ultimate reason why the hybrid model and the traditional theory which it formalizes reflect a past stage of human development: their operational principles leave no room for deliberate design of the whole. Conversely, in our groping toward the next stage in which the social process will be the manifestation of responsible action rather than an inexorable sequence of events, Political Economics as here defined may not only prove "valuable for guidance" but may even offer suggestive clues for prediction.

This guarded formulation is, of course, prompted by the per-

[30] See chap. 4, sec. 1.

petual doubts about the stringency of "social causation." But these doubts too spring from the social nature of economic processes, originating in the purposeful spontaneity of human actors rather than in the blind movement of natural forces. To render determinate the final link in the chain of instrumental inference—the link between Control and individual motivations—and thus to achieve unconditional prediction, both the macro-goal and the prescripts of Control must be affirmed by the controlled.[31] There the "linearity of cause and effect" is transformed into the "circularity of reason and consequence," namely, of external impacts which can, in principle, be accepted or rejected. This may be a high price to pay in terms of indeterminacy for a science which deals with the products of human spontaneity. Still, who but a professional manipulator or an incurable addict of "scientism" would have it otherwise?

[31] See chap. 12, sec. 3.

PART THREE

———◆———

THE HISTORICAL TREND
OF ECONOMIC SCIENCE

6

The Origin of Traditional Theory:
Adam Smith's System of
Equilibrium Growth

1. *From 1776 to 1936: Formation, Erosion, and Re-emergence of a Theoretical "System"*

In tracing the historical development of a science one expects to encounter a more or less steady progress from initial fragmentary insights to an ever more comprehensive body of knowledge in which, first, empirical regularities, then explanatory laws and more inclusive theories, and finally, a grand synthesis of all the special theories are established. The very contrary is true of the modern history of Economics. At its beginning stand the grandiose designs of classical Economics, marked by an expanse of substance and a stringency of deductive reasoning that, during the subsequent development, was achieved only once by the classical heretic Marx. Thereafter theoretical development presents itself under the curious aspect of a progressive erosion of the original system, to be partially reversed only during the present generation.

It is significant that, in the course of this process, the meaning of "theory" itself has changed. The change was described as early as 1885 in Alfred Marshall's Inaugural Lecture as the difference between a "body of concrete truth" and an "engine for the discovery of concrete truth." The same idea can be expressed as the contrast between the "magnificent dynamics" (W. J. Baumol) characterizing the work of the classical economists and the "box of tools" (Joan Robinson) forged and assembled by their neo-classical successors. It was the conviction of the former that the empirical market systems possessed a unique structure and underwent a unique evolution the essential features of which could be depicted in a *theoretical system,* permitting unconditional predictions of short-term and long-term motion. We shall discover the reasons that have led to the abandonment of this belief and, from the middle of the nineteenth century on, have replaced the theoretical system in the classical sense by a *formal framework* in which prediction is conditional on more or less arbitrary assumptions of initial conditions and behavioral axioms.

In spite of this far-reaching difference the logical structure of classical as well as of neo-classical theory can be described in terms of our hybrid model elaborated earlier. A basic configuration of the micro-units in two circular flows and the operational principles of atomism, conservation, micro-autonomy, and extremum action are common to both. And it is the resulting feedback relations that are responsible for the relative degree of determinacy of the various theories.[1]

However, as the contrast between unconditional and conditional prediction has already indicated, this determinacy varies considerably between classical Economics (including Marx) and the post-classical constructs. As a matter of fact, the former bear a deterministic character so radical that it is difficult to find an analogy for it anywhere in the realm of the natural sciences. In these systems Laplace's vision has come true: they are the product of an "intelligence" which claims to be able to "comprehend all the forces by which nature [read: society] is animated and the respective positions of the entities which compose it . . . nothing would be uncertain for it, and the future, like the past, would be present for its eyes."[2]

We shall see that even this feature of the classical systems—it is the very feature which raises them to the rank of systems as

---

[1] For the elaboration of these concepts, see chap. 4, secs. 3, 5, 7.

[2] See Pierre Simon, Marquis de Laplace, *Traité de Probabilité* (Paris, 1886), pp. vi–vii.

defined above—can be explained with the help of the hybrid model, more precisely, of the extended version of the model which integrates the regulatory factors of the environment with the motion of the core process. At the same time we have here the background on which the meaning of the subsequent "erosion" of the original system can be defined. It refers to the gradual narrowing of the scope of feedback relations and to the progressive loosening of the "coupling mechanism" in those feedbacks which neo-classical Economics still retained.

Even if this trend reflected theoretical concessions to a refractory reality, it could not help reducing the determinacy of analysis and thus weakening the predictive strength of all post-classical theory. Therefore it is not surprising that scientific interest began, slowly and sporadically, to turn from the exclusive interpretation of experience to the study of the conditions suitable to move actual states and processes toward some postulated optimum. In a word, there is an intimate historical connection between the growing frustrations of Traditional Economics and the growth of Political Economics. When finally the latter took a more definite shape in the "Keynesian Revolution," a new access to "concrete truth" was opened, holding out the promise of reconstructing a theoretical "system" on new foundations.

To trace this immanent transformation of theoretical thinking is the main purpose of our review of some of the major stages in the history of economic analysis. We start out with an investigation of the systematic principles underlying Adam Smith's *Wealth of Nations*. This work has been singled out not only because it stands at the beginning of the scientific history of Economics but because it conceptualizes more clearly than any other that stage in Western development which marks the transition from pre-industrial to industrial capitalism. It thus reveals the political and social as well as economic foundations on which traditional theory rests. Moreover, it demonstrates that certain elements of a Political Economics, as the term is here understood, are present even in a system which otherwise marks the apogee of determinism, thus pointing to an instrumental root in all scientific thinking about social affairs.

2. *The Environmental "Constants" in Smith's System*

Some constructive effort is required if one tries to distill the essence of an analytical model from the mixture of theoretical propositions, empirical descriptions, historical discourses, and political recommendations with which Smith's magnum opus presents itself to the uninitiated reader. The student interested in basic doctrine is compelled to gather the building blocks from widely scattered passages. Moreover, he will quite frequently have to unearth implicit assumptions in order to impart meaning to explicit statements, and conjectural interpretation cannot always be avoided. But since there is practical agreement on the individual premises and theorems among the experts, the risk of misconstruction is minimal.[3]

We must begin with describing the ultimate "data" on which Smith builds his model. In the typical constructs of social—and for that matter, of physical—analysis these data can be divided into constants and independent variables. Thus in the example of the thermostat the furnace, the pipes, and the "actuator" fall in the categories of constants, whereas the temperature affecting the actuator and the quantity of fuel in the storage tank belong to the independent variables. It is the singular feature of Smith's model that—with one exception—it does not contain any independent variables. In particular, all extra-systemic factors influencing the stability and growth of the system are governed by intra-systemic processes, so that the very distinction between extra- and intra-systemic motion loses its meaning.

The precise manner in which such reciprocal causation is

---

[3] The strategic passages in the *Wealth of Nations* are found in chaps. 2, 3, 8, and 9 of Book I and chaps. 3, 4, and 5 of Book II, not to forget the brief but enlightening Conclusion to Book I, chap. 11. For further details see my "The Classical Theory of Economic Growth," *Social Research*, vol. 21 (1954), pp. 127–158, and Joseph Spengler, "Adam Smith's Theory of Economic Growth," *Southern Economic Journal*, vol. 26 (1959), pp. 397–415, and vol. 27 (1959), pp. 1–12.

Numbers in parentheses given in the text refer to pages in the Modern Library Edition cited in note 7, chap. 3.

achieved will occupy us presently. But we must first enumerate the real data, namely, those natural, psychological, and institutional factors which affect the processes to be analyzed without themselves being affected by the latter. Their essential characteristic is that, though the result of a long evolution from an original "rude state of society," they are supposed to have attained their final shape in the competitive organization of the modern Western "system of natural liberty" (638). Being neither influenced by the ongoing core process nor subject to further historical development, these factors can be treated as genuine "constants" of the analysis.

Starting out with the institutional constants, we find a competitive market place under the protection of a constitutional government whose main duties consist in the preservation of law and order. Among the laws themselves, those assuring personal freedom and freedom of contract are, under the aspect of market transactions, the most important, in addition to those which safeguard private property. Smith is fully aware of the unequal distribution of such property—of the class character of society—as an essential condition for the operation of the economic mechanism as he describes it (670–672). Social mobility of the factors of production is explicitly postulated (62, 99); technical mobility, namely, smallness and non-specificity of the basic combination of factors is implicitly assumed, as we shall have occasion to observe. Finally, division of labor and free exchange are the organizational principles on which the competitive system builds.

These principles are themselves only the institutional crystallization of certain innate human propensities: the "propensity to truck, barter, and exchange" (13) and the "desire of bettering our conditions" (324) which, together with the urge to procreate, form the psychological items in the list of constants. To complete this list we must add the assumption of constant returns on natural resources, that is, an optimistic view of nature's bounty which, for all practical purposes, permits the output of agriculture and of the extractive industries to adjust itself to rising demand without any check on real output and income.

We can easily recognize in this set of constants concrete manifestations of most of the operational principles which govern the hybrid model earlier discussed, in particular those of atomism, extremum action, and of course micro-autonomy. The reason why conservation—the fourth of these principles—is not among Smith's data will presently come to light. But the constants which he does postulate fully suffice to assure negative feedback motion and the steady equilibration of the system whenever it is exposed to changes in the one independent variable included: consumers' tastes. In other words, the data fulfill all the conditions under which the Law of Supply and Demand rules supreme.[4]

3. *The Dynamic Feedback Mechanism*

However, Smith derives from the same set of constants a second feedback mechanism. There essential extra-systemic forces are integrated with the motion of the core process. This transforms the stationary setting of the latter into a dynamics of "balanced growth," which extends the range of determinacy far beyond intra-systemic motion.

It has already been indicated why the dynamic loop of the two circular mechanisms in Smith's system is significant for the motion of the core process. It regulates the stimuli which impinge on that motion in so far as they are connected with changes in the aggregate of the factors of production. What, then, is the precise manner in which the "constants" of the system influence these variables of growth, namely, the supply of labor natural resources and capital, and also technology or the order in which the productive factors are combined?

It is in the nature of the economic core process that the productive factors are continuously drained off the market by being transformed into outputs, and that they must be steadily replenished if the economic circuit is to be maintained, not to say expanded. Now, it is Smith's contention that three fundamental laws of long-term motion determine the course in which these agents, while producing

---

[4] Though Smith never formulated the law explicitly, it is fully implied in his discussion "Of the Natural and Market Price of Commodities" (55–63).

output, are themselves reproduced on an increasing scale by such output.

(1) There is, first of all, a law which governs the *supply of labor*. It is based on two complementary hypotheses. On the one hand, competitive forces are at work that tend, over the long run, to reduce the level of real wages to the subsistence level. The causal nexus is the same which later became known as the "iron law of wages." What is meant is that changes in the real wages offered evoke compensatory changes in the size of the working population because "demand for men, like that for any other commodity, necessarily regulates the production of men" (80).

On the other hand, real wages can and do rise so long as the natural and technical conditions of a country permit a steady increase in its real product. Even then the link between real wages and the size of population is not cut. Only in such a society demand for labor, as expressed in "the funds which are destined for the payment of wages" (69), can run ahead of supply. And though Smith also in this case expects that an increase in population will occur—infant mortality is likely to fall when real wages rise (79) and procreation is stimulated since children are an asset in a seller's market for labor (70–71)—a rising wage fund can keep wages above subsistence for an indefinite period.

Thus at any moment the supply of labor is governed by two balancing forces: the propensity to procreate, which itself is a composite of a biological urge and a calculation about the "value of children," and the available wage fund. The former is, as we saw, a constant, but one which by itself would cause the system to "run down" to a stationary level of labor supply and thus of output. This tendency can be counteracted only by the latter force—the wage fund—which is a variable. How is it determined?

(2) This leads us to a law of *accumulation*. The funds which govern the demand for labor result from saving, which is the outward expression of another psychological constant: the desire of bettering our conditions. Of course, it is not by saving as such but by the use people make of their savings that conditions can be bettered. Accumulation, which for Smith and all classical writers in-

cludes both saving and investment, "is the most likely way of aug-
menting their fortune" (325), provided that a "neat or clear profit"
(96) can be earned.

The level of profit and interest, however, is as precarious as the
level of wages, because competition among manufacturers and
lenders increases with the rise of a country's capital stock (87, 336).
Once more the system would "run down" if the tendency of profits
to level out were not counteracted by another variable element. As
is the case with wages, "it is not the actual greatness of national
wealth, but its continuous increase" (69) that favors profits. Such
a rise of "national wealth" (synonymous with what today we call
national income) can be stimulated only by a rise in productivity.

(3) In the concept of *productivity* we encounter the strategic
variable of the whole system. Productivity depends, first of all, on a
country's geographic position and its supply of natural resources.
The latter, as we have already seen, is treated as a constant over
the practically relevant time span. Therefore the true source of a
rise in productivity is technical progress. We must not, however,
equate Smith's notions of technical progress with the large-scale
innovations which characterize a fully developed industrial system.
What he has in mind he defines as progressive "division of labor,"
so impressively described in the first three chapters of the work. It
comprises the economies of specialization, and also the use of such
machinery as serves to "facilitate and abridge labor" (17).

Now, it is essential for the understanding of the dynamic mechanism to realize that in this conception technology, and in particular
the introduction of machinery, is regarded as a complement of
rather than a substitute for labor. In other words, far from dis-
placing labor and thus exerting a potential pressure on employment
and wages—the major variable in Marxian dynamics, as we shall
see—division of labor in this inclusive sense is itself conditional on
a prior increase in labor supply. "The number of workmen in every
branch of business generally increases with the division of labor in
that branch, or rather it is the increase in their number which
enables them to class and subdivide themselves in this manner"
(260).

Strange as these ideas may sound to a modern reader, they make good sense as soon as we remember that the *Wealth of Nations* appeared in the early years of the Industrial Revolution and, in fact, describes the conditions of the small-scale manufacturing system that preceded full-scale industrialization. But this identification of technical progress with labor-attracting forms of specialization has far-reaching consequences for the entire model. Rises in productivity on which, as we saw, a satisfactory level of both wages and profits depend, cannot take place spontaneously. They are conditional on a prior increase of aggregate demand since, as the title of the famous Chapter 3 of Book I puts it: division of labor is limited by the extent of the market (17). Far from being treated as an independent variable, technical progress for Smith can only develop "in proportion to the riches and populousness" (19) of the country in question and in proportion to its trade with other countries. Therefore, and this is Smith's third law of dynamic motion, it is the rate of increase in aggregate demand that governs the rate of increase in productivity.

Smith is quite outspoken as to the principal source of such steady increase in demand. Though he is renowned as the protagonist of international division of labor, "according to the natural course of things . . . the greater part of the capital of every growing society is first directed to agriculture, afterwards to manufactures, and last of all to foreign commerce" (360). Thus pride of place belongs to the domestic market, that is, to a steady increase in population equipped with sufficient "effectual demand"—our argument has turned a full circle.

It may be helpful to retrace the sequence of this circular or rather spiral process and to emphasize once more the strategic spots where the constants exert their recurring influence. We should remember that we contemplate a process in motion. In order to follow up the sequence of events we must break into the chain of interdependent links artificially at some point. The most opportune place to do so is the point where a prior increase in aggregate employment, stemming from the preceding "turn of the spiral," has raised aggregate demand, thus providing new investment opportunities for further division of labor. These opportunities raise profit expectations and thus demand for savings, in this manner keeping the level of the rate of interest above the minimum and, considering the propensity for "betterment," stimulating the supply of savings. Such savings offered for investment represent demand for additional labor and maintain real wages above the subsistence level. Under the influence of the propensity to procreate, labor supply responds, even if with a time lag, to the wage stimulus so that the original investment opportunities can be realized through rising employment. This raises payrolls and market demand above the level expected when the spiral under observation first began to turn, creating new investment opportunities and the opportunity for another turn.[5]

It should be emphasized that the long-term feedback mechanism, which underlies this spiral process, is "positive," that is, self-enforcing rather than compensatory. But the "coupling" is such as to preclude any "runaway," the biosociological period of human maturation setting an upper limit to the rate of change of the system.

4. *Stationary and Dynamic Feedbacks in Joint Operation*

In order to comprehend the structure of Smith's model in its entirety, we must now relate the stationary feedback, which maintains taste-adequate equilibrium of goods production for a fixed aggregate of inputs and outputs, with the dynamic feedback, which governs the expansion of this aggregate. In this all-inclusive construct the following characteristics stand out.

We note, first of all, that the sectoral adjustments of supply to demand, which sustain the equilibrium of the market, are only minor oscillations in a steady process of aggregate expansion. Owing to the mechanism of specialization, reproduction of inputs and outputs coincides with their increase. Therefore—and this distinguishes all classical systems from the models of neo-classical theory—the

---

[5] A lucid exposition of the model has been given in W. O. Thweatt, "A Diagrammatic Presentation of Adam Smith's Growth Model," *Social Research*, vol. 24 (1957), pp. 227–230.

equilibrium of the aggregate is never truly stationary, but always dynamic, making growth the frame of reference for all sectoral movements. Only in the distant future, when a country has "acquired that full complement of riches which the nature of its soil and climate, and its situation with regard to other countries, allowed it to acquire" (94), will nature's latent stinginess manifest itself and the system tend toward a stationary state.

No less important than growth as such is its steady nature. Distortions are excluded from the system by the stationary as well as by the dynamic feedback mechanism. The former assures the prompt adjustment of the qualitative order of supply to the one independent variable in the system: consumers' tastes. The latter, by continuously "transforming" commodity output into factor input and thus into new commodity output, keeps the spiral of expansion closed and at the same time reduces the rate of expansion to the slow growth rate of population. The crucial factor in all this is technology, namely, the small-scale organization of production, the adaptation of machinery to labor rather than conversely, and the unlimited possibilities of rising productivity rooted in progressive division of labor. Without such technical progress the system would run down to a stationary level long before nature itself sets a limit to expansion. But ultimately it is the labor-attracting character of the postulated technology which assures dynamic equilibrium. There can never be any discrepancy between factor demand and factor supply. Rising productivity by inducing rising employment and income creates its own demand.

It should now be clear why, with the exception of consumers' tastes, Smith's system does not contain any independent variables. Once the dynamic process is set in motion, the linkage of the variables with the natural, psychological, and institutional constants creates a reciprocity of cause and effect—though at any given moment cause and effect are clearly distinguishable—which excludes any influence from outside the mechanism. This, together with the slow rate of growth, bestows on the system, and thus on the analysis of its movements, a degree of determinacy which in other fields is attained only under strictly circumscribed laboratory conditions.

The postulate "other things remaining equal," conventionally taken as a methodological rule, here gains empirical significance: it describes the actual state of affairs as controlled by a double feedback mechanism. Only changes in taste fall outside their "loops" but the bipolar nature of these changes evokes a compensatory motion of its own. All other changes are channeled through circular mechanisms and are as such strictly calculable.

Still another feature of the model is worth mentioning. The major stimuli being strictly controlled, there is no room left for "uncertainty of expectations." Moreover, prevailing expectations, based on the past and present experience of equilibrium, cannot be other than equilibrating. Consequently the scientific observer can disregard expectations altogether, as Smith and the other classical writers in fact did.

What cannot, of course, be disregarded is the nature of the prevailing action directive. It stands outside the circular mechanisms, but is no less determinate: it forms an essential part of the system's constants. Actually it is the fundamental force which impels and unifies the motions of the socioeconomic process. In applying the extremum principle not only to the commodity market but also to the factor markets and, above all, to the "production" of men, Smith raises the pecuniary motive which rules the market to the universal motive power in society at large. On empirical as well as philosophical grounds we may have good reasons for repudiating an interpretation of social relations in the image of market relations. But we must realize that only by an all-encompassing hypothesis in which economic relations are presumed to govern the wider social process—a truly materialistic conception of history—did Smith succeed in making the economic process truly "circular" and thus fully determinate.

5. *Instrumental Roots of Smith's Premises*

The constants of Smith's model are the data from which the unbreakable spiral of the steady process of growth is derived. But data and resulting process are related in still another and more subtle manner about which a word must be said in conclusion.

Though the growth process once it is set in motion pursues its course with the inexorability of a law of nature, Smith is interested not only in the reciprocal "causes" of the growing "wealth of nations" but also in its "nature." More precisely, he by no means accepts the outcome of the secular process of production with indifference. Rather he singles out two specific goals as the "distinct objects" of a "political economy," understood as "a branch of the science of a statesman or legislator." These goals are "first, to provide a plentiful revenue or subsistence for the people . . . and, secondly, to supply the state or commonwealth with a revenue sufficient for the public services" (397). In other words, the effectiveness of the growth process, in terms both of aggregate output and of its distribution among the social strata involved in its production, is subject to a value judgment, the criterion of which is the welfare goal just stated.

Now, and this is the miracle performed by the "invisible hand," the spiral of unplanned economic growth, which the initial set of natural, psychological, and institutional constants releases, propels society toward this very goal: maximum wealth through the steady increase of the annual produce of land and labor, benefiting equally those who live by rent and wages.[6] Thus the dynamic laws which map out the path of economic evolution are themselves the vehicles which carry society toward what for Smith is the "good life."

But this coincidence between that which "inevitably occurs" and that which is "good" is not assured by just any set of data. It is clearly restricted to the framework of constants as outlined above. True, some of these constants, namely, the natural and psychological ones, are regarded by Smith as unalterable, describing the external and internal endowment of Man. But this is by no means the case with the institutional constants which are summarized by him in the concept of a "system of natural liberty" (651). Outside

---

[6] It should be noted, however, that Smith has considerable doubts whether this harmony between the "general interest" of society and the sectional interests of its components includes also "those who live by profits," since the rate of profit "is always highest in the countries which are going fastest to ruin" (248–250).

of this form of political organization even the psychological propensities remain *dormant,* and the force symbolized in the extremum incentive, which alone can steer the process of development in the proper channels, will be frustrated. Inexorable as is the process of growth, the political and social conditions from which alone it can take off and by which it is sustained are not themselves preordained. They are the product of history, but of a history in which human choices in the form of political decisions play a decisive role.

How central this idea is for Smith can be gauged from the fact that one third of the book is devoted to a description and critique of the possible alternatives to the institutional order of natural liberty. Mercantilism, and the ancient and modern systems devoted to the one-sided furthering of agriculture are denounced because each is "subversive of the great purpose which it means to promote" (650–651). Only the cooperation of free men left to themselves in pursuing their interests under a government protecting law and order will succeed in promoting that purpose: steady increase in wealth and welfare.

In speculating about the origin of the spatio-mathematical order of the universe, the metaphysicians of the seventeenth and eighteenth centuries came up with a version of the engineering model which helps to elucidate the synthesis of "determinism and freedom" in Smith's doctrine. Once the world machine has been constructed its motions are found to be fully determined by the laws of Mechanics, and to proceed in full autonomy. But the divine engineer or heavenly clockmaker who established the initial conditions and gave the system the initial push was a free agent not himself subject to mechanical laws. By the same logic the determinist motion of Smith's model presupposes a prior free decision on the part of the political sovereign in favor of one rather than another set of institutions.

But what is the criterion for his choice? In deciding against the arbitrary "preferences" and "restraints," which dominated the political systems of the past, in favor of a system of natural liberty the sovereign adopts the macro-goal of maximizing welfare by maximizing wealth. The reason why a system of natural liberty is the suitable means for the attainment of that socioeconomic end is its consequences for individual economic behavior. It activates the dormant force of the extremum incentive for the motion of economic growth through which alone the welfare goal can be approximated.

Thus we arrive at the important conclusion that Smith's theoretical construct rests on an instrumental foundation. Steady progress toward maximization of wealth benefiting all major strata of economic society is postulated as the macro-goal to the attainment of which the productive effort is directed. The spiraling path of growth, the laws of behavior which impel its pursuit, the extremum incentive which shapes such behavior, and last but not least, the institutional environment in which alone such behavior and motivation can assert itself, all these events and underlying forces are more than just factual occurrences. They are at the same time the means to an end, an end which the philosopher Smith prescribes to the economist Smith as the *terminus ad quem* for his inquiry, and which the economist Smith enjoins the "statesman or legislator" to adopt, as maxims for his political decisions.[7]

But when all this has been said, it must be stated with equal emphasis that nowhere in Smith's model do instrumental arguments penetrate into the chain of economic reasoning itself. Once he presides over a regime of natural liberty, Smith's sovereign is reduced to a guardian of law and order. Again like the divine engineer, he stands aloof from his creation and is "completely discharged from . . . the duty of superintending the industry of private people" (651). To build the "economic machine" required for the attainment of the postulated social goal is an act of political will. Once it operates it obeys, as does the Newtonian cosmos, nothing but the laws of a deterministic order.

---

[7] It need hardly be mentioned that the source upon which the philosopher Smith draws is the Natural Law doctrine in the peculiar synthesis of Stoic and Epicurean elements, which is achieved in his *Theory of Moral Sentiments* (1759).

7

An Alternative to the Original System: Karl Marx's Theory of Cyclical Transformation

1. *The First "Cracks" in the Dynamic Feedback Mechanism— Malthus and Ricardo*

Smith's optimistic vision was not to survive for more than one generation. A little over twenty years after the publication of the *Wealth of Nations,* Malthus' *Essay on the Principle of Population* appeared, to be followed after a similar interval by the third edition of Ricardo's *Principles of Political Economy.* It is the pessimistic tenor of these two books which turned Economics into a "dismal science." And interestingly enough, the arguments which shattered the optimistic complacency of the preceding generation are at the same time the first breaches in the formal structure of an all-inclusive circular mechanism.

We shall not linger over these initial departures, but shall only indicate their general direction. From our point of view the more important of the two writers is Malthus, who was the first to inject an instrumental idea into the conception of the evolutionary path itself. Originally his notions were no less deterministic than Smith's, the difference referring only to the trend of social development. Where Smith saw an ever-brighter future, Malthus predicted inevitable misery owing to the fateful conjunction of the Iron Law of Wages with the Law of Decreasing Returns on Land. In the second edition of his Essay, however, he broke the iron clamp by pointing to "moral restraint" as a voluntary check on the supply of labor. When shortly afterwards Jeremy Bentham and James Mill interpreted this notion as including birth control, an alternative mode of behavior was shown as feasible, capable of subverting the deterministic mechanism and leading society after all toward a self-chosen goal of collective well-being.

Even so Malthus did not fully restore the original chain of beneficial economic movements. By denying that accumulation necessarily creates additional demand, he broke the link that in Smith had fastened increasing employment and output to the "extent of the market," admitting the possibility of excessive savings and overproduction. As a result the steady course of development foreseen by Smith was transformed into a succession of industrial fluctuations. Nonetheless Malthus' variant altered only the equilibrating form without reversing the upward trend of economic development.

Ricardo's modification of Smith's model went into another direction. He was the first to build his entire system on the Law of Decreasing Returns on Land, on which Malthus had based his population theory. This was bound drastically to modify Smith's optimistic prognosis by shortening the interval between the present and a future in which the stinginess of nature would assert itself. In fact, Ricardo moved that dismal state right up to the present, and the system now stood under the constant threat of "running down" unless technical progress gave it a temporary respite.

Still, radical as this modification was in changing the *trend,* it again did not affect the *steadiness* of the secular process which, in Ricardo's original conception, was as firmly determined as in Smith's. But this too was changed with the insertion of the famous chapter "On Machinery" into the third edition of the *Principles.* By taking note of the potentially labor-displacing effects of industrial technology Ricardo removed the cornerstone from the Smithian structure. Even if the prospects of innovation profits continued to stimulate savings and investment, there was no longer any assurance of the steady growth of aggregate employment and thus of demand.

Though the cause of instability which Ricardo emphasized greatly differed from the cause adduced by Malthus, the anticipated effect was the same: contraction of the "extent of the market."

The stage seemed now to be set for a radical break in the circular mechanism and for the abandonment of economic determinism altogether. Ricardo himself drew no conclusions from his revolutionary findings. This was left to his greatest pupil, and the conclusion he drew was startling indeed.

2. The Formal Characteristics of Marx's Model

If one takes the shocks arising from technological unemployment seriously,[1] the notion of a self-balancing process seems at first sight quite incompatible with industrial technology. Marx's analysis is an impressive demonstration that this need not be so. By substituting the cyclical rhythm of upswings and downswings for the classical oscillations about a dynamic equilibrium he discovered a new and more realistic frame of reference for short-term movements. Moreover, by joining successive cycles in a comprehensive secular process he succeeded in constructing a long-term feedback in some ways even more deterministic than Smith's model.

Formally this dynamic feedback, which Marx calls the "general law of capitalist accumulation" (I, 23),[2] is built from the same components as Smith's: a law of population interacts with a law of accumulation and, above all, with a law of technical progress. But the social forces which are subject to these laws operate in quite a novel manner. On the one hand, technology and its changes dominate the system's motion even more strongly than in Smith's model, so strongly in fact that the laws of population and accumu-

---

[1] For the checkered history of this important concept of dynamic theory, see my "Technological Unemployment Re-examined" in *Wirtschaft und Kultursystem* (Erlenbach-Zurich, 1955), pp. 229–254.

[2] Since there is no standard edition of *Das Kapital* available in English, all references are to the original German edition published in Hamburg: Vol. I, 1867; Vol. II, 1885; Vol. III, 1894. To facilitate comparison with English translations, volume and chapter rather than pages are cited. For further details on the Marxian model see my "Classical Theory of Economic Growth." *Social Research,* vol. 21 (1954).

lation are only secondary consequences of the law of technical progress. On the other hand, this technical dynamics involves in its changes not only the customary variables, namely, supply and demand for commodities and factors, but also the psychological and institutional conditions which the classical writers had treated as constants. Thus Marx's conception of capitalist development transforms not only the determinants of the market process, but also the forces which create and change these determinants, into variables which are reciprocally related to the cyclical fluctuations of the secular trend.

This does not, of course, exempt him from postulating a "set of data," psychological, institutional, and technological, from which the course of capitalist development is supposed to have initially taken off. These data are described in great detail under the heading of Primitive Accumulation (I, 24) and much resemble Smith's social frame of reference, even if they are very differently evaluated. The main new element in the set is industrial technology, reflecting the fact that the Industrial Revolution, of which Smith had only sensed the beginnings, was by then in full swing.

3. *A Double Feedback Mechanism Transforms Society*

We remember that, before Marx, technical progress was regarded not only as the vehicle of economic and social progress but also, with the exception of the later Ricardo, as fully compatible with market stability. By extending the market it was supposed to create additional employment; by stimulating investment it would banish the specter of oversaving. Marx does not simply reverse this argument; rather, his is a "dialectical" position in which technology displays both a constructive and a destructive tendency at the same time. It continues to sustain accumulation and growth, but through its displacement effect it worsens the historically inherited misery of the masses and blocks the extension of the market, thus destroying stability and even jeopardizing profits.

One aspect of this destructive tendency is Marx's law of population or of labor supply. The state of the labor market is no longer left to the play of a biological urge. What really determines wages is "relative surplus population," created by technological displacement. Yet it is not moral turpitude that makes the capitalist-entrepreneur use the whip of innovation in this manner but an equally inexorable special law of accumulation. And in subjecting himself to its commands he does not surrender to some innate propensity but to the pressure of a competitive market which compels him "to keep continuously expanding his capital, in order to preserve it" (I, 22).

This obviously is a different kind of competition from the one which Smith had visualized. The reason is that we deal with a different kind of accumulation. Marx agrees with Smith that accumulation which does not at the same time raise productivity ("accumulation with constant organic composition of capital" [I, 23]) is self-defeating, since it tends to raise wages. Though such a mere "widening" of the capital structure does sometimes occur, only capital-intensifying technical progress ("accumulation with rising organic composition of capital") assures to the individual entrepreneur competitive superiority. But the displacement effect which is inseparable from this kind of accumulation at the same time destroys the equilibrium between aggregate supply and aggregate demand.

It is this "contradiction" inherent in industrial progress[3]—between an expanding output due to continuing accumulation and a less rapidly rising or even contracting mass demand owing to technological unemployment—which creates the cyclical rhythm of economic motion in Marx's system. To depict this new and more complex form of a circular mechanism we again break into the continuous process at the same point where we broke into Smith's chain of interdependent sequences, namely, where the availability of new technical inventions offers new investment opportunities. In sharp distinction from the earlier model, this is not a point on the steady path of a dynamic equilibrium but the characteristic depression phase of a cyclical disequilibrium, which is defined by

[3] Enhanced by the alleged tendency of the rate of profit to fall whenever capital per man rises.

large supplies of idle labor and capital inherited from the preceding turn of the cycle.

As a consequence of new investments—through the interaction of multiplier and accelerator, as we would say today—a new upswing toward the state of full resources utilization sets in. What course this upswing takes, and in what manner it ends, depends on the relative weight of merely "widening" projects and of technical improvements, respectively. If the former predominate, the labor pool inherited from the depression will be gradually exhausted and wages will rise. This, then, creates what modern theory defines as the "disproportion" dilemma of "overinvestment," eventually resulting in cutthroat competition (I, 23; III, 15). Conversely, a sufficiently large share of genuine improvements in total investment will, during the upswing, continually refill the labor pool, thus preventing wage rises and favoring profits. However, the pressure on payrolls which the low level of unit wages exerts must in this case drive the system gradually toward the "underconsumption" dilemma (III, 15). What is common to both types of upswing is the inevitable decline of profits which brings accumulation to a stop, initiating a general contraction of output and the re-creation of large pools of idle factors, the potential bearers of a new upswing.

The main significance of this mechanism for Marx's model lies in the fact that, once the first cyclical movement has been generated as a consequence of the Industrial Revolution, the cycle as such operates as a law of circular motion according to which the factors of production are drained off and replenished. In principle, no additional channels are required to feed outside forces—biological or psychological—into the economic system. The short-term mechanism itself periodically creates changes in the supply of the agents that sustain its motion, especially of capital and labor, though it does so by creating temporary idleness of already existing factors rather than by inducing actual increases.

For this reason the short-term feedback mechanism operating through the fluctuations of the business cycle fulfills the same function as the stationary feedback mechanism in Smith's model: the production and circulation of outputs created by a given stock of inputs. True, cyclical swings in the aggregate level of employment of this stock take the place of the bipolar shifts within a steady equilibrium of full employment. But we still deal only with the core process of the market. Or to use a term which has received currency in connection with Keynes's analysis of the capitalist process: so far we have been discussing nothing but changes in the "level of activity" isolated from the influences of the environment, and not with the long-term effects of the stimuli emanating from the environment itself, that is, with growth. Nor is it obvious from what has so far been said that the long-term process should be anything but a steady sequence of cycles, each subsequent one more or less resembling all those preceding it, without any definite trend of development.

That Marx arrives at the very opposite conclusion follows from his most original contribution: the linking up of the institutional environment itself with the cyclical process. The decisive link is a property of industrial improvements which has not yet been mentioned, namely, the organizational consequences of the "rising organic composition of capital" (I, 22). The ensuing capital intensification is bound to raise the degree of "concentration," that is, the average quantity of capital per firm, from cycle to cycle (I, 23). And even more important for secular development, it promotes also the "centralization" of production (*ibid.*), namely, a continuous increase of the share of large concerns in capital stock, output, and employment. This change in industrial organization is brought about by the periodic downswings, during which it is the larger and therefore more efficient units that prove capable not only of surviving but also of absorbing their weaker competitors.

And only now does the historical function of cutthroat competition come into the open. Through the medium of capital-intensifying technical progress it gradually transforms a widely stratified society, originally composed of many independent producers, into two starkly antagonistic classes. Ever fewer capital magnates confront the large mass of the proletarized people, whose misery mounts under the impact of crises that their very underconsumption speeds along and deepens.

Yet at the same time centralization furthers the rationalization and planning of all economic activities. It even helps train the working masses in the "cooperative form" of production and arouses in them the will to active defense. In Marx's famous words: "Centralization of the means of production and socialization of labor at last reach a point where they become incompatible with their capitalist integument. This integument is burst asunder" (I, 24). Thus the long-term "runaway" feedback of capitalist growth, caused by the defective "coupling" of industrial technology with the consumption power of society, ends in explosion—the deterministic process of historical development comes to an end.

4. Gaps in Mechanical Linkage

As is the case with Smith's model, the closed spiral linkage of events in Marx's system is due to the absorption of the social into the economic process. However, the reciprocal relations are now much more comprehensive. They are not confined to the realm of motivations, where one and the same innate force, the extremum principle, is supposed to impel social as well as economic behavior. The institutional framework is no longer seen as a constant but as subject to a predictable process of transformation under the impact of that very motivational force which, in turn, gains growing strength through the increasing pressure of the environment. Once capitalist evolution is set on its fateful course nothing can remain invariant. In methodological terms, no independent variables are left; a cyclo-dynamic feedback mechanism has swallowed up the "knowns" as well as the "unknowns" of the problem.

It is easy to understand why prevailing opinion sees in Marx rather than in Smith the culmination of economic determinism. Not even the one opening in the circular mechanism which orthodox classical theory had acknowledged, namely, the presence of rival economic regimes between which a political choice must be made, is admitted any longer. Competitive capitalism and bourgeois society, its field of battle, are seen as the product of an inexorable process propelled by the class struggle, the same spring that drove the clock of all past history. Needless to stress that such a world leaves no room for "welfare" postulates; Hegel's "cunning of historical evolution" has replaced the precepts of Natural Law.

However, this secular or rather millennial process slowly approaches its end. As a matter of fact, Marx does not expect that, even under communism, the economic sphere will ever belong to the "realm of freedom" which the socialist revolution is otherwise supposed to usher in. Man will forever be subjected to the laws that regulate the "metabolism between human and natural energies." But under the communist regime of "rational control" he will choose the "most worthy and adequate conditions" under which to attain his ends (III, 48). In a word, whereas a political decision, that is, a choice among alternatives of political-economic systems, is required to release the two Smithian feedback mechanisms which then roll on to the end of all days, for Marx the time for such a decision lies not at the beginning but at the end of the historic process. In his view Man, once he emerged from the animal-like organization of primitive communism, became the puppet of the "material forces of production." But these very forces carry him to a final stage of history in which the puppet is transfigured into a genuine human being capable of deciding not only "adequately" but "worthily" forever after.

It is interesting to note in this context that, though a revolution is to separate the institutional worlds of communism and capitalism, no such sharp break is implied in the transition from purely mechanical response to purposeful action. While still suffering under their proletarian misery the workers are supposed to learn the cooperative forms of production, to organize in unions, and, finally, to rise in wrath against their exploiters. The mediating element is their growing "class consciousness." But though for Marx it is the "social existence" of men that "determines their consciousness," the call: "Workers of the World, Unite!" is obviously directed to beings capable of decision rather than to molecules exposed only to push and pull.

Of greater importance for the entire course of capitalist development is another gap in the sequence of feedbacks, which concerns Technology. Marx's assertion that innovations, the economic *application* of scientific and technical inventions, can be related to the phases of the business cycles is plausible. But it seems difficult to demonstrate that the types of invention itself should be strictly geared not only to the requirements of profitable investment but also to the historical function of capitalism. In this respect it is indeed essential for the Marxian growth process that the technological trend be in the direction of increasing capital per worker. His cyclical analysis and, above all, the growth of the new order in the "womb of the old society" through concentration and centralization is conditional upon such a trend.

Historically the postulate is not unrealistic, since growing capital intensity of production is a main characteristic of the industrial development over the past century. But this development is in all likelihood related to a factor which itself is at variance with the fundamentals of Marx's theory: the steady rise of wages which put a premium on the substitution of capital for labor.

Still more significant is the weakening of the deterministic rigor in the behavior of the protagonists of capitalist evolution. Considering the innumerable appeals to profits and accumulation as the ultimate motive power—"this is Moses and the Prophets!" (I, 22)—one might expect that Marx retains, at least, the extremum principle in its classical simplicity and determinacy. But when we examine the reasons given for both the overinvestment and the underconsumption crises we realize that this is not so. In either case the general contraction of output is conditional on a universal change of optimistic into pessimistic price and quantity expectations, which may well occur while profits are still a positive magnitude.[4] Even if maximization of profits over *some* time span remains the dominant action directive, it is no longer short-run profits as in Smith's model that govern the market process. Rather

[4] The rather vague statements of Marx himself (III, 15, and *Theories on Surplus Values* [Stuttgart, 1910], vol. II, Part 2, pp. 265–268) have been rendered more precise in Paul M. Sweezy, *The Theory of Capitalist Development* (New York, 1942), pp. 141–145.

anticipations of future changes are supposed to affect today's decisions of the capitalist-entrepreneur, and his behavior is no longer treated as a mechanical response to past and present events.

This modification of the orthodox classical behavior pattern introduces another cause of instability into the system. Rise and fall of investment and output and thus the degree of resources utilization now depend on the evaluation of future demand rather than on the registration of its present size. And those two levels are indeed likely to differ whenever changes in taste or technology intervene. In the Smithian model the stationary feedback was supposed to eliminate such disequilibria and to restore full utilization of resources through short-term bipolar adjustments. Now, the large-scale organization of modern industry, its fixed investments and long-term financial commitments, and the specificity of its stocks of capital goods, prevent speedy conversion of the factors of production to new profitable uses, in particular when a new capital stock must be built to absorb technologically displaced labor.

In the Marxian system such adjustment delays combine with the prevailing pressure on the level of mass income to cause periodic reductions of aggregate mass demand, and thus form the objective basis for the subjective volatility of expectations. There for the first time recognition is given, even if only implicitly, to the destabilizing effect which growing immobilization exerts on the behavioral and motivational patterns of the leading economic strata.[5]

This "viscosity" effect of industrial technology must be clearly distinguished from its "transformation" effect. Whereas the latter impels and gives direction to the long-term feedback, the former contributes to destabilizing the short-term mechanism. Not that Marx substitutes chaotic crisscross movements for the orderly oscillations of classical analysis. Notwithstanding some loose talk about "anarchy of capitalist production," the sequence of cyclical

[5] Twenty years before Marx, J. S. Mill (*Principles of Political Economy,* Book III, chap. 12, par. 3) had assigned a strategic role in generating "commercial crises" to profit expectations. But in relating them, as did the popular literature of his time, to speculation supported by credit extension, he failed to see that the ultimate responsibility also for excessive fluctuations of credit reposed in the viscous structure of industrial capital.

phases which takes the place of short-term equilibrium is itself determinate. Even the length of the cycle as a whole is set, in accord with an alleged period of physical depreciation of capital, at ten years.

But there *ex ante* determinacy and thus predictability end. The amplitudes of successive cycles and also the relative length of the individual phases are open to variation. Between the extremes of full and zero utilization of resources any position is, at least in principle, possible. In contrast with the rigorous determinacy of every bipolar movement in the stationary feedback of classical theory, all that is predictable of the short-term aggregate motion in Marx's model is the ordered sequence of phases forming some cyclical "wave."

5. *The Basic Flaw in Marx's Deterministic Model*

Thus closer scrutiny reveals quite a number of gaps in the mechanism of cyclical transformation which Marx claims to be fully determinate: the abandonment of the stationary feedback and its replacement by cyclical waves of changing amplitude and duration; the variability of entrepreneurial behavior patterns in response to the growing viscosity of the system; a widening range of choice for the behavior of the organized proletariat; and finally the voluntaristic breakthrough into the communist realm with its alternatives for collective action.

Significant as these defects are in the context of a methodological critique, they are hardly more than minor blemishes on a body of doctrine which must command admiration for the grandiose sweep of theoretical imagination from which it sprang. However, what is the verdict when the inferences drawn from the model are tested against the development of the industrial systems during the past century?

We have not even tried seriously to apply this test to Smith's system. It is evident from its institutional and technological starting point that, even if all other premises were admitted, Smith's conclusions could only refer to a sort of Jeffersonian world, inhabited by freehold farmers and small artisans, but never to a modern industrial economy. This is not so with Marx. Industrial technology, large-scale organization, and other features of a mature capitalism form the main building blocks from which his model is constructed. From these premises he has been able to predict with amazing accuracy the transformation of the classical and neo-classical stages of atomistic competition—the exclusive field of his own experience —into the contemporary stage in which concentration and centralization of capital and the self-organization of labor are indeed major features. But what has become of the progressive "immiseration" of the masses, the polarization of classes, and the inexorable drift toward social revolution?

In searching for the critical flaw in Marx's reasoning, which made him misread the social trend of Western development, the gaps and inconsistencies in his argument and even his explicit premises are of small moment. The fault lies with the disregard of essential facts which, properly considered, would have not only further loosened but entirely destroyed the postulated chain of reciprocal socioeconomic causation. Imposing as the vision was of a fully deterministic evolution toward the great divide at which the "prehistory" of the past and present was supposed to pass into the "true" history of a classless society, it blinded Marx to the radical transformation which the relationship between the economic and the political forces was undergoing before his own eyes.

While evaluating the early stages of capitalist development Marx was not too far from the truth when he asserted that the active forces impelling evolution were mainly economic and technological, and that the institutional environment adjusted itself more or less passively to these exigencies. But the very consequences of this evolution: the change in social stratification with the shift of political power to the middle classes, the rise of strong labor unions with a membership intellectually disciplined by general education and capable of making their growing aspirations felt under a system of widening franchise, not only democratized the spirit of modern government but created the new administrative key positions for a progressive Control of economic by political forces.

By failing to realize the potentialities of this radical transformation, Marx could not grasp the alternative of a peaceful revolution which was to set Western society on the path toward his own humanitarian goals. The ultimate reason for this failure was his attitude toward the function of democratic government. Though he did not follow Smith in conceiving this function as little more than that of a "night watchman," he saw in it only the subservient tool of upper-class interests. Moreover, in the eyes of Marx's followers it is the very partiality of modern governments, manifesting itself in the support of "monopoly capitalism" and "imperialism," which is supposed to accelerate the course of history toward that final stage when political organization will itself wither away like all the other institutions of "prehistory." Thus it was ultimately his anarchist conception of "true" government that prevented the greatest system builder in modern social science from recognizing the potentialities of a Political Economics.

8

The Erosion of the Original System:
The Post-Classical Pure Economics

1. *The Trend of Post-classical Theory*

It is an ironic fact that Marx's model of the socioeconomic process was, methodologically speaking, an anachronism. When the first volume of *Das Kapital* appeared its prototype in determinism, the orthodox classical system, was already rapidly disintegrating. The process had started among Ricardo's disciples, Nassau Senior's *Introductory Lecture on Political Economy* (1827) marking the turning point. The critical assault gathered momentum in J. S. Mill's several "conversions," and is supposed to have swept away the old framework in the "utility revolution" of the 1870's, from which the so-called neo-classical doctrine emerged.

In an earlier quotation of Marshall the deeper meaning of this trend was already stated: a body of concrete truth was transformed into an engine for the discovery of concrete truth. More specifically, in place of a model of a particular socioeconomic system and its motion, a set of principles was to be substituted general enough to serve as passkey to the understanding of any conceivable economic event, independent of place and time and without regard to the institutional environment in which it occurred.

In order to attain this level of seemingly universal validity, economic theory had to divest itself of three properties that had characterized all classical constructs: involvement with the structure and evolution of a distinctive society; commitment to a particular welfare goal; and last but not least, adoption of a specific motivational pattern. Economics had started out as a theory of society, at the same time normative and positive, and tied to a pecuniary version of the extremum principle. Now it was to be transformed into a "pure" theory, radically positive, and broad enough to accommodate any economic motivation. The programmatic formulation of the first two steps was set forth by Mill; the third was attempted in the utility revolution, and received its most fruitful exposition by Walras.

2. *The Turn toward Pure Theory—J. S. Mill*

Development of economic theory since the middle of the nineteenth century has been described earlier as a steady process of erosion of classical determinism. Though not himself the originator of this transformation, J. S. Mill formulated the new tendencies in a representative statement. In 1843, more than twenty years before Marx submitted his *scientia generalis,* Mill had this to say about the manner in which Economics should be constructed:

Notwithstanding the universal *consensus* of the social phenomena, whereby nothing which takes place in any part of the operations of society is without its share of influence on every other part . . . it is none the less true that different species of social facts are in the main dependent, immediately and in the first resort, on different kinds of causes. . . .

There is, for example, one large class of social phenomena, in which the immediately determining causes are principally those which act through the desire of wealth; and in which the psychological law mainly concerned is the familiar one, that a greater gain is preferred to a smaller. . . . By reasoning from that one law of human nature, and from the principal outward circumstances (whether universal or confined to particular states of society) which operate upon the human mind through that law, we may be enabled to explain and predict this portion of the phenomena of society, so far as they depend on that class of circumstances only; overlooking the influence of any other of the circumstances of society; and therefore neither tracing back the circumstances which we do take into account, to their possible origin in some other facts in the social state, nor making allowance for the manner in which any of those other circumstances may interfere with, and counteract or modify, the effect of the former. A science may thus be constructed, which has received the name of Political Economy.[1]

In isolating a set of "outward circumstances" as data, in abstracting "one large class of social phenomena" from all other circumstances (including the more remote circumstances which influence the data themselves), and finally in introducing as major premise the traditional extremum principle, a syllogism can be formed which is supposed to bestow on economic explanations and predictions a "nearer approximation . . . than would otherwise be practicable to the real order of human affairs."[2] In this manner Mill elevated Economics to the rank of an independent specialty within the larger body of the social sciences,[3] and thus proclaimed a scientific trend that was to determine the direction of research for subsequent generations.

However, it would be a mistake to assume that it was primarily considerations of methodology which brought about this turn. The change was rather the outgrowth of the general disappointment with the empirical failures of the classical model, and in particular of its dynamic feedback. The alleged laws of population, accumulation, and technical change, which were supposed to regulate the supply of the agents of production and thus to assure dynamic equilibrium in the commodity markets, were clearly refuted by nineteenth-century experience. This was true not only of the Iron Law of Wages and its derivative, the wage-fund theory, but also of the naïve theory of accumulation which Malthus had already disputed. Mill himself tried to qualify Ricardo's pessimistic interpretation of industrial progress, but was unable to recapture the earlier optimism about the self-regulatory powers of the market. The

---

[1] See *A System of Logic,* Book VI, chap. IX, par. 3.

[2] *Ibid.*

[3] The statement is all the more significant since Mill expresses doubts whether any other branch "may admit of being carved out of the general body" and expressly denies such a privilege to the "Science of Government." *Ibid.,* par. 4.

reality of business cycles could no longer be denied, even if so far no one had succeeded in explaining them on the basis of the prevailing theory of price and distribution. Anyhow, what to Smith and Ricardo had appeared as a uniform process of stark simplicity revealed itself to Mill as the outcome of a multitude of conflicting tendencies, the relative strengths of which could not be ascertained by deductive analysis.

This crumbling of the classical foundations, especially the abandonment of the idea of a long-term feedback, can be studied in Mill's economic treatise published five years after his *Logic*. In discussing the "influence of the progress of society on production and distribution,"[4] he analyzes in thoroughly neo-classical fashion five hypothetical cases concerning the supply of the agents of production. In each case another set of dynamic stimuli is supposed to operate. Constant or increasing population is combined with constant or increasing capital supply and constant or increasing productivity, in a "catalogue of permutations" which suggests the equi-probability of each set of combinations. No longer is any attempt made to investigate the forces that make the supply of the agents themselves change—the "data" have become independent variables the behavior of which must be established by empirical observation rather than from general principles. There are occasional relapses, e.g., when a fairly attractive stationary state is deduced as the "ultimate point" toward which "society is tending by its industrial progress."[5] But the drift of his analysis is toward the "box of tools" approach, resulting in a neutral tabulation of hypothetical processes deduced "ceteris paribus" from freely chosen premises.

Thus it was the renunciation of the classical long-term feedback mechanism, owing to a more realistic appraisal of the underlying forces, that led to the rise of a "pure" Economics, that is, to a theory which treated the economic core process in isolation from the forces of the environment. At the same time, the analysis of

[4] See his *Principles of Political Economy,* Book IV, chap. III.
[5] *Ibid.,* Book IV, chap. VI.

the core process itself remained faithful to the classical tradition. Not only the extremum principle as a "law of human nature" but also the postulate of social and technical mobility was upheld, thus assuring the equilibrating motion of the short-term feedback. It is true, once the constraining influence of the long-term feedback on changes in factor supply was eliminated, neither the nature nor the relative strength of the dynamic stimuli could any longer be predicted, and the precise structure of the ensuing intra-systemic process could not be calculated in advance. But so long as perfect mobility prevailed *some* sort of short-term production equilibrium was assured.

What, however, could no longer be taken for granted was that, out of this process of equilibration, an order of distribution would arise which necessarily conformed to the original welfare norms. Already Ricardo had given warning of the growing conflict between the interest of landowners and that of all other productive classes, to be aggravated by the competition between labor and machines. But considering the iron grip in which the long-term feedback mechanism was supposed to hold the motion of the market, few practical consequences could follow from his pessimistic view.

Paradoxically, the new understanding of the relationship between the core process and its extra-systemic variables led to a much more optimistic conclusion. While the renunciation of the long-term feedback greatly limited the range of theorizing, it opened a path for economic-political action. Once factor supply was no longer tied to factor demand by inexorable laws, it seemed possible, and even legitimate, to modify the institutional environment and the distribution of wealth and income in accord with politically postulated welfare goals.[6] Though laissez-faire was to

---

[6] These goals did not essentially differ from the Smithian prescripts, though they were now referred to a rather different source: the philosophy of Utilitarianism. Already Ricardo argued from this position against the one-sided benefits which the process of development bestowed on a landowning minority. The practical implications of Bentham's teaching for economic as contrasted with political reform were fully grasped only by Mill.

Utilitarian notions, though with a progressively watered-down content, have dominated normative reasoning in Economics right down to the present. They

remain the general rule, it was regarded as "liable to large exceptions" (Mill), for which factory acts, tax reform, educational tariffs, and other interferences with the automatic order were characteristic examples.

With these considerations, discussion of which abounded after the middle of the nineteenth century, a turning point seemed to be reached. Rather than moving further in the direction of a positive science, devoid of all normative postulates, the logical step was to give pride of place to such postulates as first principles of the analysis, and to investigate which micro- and macro-processes would prove suitable for their realization. What actually happened was that Senior, Mill, and their neo-classical successors stopped short halfway. Instead of adopting the viewpoint of instrumental analysis they divided Economics into two compartments. In one it was supposed to perform as a "science" describing the autonomous tendencies of market relations. In the other it had the function of an "art" prescribing goals for public policy and the institutional arrangements necessary for their attainment.

In order to understand the meaning of this methodological bifurcation, one must focus on the precise relationship in which the science and the art of Economics were supposed to stand. Mill has analyzed this relationship minutely and has come up with statements that at first sight read like a program of Political Economics:

The relation in which rules of art stand to doctrines of science may be thus characterized. The art proposes to itself an end to be attained, defines the end, and hands it over to the science. The science receives it, considers it as a phenomenon or *effect* to be studied, and having investigated its causes and conditions, sends it back to art with a theorem of the combination of circumstances by which it could be produced. Art then examines these combinations of circumstances, and according as any of them are or are not in human power, pronounces the end attainable or not. The only one of the premises, therefore, which Art supplies, is the original *major premise,* which asserts that the attainment of the given end is desirable. Science then lends to Art

lie at the root of the so-called Pareto optimum (see chap. 2, sec. 4), and "modern welfare economists merely revive the Benthamite tradition" (Schumpeter, *History of Economic Analysis,* p. 1069).

the proposition (obtained by a series of inductions or of deductions) that the performance of certain actions will attain the end. From these premises Art concludes that the performance of these actions is desirable, and finding it also practicable, converts the theorem into a rule or precept.[7]

There is only one equivocal passage in this otherwise exemplary formulation. It concerns the service which science is to render to art in making sure that "the performance of certain actions will attain the end." All would be well if such "actions" were to refer to the behavior of the micro-units, and if this behavior were in the center of the scientific investigation. However, what Mill has in mind are the actions of the policy-makers when they reshape the environment. In doing so the guardians of the "desirable end" are to accept micro-behavior as preformed once for all by the "psychological law . . . that a greater gain is preferred to a smaller."

Thus in unison with subsequent writers on economic policy Mill limits the domain of "art" to rearranging the stage sets, trusting that the performance can be perfected without any interference with the spontaneous behavior of the actors themselves. Such dogmatic elimination of micro-behavior as a source of disequilibrium indeed makes the new model of the core process stable, but negates at the same time its predictive claims. By having short-term equilibration, even if not harmony of interests, built into his motivational axiom, Mill in spite of all his heresies remained a partisan of the classical tradition.

3. The "Utility Revolution"

It is generally taken for granted that this last classical bastion fell in the early 1870's, when the famous triumvirate of iconoclasts, Jevons, Menger, and Walras, replaced the original extremum principle by the utility principle. In subjecting this belief to some scrutiny we shall discover that Walras occupies a special place in our survey, since he was the first to formulate an economic law in

[7] See *System of Logic*, Book VI, chap. XII, par. 2 (italics added).

instrumental terms. But before taking up this issue we must acquaint ourselves with those basic propositions on which all the pioneers of the Utility School agree.

What is at stake is not any startling proposition about economic *behavior*, but a new *motivational* principle which is to explain the manner in which marketers and, incidentally, the members of all other socioeconomic organizations make their choices and, by so doing, establish orderly macro-states and -processes. Thus it is not a question of replacing the Law of Supply and Demand by any other behavioral rule. Rather the conventional law, instead of being related to the classical incentive of maximizing receipts and minimizing expenditures, is now to be derived from the aim of maximizing utility or satisfaction, an aim which is said to describe a universal and constantly present state of marketers' minds.

The new theory starts from the premise that satisfaction of wants is both the welfare norm of any economic organization and the universal incentive for individual economic action. As originally conceived such wants express themselves as desires for goods and services on the part of the householders or final consumers. It is their state of mind that is raised to the ultimate datum from which economic behavior is to be derived.

In defining that state of mind the founders of the Utility School had recourse to an alleged psychological law. The law in question —commonly known as Gossen's First Law—postulates that the amount of one and the same enjoyment diminishes continuously as we proceed with that enjoyment without interruption, until satiety is reached. As a consequence, to use Marshall's formulation, "the total utility of a thing to anyone (that is, the total pleasure or other benefit it yields him) increases with every increase in his stock of it, but not as fast as his stock increases."[8]

From this fundamental proposition another one—usually denoted as Gossen's Second Law—has been derived. It states that, given a good like money capable of satisfying different wants, maximum total utility will be obtained if this good is allocated among

[8] See Marshall, *Principles of Economics,* p. 93.

its different uses in such a manner that the marginal utilities, that is, the utilities obtainable from the last unit allocated to any one use, tend toward equality. In other words, maximum satisfaction requires that the last dollar spent in each direction adds the same increment of utility, which is only another way of stating that the marginal utilities to the buyers of the various goods acquired must be proportional to the prices they are willing to pay for them.

Now, here a principle of resource allocation is enunciated which seems to relate the interplay between supply and demand to one and the same overriding consideration motivating the participants on both sides of the bargain. What the haggling of buyers and sellers achieves is an exchange value or price, at which one and the same quantity of the good in question yields to either party maximum utility, and is therefore actually demanded and supplied.

Certainly the classical writers too tried to build an explanatory substructure under their theories of exchange value: cost-of-production or labor-quantity theories. We need not dwell on the analytical deficiencies of these notions. What is essential is the fact that they never were, and never could be, used as criteria for behavior under conditions of *change*. It is precisely this function which the utility theory of value claims for itself, by interpreting changes in the quantities demanded and supplied and the response to such changes, as the result of a change in the respective utilities as experienced by competing marketers.

Still, before the utility principle can be accepted as a general explanation of market behavior, it must be shown that it applies not only to the markets for consumer goods but also to the factor markets. This is to say that those quantities and prices which ensue from the bargaining between agents of production and their employers must also be related to some version of Gossen's laws operating on either side of the bargain. This does not appear difficult as far as the supply quantities and supply prices of the factors are concerned. A worker's idea of what his hourly wage should be might well be related to the satisfaction he expects to obtain from the consumer goods which he is subsequently going to buy or—in a different version—to the "disutility" he experiences in expending effort. But whose utility schedule is to be consulted when we try to establish the hourly wage which a prospective employer is willing to pay?

The Austrian members of the Utility School made the attempt to demonstrate that the prices which perfect competition in fact establishes coincide with the prices that would result if employers were to evaluate the services of the productive factors in terms of the satisfaction which their output bestows on the ultimate consumers. It is noteworthy that this methodological fiction never carried much conviction, and that the explanatory gap was filled in a rather startling manner. What happened was that most neoclassical utility theorists—among them Marshall, Pareto, and Hicks —have confined the range of the utility principle to the actions of householders, while resurrecting the classical principle of *profit maximization* for the behavior of firms as sellers of commodities and buyers of services. We shall soon discover that this apparent inconsistency offers an important clue to the understanding of the utility principle itself.

4. *Maximization of Utility—An Operational Principle or a Tautology?*

The major achievement of utility theory has often been defined as its capacity for deriving "value of exchange" or price from "value in use." Or, to express the underlying idea in the terms used earlier: by raising maximization of utility to the rank of a universal action directive (at least for consumers) the "modal" micro-goal—a quantitative concept—appears linked up with the set of "final" micro-goals—a qualitative concept. If this claim can be sustained, genuine progress has been made in the direction of scientific unification and simplification. At the same time it is not intuitively obvious how, from the free interplay of qualitative choices, patterns of behavior can emerge that are sufficiently regular to uphold the good working order of an economic system. This issue—the key question of any theory of the market—will provide the viewpoint under which we are now going to examine the new axiom more closely.

In doing so, we must brush aside a host of controversies which, though interesting in themselves, do not touch our central problem. Thus we shall skirt such time-honored questions as to whether the utility experienced by a consumer can be directly ascertained or can only be inferred from his overt behavior; whether utility is measurable and thus commensurable with price magnitudes, and if so, in cardinal or only in ordinal terms, and many other subjects of a debate which by now has extended over almost a century. All we ask is this: does the principle of utility maximization, while admitting "free" qualitative choices, yet place a constraint on the ensuing behavior strict enough to permit the prediction of micro-actions and the ensuing macro-states and -processes? And will the actions thus predicted conform to the conventional Law of Demand, postulating an inverse relationship between changes in price and changes in demand, as utility theory asserts?

There is good reason to pose the problem in this fashion. Critics have repeatedly asserted that the notion of maximizing utility is much too general to have any operational meaning. And suspicion grows if we are told that it "does not affect the formal theory of demand in the least whether the individual maximizes wealth, religious piety, the annihilation of crooners, or his waistline."[9] Does this really say more than "that people behave as they behave, a theorem which has no empirical implications, since it contains no hypothesis and is consistent with all conceivable behavior, while refutable by none"?[10]

In order to make this abstract query concrete, we need only consider the possible responses of a buyer to a fall in price. Supposing that all we know about his motivations is his wish to maximize utility, we can predict no more than that he will raise his demand or reduce it or leave it as it is. If he raises his demand

[9] See George J. Stigler, *The Theory of Price*, 1946, p. 64.

[10] See P. A. Samuelson, *Foundations of Economic Analysis*, pp. 91–92. Also T. W. Hutchison, *The Significance and Basic Postulates of Economic Theory* (London, 1938), pp. 112, 115.

he will indeed respond in accord with the predictions of the conventional Law of Demand. In accord with Gossen's laws, he apparently adds to his total satisfaction by buying more units which can now be obtained, in proportion to their diminishing marginal utility, at the smaller sacrifice made possible by lower prices.

But there is no doubt that the other modes of behavior, though conflicting with the conventional Law of Demand, can be interpreted equally well as utility-maximizing. If demand falls as a response to a price fall, we may deal with the Veblenesque case of ostentatious expenditure, in which expensive goods are valued more highly than cheap ones. Or the good in question may be regarded by the potential buyer as an "inferior" good on which he spends less when its price falls, to devote the gain in purchasing power to increasing purchases of more highly valued goods.[11] Finally he may read into the price fall the beginning of a trend indicating a further price fall to follow, so that postponement of purchases to some future date promises still greater satisfaction.

Turning to the third case in which the price fall has no effect whatever on demand, we can interpret even such abstention from action as utility-maximizing. Either the buyer does not care at all for the commodity concerned and would not buy it even at zero price or the amount so far acquired already yields him maximum satisfaction—a case of consumer's homeostasis.

If in the face of such plain objections the protagonists of utility theory maintain their claim of being able to predict behavior in accord with the conventional Law of Demand, we must suspect that they have somehow introduced a limiting assumption into what so far really looks like a mere tautology. This surmise is fully confirmed when we examine the writings of the early marginalists. As a matter of fact, we find there not one but three special conditions for the validity of the new theory.

The first concerns the nature of the "things" the utility of which is to be maximized. There is no doubt whatever that Jevons, Menger, and Walras—or, for that matter, Marshall—were not concerned with piety or waistlines but with the disposal of priced

[11] For details, see Hicks, *Value and Capital*, pp. 28–29.

goods and services. Second, the consumer who tries to maximize his satisfaction with such goods and services is supposed to find himself in a state of "undersatiation."[12] Third, the time span over which the consumer maximizes utility and acts accordingly is supposed to be fixed once and for all.[13]

It is easy to see that acceptance of these conditions excludes all the exceptions from the conventional Law of Demand enumerated above—the Veblen case where ostentation rather than goods disposal is to be maximized; the homeostasis case where full satiation has already been reached; the case of inferior goods where the consumer is virtually "oversatiated" with, say, margarine, and therefore applies the increment in real income owing to the price fall to the purchase of butter with which he is undersatiated; and finally the case of elastic price expectations, because it conflicts with the fixity of the period of disposal. If we wish we can even classify the first and the last case under the aspect of satiation: ostentation leading to oversatiation with low-priced goods, whereas elastic expectations express oversatiation with "present" goods.

Such formulation of the various alternatives of behavior in terms of degrees of satiation has the advantage that it throws the conventional case into relief. In particular, it makes clear why the state of undersatiation with goods and services stimulates an increase in the quantity demanded if price falls. To see the salient point one must realize that undersatiation implies more than the painful experience of a discrepancy between the range of our wants and the range of the means at our disposal. It carries with it the desire to attain full satiation, and thus the incentive to transcend the present state in the direction of larger provision, that is, of acquiring *larger quantities* of the items which constitute our basket of consumption.

[12] The condition is explicitly postulated in Gossen's First Law, already quoted, and is implied in all practical applications of the theory. It has recently been formalized in the so-called "convexity postulate," on which the most advanced version of utility theory—indifference analysis—has been found to rest. (See Koopmans, *Three Essays* . . . , pp. 23–28.)

[13] See, e.g., W. Stanley Jevons, *The Theory of Political Economy*, chap. III, or P. N. Rosenstein-Rodan, "Grenznutzen" in Handwoerterbuch der Staatswissenschaften (Fourth Ed., Jena, 1927), vol. 4, p. 1197: "The economic period must be determinate—if economic calculation is to lead to an unambiguous result" (my translation).

This incentive has nothing whatever to do with the value in use of the particular goods desired. If, as a consequence of a price fall, the degree of satiation is increased, no change in the qualitative order is involved. What changes are the quantities bought, because non-satiation creates a preference for the larger over the smaller amount. Thus in the conventional case maximization of utility is achieved by maximization of provision. In other words, whenever the Law of Demand can be derived from it, maximization of utility amounts to maximizing the quantity of purchases per unit of expenditure, or to minimizing expenditure per unit purchased.

5. Utility Maximization and "Scarcity"

We have arrived at the result that, in its nontautological inter-pretation, the utility principle fully coincides with the extremum principle. True, by pointing to the "dynamics of undersatiation" which induces a constant striving for fuller satiation, one may con-strue the former as a psychological explanation of the latter (though only the latter spells out the specific pattern of market behavior through which the goal of fuller satiation can be attained). Even so, the original claim that the "new" theory of exchange based on the utility principle is more general than the old one based on the extremum principle[14] cannot be maintained.

Neither is it true that value in exchange can be explained in terms of value in use or, what amounts to the same thing, that the action directive of a buyer can be derived from his scale of prefer-ences. It is the preference for more shoes over fewer shoes, and not the preference for shoes over hats, that underlies the conventional Law of Demand. And the plain fact that there are exceptions from such "quantitative" preferences even if the qualitative preferences are unchanged is sufficient proof that the former cannot be reduced to the latter.

Nor is the utility principle better equipped for dealing with such

---

[14] For a contemporary assertion of this claim, see, e.g., Schumpeter, *History of Economic Analysis,* pp. 911–912.

"exceptions." At first sight it indeed appeared as if the deviations on the part of homeostatic consumers or of buyers with elastic expectations could be "explained" by reference to a universal striving for maximizing utility. But we had to realize that, stripped of the restrictive assumptions of the conventional case, the utility concept loses all operational significance. It has meaning only in a timeless world of undersatiation.

If in spite of these limitations neo-classical theory treats the nontautological utility principle and the conventional Law of Demand derived from it as "almost infallible in its working" and the exceptions as "rare and unimportant,"[15] the reason is not far to seek. Is not undersatiation the psychological reflection of the state of scarcity, which is Man's existential and unchangeable condition in this world? Even if for a fleeting moment one or the other particular want should be fully satisfied, is not nonsatiation and therefore conventional behavior the iron rule for the aggregate of a consumer's basket?

Once before we were faced with the ambiguity which besets the notion of scarcity.[16] It then became clear that, in order to define those resources which are objectively and unalterably scarce, two realms of human activity must be distinguished: a primary realm of final activities concerning the actual attainment of our vital, interpersonal, political, aesthetic, moral, etc. goals, and a secondary realm of modal activities—the economic realm—through which the material means are provided which are necessary for the attainment of *some, but by no means of all* our final goals. What the two realms have in common is that both kinds of activities are conditional on the expenditure of the actor's energy and time, which thus acquire the rank of basic resources. And assuming that there is no limit to the totality of our wants—including both those which require material means to their realization and those which do not —these basic resources are indeed objectively and unalterably

[15] See Hicks, *op. cit.,* p. 35. Also Samuelson, *op. cit.,* pp. 115–116, where only the case of inferior goods is admitted as exception; and Schumpeter, *op. cit.,* p. 1067: "Faced with a given set of prices and a given 'income,' everybody chooses to buy (or sell) in a uniquely determined way."

[16] See chap. 1, sec. 2.

scarce. In this sense we find ourselves always in a state of under-satiation in relation to the totality of our wants.

However, in trying to derive a universal *economic* action directive from the postulate of objective and unalterable scarcity, traditional theory goes much further. It assumes that not only the actor's "internal" resources—energy and time—but also his "external" resources—natural resources and services of others—which are necessary to provide him with the material requisites for his means-requiring ends bear the stigma of irremediable scarcity. If this were true, the same stigma would attach, of course, to those "economic," as opposed to free, goods which are the joint product of internal and external resources. But it is true only in circumstances in which *not merely the totality* of our wants *but also that part which requires material means* to their satisfaction cannot be fully satisfied.

It has repeatedly been emphasized here that states of irremediable scarcity of material means do in fact exist.[17] The most obvious case concerns a state of *destitution* in which the available stock of such means does not rise above the threshold that assures physical survival. At the other end of the scale is a state in which even the largest conceivable stock of means fails to satisfy the means-requiring wants, because the latter are felt as *insatiable*. However, far from reflecting unalterable natural constraints or intrinsic human propensities, destitution and unlimited appetition are historical experiences, related to particular stages in the technological and cultural evolution of mankind. More precisely, chronic and universal nonsatiation of means-requiring wants and the scarcity of material inputs and outputs from which such nonsatiation springs can be traced back to the same historical conditions within the limits of which the extremum principle is valid.[18]

Between these extremes of destitution and unlimited appetition fall most of our actual experiences, including the "exceptions" discussed, above all the cases of elastic expectations and of homeostatic behavior. And ample evidence has been given earlier that, far from being "rare and unimportant," these particular exceptions are, if

[17] See, e.g., chap. 1, sec. 2.
[18] See chap. 3.

not the rule, certainly accessory features of the motivational patterns which govern wealthy industrial societies.

Under the aspect of a theory of economic motivations homeostasis is the more interesting case. First of all, it demonstrates the possibility of permanent and not merely transient full satiation of means-requiring wants. And this possibility concerns not only some single want but an individual's and even a society's aggregate "basket." Moreover, it brings into prominence the ever-present potentiality of a "spill-over" of the basic resources—energy and time—from final to modal activities and conversely. If, e.g., a homeostatic consumer does not increase his demand when price falls, energy and time hitherto employed in procuring the material means in question at the higher price are now released into the realm of "direct" want satisfaction, e.g., for more frequent visits to church or for hissing crooners. The reverse spill-over must happen when prices rise and the old level of demand is to be maintained.[19] Maximization of piety and steadfast loyalty to a particular seller—an example cited by Professor Robbins—are certainly possible microgoals in a society which has risen above the subsistence level. However, if in such a society a price fall of material means is responded to by more frequent visits to church or by favoring sellers who stick to the higher price, this may be a better world to live in, but not one that can be understood in terms of the "formal theory of demand."

6. *Neo-classical Vestiges of Instrumental Inference*

Once the practical identity of the utility principle with the extremum principle is seen, it can no longer surprise that neo-classical theory was able to retain the short-term feedback mechanism of classical Economics, and to deduce the same equilibrating tendencies of the economic core process. It is this coincidence between the basic motivational hypotheses which assured the con-

---

[19] Obviously such response implies a systematic variation of aggregate expenditure with change in price.

tinuity of analysis from Senior and Mill to Marshall and beyond. In the light of this uninterrupted tradition, what posed in the 1870's as a "revolution" was no more than a surface ripple. If a caesura exists, it separates Mill from his predecessors rather than from his successors. His abandonment of the long-term feedback mechanism, in isolating the core process from its environment, marked the beginning of modern "pure" Economics, and can with good reason be called the birth of Neo-Classicism.[20]

But this very affinity with ideas of the past destroyed the usefulness of Neo-Classicism as a tool for the explanation of mature industrialism. Not only did its followers imitate the classical pattern of deriving the equilibration of the core process from dogmatically stated behavioral premises, but they tried to force into this framework the new institutional and technological experiences. They covered up the ever-widening gap between theory and facts by distinguishing between "pure" and "applied" Economics—a variant of Mill's distinction between "science" and "art." This made it possible to play down the undeniable disequilibria, cyclical and secular, as the obvious deviations which any empirical phenomenon shows when contrasted with the simplified structure of a theoretical model, or to subject them to *ad hoc* explanation.[21]

The idea of surrendering altogether the positive claims of theory hardly ever arose, and when it did it was quickly abandoned again. A very enlightening example of this attitude is the rumination which Hicks, the leading exponent of modern utility theory, has been

[20] We arrive at a different evaluation if "marginalism"—a postulate concerning the economic calculus—rather than "utility"—a postulate concerning economic motivation—serves as criterion for the "revolution" of the 1870's. "Marginal utility" marks, then, the beginning of a more refined interpretation of the extremum principle in terms of the differential calculus.

[21] The immunity of the short-term feedback mechanism to any extra-systemic shock was assured through a technological postulate: the free variability of the coefficients of production—the neo-classical conceptualization of perfect mobility. Specifically it was assumed that any increase in labor supply or change in technology could be accommodated by the existing "capital stock," so long as factor prices freely adjusted to the ensuing change in marginal productivity. In fact, such unlimited variability of the employment capacity of a given capital stock is incompatible with the structure of modern industrial technology. More about this in chap. 11, appendix to sec. 8.

carrying on in order to justify the "nonsatiation" postulate (in the form of a diminishing rate of substitution) as the foundation of the theory of demand.[22]

Hicks is not satisfied with a purely empirical test of this postulate, but searches for a "more general validity than that." And his argument takes an unexpected turn when he suddenly begins to reflect on "the *purpose* for which we *require* our principle," which turns out to be that we "want to deduce from it laws of market conduct." And indeed the principle lends itself very well to this purpose. But, in order to pass over from what is suitable for a purpose to what prevails in fact, we must "rule out" all deviating "oddities," assuming that "there is a sufficient degree of regularity in the system of wants." "Again, this assumption may be wrong; but, being the *simplest assumption possible,* it is a good assumption to start with; and in fact its accordance with experience seems definitely good" (italics added).

What makes this soliloquy such fascinating reading is its drift of "free association" in the direction of an instrumental interpretation of the principle concerned, but stopping short before the decisive step.[23] It all culminates in Hicks's famous dictum that "Pure Economics has a remarkable way of producing rabbits out of a hat— apparently *a priori* propositions which apparently refer to reality." In fact, as elsewhere in empirical science, all a priori propositions in Economics are nothing but tautologies. And the "reality" to which a nontautological proposition such as the principle of a diminishing rate of substitution refers is not the observed reality of randomly chosen facts of experience, but a "potential" reality only: a postulated state of affairs for the realization of which choices in accord with a diminishing rate of substitution are the suitable means.

Hicks's reluctance to draw the final conclusions from his advanced position is in a way surprising. More than half a century

---

[22] See *Value and Capital,* pp. 22–24.

[23] Professor Stigler's musings on the empirical validity of the profit incentive (*Theory of Price,* pp. 148–149) offer a striking parallel.

earlier Walras had encountered the same problem and had given it a much more constructive solution. It is not for this that Walras is generally credited with the outstanding performance among the founders of utility theory. His reputation is based on his description of the general equilibrium of the market by a system of simultaneous equations. Without detracting from this achievement, one may see in it primarily a work of synthesis presented in the transparent language of mathematics, work for which the ground had been prepared by three generations of classical and post-classical writers.

For our purpose Walras' theory of general equilibrium is interesting because it represents the most advanced model of integrating micro-actions into macro-states, which neo-classical theory has produced. Still, there is today general agreement that the Walrasian equations defining market equilibrium do not offer a solution to the problem of how the system adjusts itself to conditions of change. More precisely, they do not contain any restrictions from which a specific action directive can be derived, which would bring about equilibrium if the system started from a state of disequilibrium or would restore equilibrium had it been disturbed.

Walras himself was quite aware of this problem when he introduced his peculiar concept of "prix criés." In doing so he postulated that buyers and sellers meeting simultaneously in the market go on crying prices, continuously revising their list of offers, but not entering into actual exchange until they hit upon a system of prices which secures equilibrium for everybody and in all parts of the market (242).[24] But even this "pseudo-auction" will never achieve an equilibrium position unless the successive prices cried gradually reduce the original gap between potential purchases and sales, and finally converge to a level at which the market can be cleared. This, in turn, presupposes that there is a behavioral rule, adherence to which will bring about the desired effect.

As we know by now, no such rule can be extracted from "unconstrained" utility functions. The actual functions on which Walras' equation system builds are by implication constrained. They presuppose that state of undersatiation from which the behavioral

---

[24] Numbers refer to the English translation as *Elements of Pure Economics*.

rule of the classical Law of Supply and Demand can be derived
(180–181). But what interests us more in the present context is
the interpretation which Walras places on this constraint. Curiously
enough, he offers not one but two such interpretations.

One, based on the famous notion of "tâtonnements," is on the
level of positive Economics, which treats the rule as a formalization
of actual behavior. "The upward and downward movements of
market prices in conjunction with the effective flow of entrepreneurs
from enterprises showing a loss to enterprises showing a profit is
purely and simply a method of groping toward a solution of the
equations involved in these problems" (to wit: exchange, production, capital formation, and circulation) (44).

There we have the conventional answer based on the "dynamics
of nonsatiation," which impels buyers and sellers to move to positions of more satiation whenever the state of the aggregate permits
it. But for this very reason the same doubts hover over the realism
of Walras' theory of tâtonnements which becloud all other uses of
the utility principle in traditional reasoning. Therefore a second
answer which Walras offers to the question of what the classical
behavior rule really signifies is of much greater significance. It is
contained in his so-called laws for the *establishment* of equilibrium
prices in both exchange and production—well to be distinguished
from his much-discussed conditions for the *stability* of equilibrium:

Given several commodities, which are exchanged for one another
through the medium of a numéraire, for the market to be in a state
of equilibrium or for the price of each and every commodity in terms
of the numéraire to be stationary, it is *necessary and sufficient* that
at these prices the effective demand for each commodity equal its effective offer. When this equality is absent, the attainment of equilibrium prices *requires* a rise in the prices of those commodities the
effective demand for which is greater than the effective offer, and a
fall in the prices of those commodities the effective offer of which is
greater than the effective demand (172).

And subsequently:

Given several services by means of which various products can be
manufactured and assuming that these services are exchanged for their

products through the medium of a numéraire, for the market to be in equilibrium, or for the prices of all the services and all the products in terms of the numéraire to be stationary, it is *necessary and sufficient* (1) that the effective demand for each service and each product be equal to its effective supply at these prices; and (2) that the selling prices of the products be equal to the cost of the services employed in making them. If this twofold equality does not exist, in order to achieve the first it is *necessary* to raise the prices of those services or products the effective demand for which is greater than the effective supply and to lower the price of those services or products the effective supply of which is greater than the effective demand; and in order to achieve the second, it is *necessary* to increase the output of those products the selling price of which is greater than the cost of production and to decrease the output of those products of which the cost of production is greater than the selling price (253–254). [Italics added.]

The importance of these passages lies in the fact that they represent the first explicit statements of instrumental analysis. There it is no longer claimed—as Walras does in many other passages (180, 260)—that the forces of competition *in fact* make the system approach the state of general equilibrium. Rather certain behavioral *requirements* are established which are regarded as prerequisites for maintaining general equilibrium once it exists, and for bringing it about when it is absent. In these propositions the Law of Supply and Demand is deprived of its positive meaning as an empirical generalization (although once more it should be said that there are explicit statements in which Walras claims the Law to be exactly this). Instead it is transformed into an instrumental rule postulating the means, namely, a specific micro-behavior suitable for the attainment of the end: macro-equilibrium. No prediction is implied concerning the behavior that will actually materialize in the circumstances contemplated.

This is indeed a legitimate procedure for putting the rabbit of behavior constraints into the hat of market theory. At the same time the classical Law of Supply and Demand is resurrected in a manner which does not simply take us back to the argumentation of the past but lifts us off the horns of the dilemma of making statements on behavior which are either empirically untenable or so general that they are meaningless. In these passages general equilibrium is for the first time postulated as a goal attainable only by specific action, and no longer as the product of a "blind mechanism so constituted that it automatically makes continual trial and error adjustments toward equilibrium."[25]

[25] See William Jaffé in "Translator's Notes" to Walras' *Elements*, p. 520.

9

Emergence of a New System:
J. M. Keynes's Rudiments
of Political Economics

1. The "Keynesian Revolution"

Walras' traces of instrumental analysis went unnoticed among his neo-classical contemporaries and successors.[1] More than two generations were to pass before the quest for the conditions suitable for the attainment of certain macro-goals was renewed.

In looking back to the publication of Keynes's *General Theory of Employment, Interest and Money* from the distance of another generation, one realizes that the instrumental developments which can be related to this work are at best secondary consequences of its major theme. In spite of drastic breaks with tradition, such as the repudiation of Say's Law or of the conventional theory of interest, and though it substitutes as its main building blocks macro-economic aggregates for the customary micro-economic particles, the General Theory as a logical construct is a product of neo-classical thinking. What distinguishes it from the orthodox version is a different set of motivational and institutional premises rather than a different technique of analysis.

It is all the more instructive to study the consequences, methodological as well as practical, to which Keynes is led from his tra-

[1] An allusion to it may be found in Gustav Cassel's "normative" interpretation of market prices. See his *Theory of Social Economy* (New York, 1931), chap. 3.

ditional starting point. Though his immediate problem is the disequilibria and pseudo-equilibria engendered by lapses of the market from the state of full employment, he does not confine himself to merely explaining and predicting these events which have no place in the orthodox model. By demonstrating that equilibrium and equilibration in the traditional sense are the exception rather than the rule in the real world, he has restored awareness of the normative character of these notions. And the entire analytical effort reveals itself as ultimately devoted to the task of determining the requirements for the attainment of a macro-goal—full employment which is postulated independently of actual experience. Moreover, when the major condition for such attainment turns out to be the substitution, in the sphere of investment, of a novel behavioral force for the traditional decision-making of the micro-units, the realm of instrumental analysis has been entered.

It will be our main task to trace this subtle transmutation of a "pure" into a "political" Economics. For this purpose it is necessary, first of all, to summarize the explanatory-predictive argument of the General Theory and to contrast it with the orthodox neoclassical model. This will yield us also some insight into the true nature of a "general" theory of the industrial market process. In particular we shall discover that the model elaborated in the General Theory rests on very special assumptions rather than on a "necessary principle" (254).[2]

2. Data and Unknowns[3]

Like all post-classical theories the General Theory presents a model of the economic core process isolated from any changes in the extra-systemic variables. Thus what it offers is a novel version of the short-term feedback mechanism. "Occasional digressions"

---

[2] All references in parentheses are to the *General Theory of Employment, Interest and Money* (New York, 1936).

[3] The exposition of this and the subsequent section follows closely that in chap. 18 of the *General Theory,* in which the constants, independent variables, and the dependent variables or unknowns of the model are systematically discussed.

dealing with the "effect of secular progress" (109) do not alter this limited scope, nor do the interesting attempts at building a theory of economic growth on Keynesian foundations, which some of his disciples have undertaken in recent years. As we shall see, rather than restoring a long-term feedback mechanism along classical or Marxian lines, and with it the predictability of the secular socioeconomic process, these extrapolations from the Keynesian model have an instrumental flavor.

Keynes leaves no doubt about the short-term nature of his analysis. Besides consumers' tastes, the degree of competition, and the social structure generally, he explicitly takes the supply of labor and equipment as to both quantity and quality, and thus the technique of production as constant over the range of the investigation (245). This investigation itself is concerned with discovering "what determines at any time the national income of a given economic system and (which is almost the same thing) the amount of its employment" (247).

Still the very formulation of his central problem places Keynes in opposition to the orthodox tradition, since it implies that aggregate income and employment are liable to short-term changes. Trusting in the extremum principle as action directive and in social as well as technical mobility, classical as well as neo-classical theory knows only one level of aggregate employment: the full employment level and the level of national income corresponding to it. With technical progress eliminated from the analysis, even Marx could not have arrived at any other conclusion.

In defense of his heresy Keynes appeals to experience. There he finds as "an outstanding characteristic of the economic system in which we live that . . . it is subject to severe fluctuations in respect of output and employment" (249). At first sight one might want to interpret this diagnosis as the springboard for just another theory of business cycles. That this would be wrong can easily be seen when we remember the two characteristics which all traditional business cycle theories share between themselves: incompatibility with the ruling theory of price, distribution, and resource utilization, and the appeal to extra-systemic factors as causes of industrial fluctuations—from sunspots to credit inflation and technical progress.

In striking contrast with this it is the claim of the General Theory that it has overcome the vexing dichotomy in the modern body of doctrine and, moreover, that it is capable of tracing the instability of income, output, and employment back to the fundamental psychological and institutional order of the core process itself. And though the bulk of the book is concerned with "a study of the forces which determine changes in the scale of output and employment as a whole" (vii) rather than with a detailed exposition of the path of the system as created by these forces, the feedback mechanism which is supposed to steer the system through cumulative ups and downs can easily be demonstrated.[4]

Before turning to this central issue we must take note of another property of the General Theory—its macro-economic form. In contrast with neo-classical usage and, in particular, with the Walrasian model of general equilibrium, its major components are aggregates of the micro-economic elements and not these elements themselves. There are obvious pitfalls in such a procedure. Not only does it presuppose the solution of difficult index problems, but it depicts the course of the actual macro-processes accurately only to the extent to which conflicting sectoral movements within the aggregates can be disregarded. However, within these limits its operational significance is very great indeed. By substituting for the innumerable micro-relations of the Walrasian model a few basic macro-relations, the General Theory arrives at propositions which easily lend themselves to statistical testing and, no less important, are handy tools for policy-making.

3. *The Independent Variables and the Skeleton of a "General" Theory*

The essential part of the theory is the strategic factors or independent variables which, together with the constants, serve as the

---

[4] Only the Notes on the Trade Cycle (chap. 22) are explicitly devoted to this task. But the earlier chapters and, especially, the summary in chap. 18 abound in references to the macro-dynamics that logically follows from the macro-statics of the basic model.

determinants of the level of income and employment. We shall describe them first in their macro-economic appearance, though Keynes leaves no doubt that in this form they are only the proximate causes of the system's motion.

There is, first of all, what in more recent writings goes by the name of the "consumption function," which measures the total value of consumer goods demanded at different levels of aggregate income. There is, secondly, a corresponding investment function, describing the total value of capital goods demanded at different levels of expected profits. And there is finally the rate of interest.

No argument is required to demonstrate that aggregate output and employment are necessarily influenced by the aggregate demand for consumer plus capital goods. But a word must be added concerning the manner in which Keynes relates the demand for capital goods, his second independent variable, to the third: the rate of interest.

He measures the profitability of an investment with the help of the concept of the "efficiency of capital," nowadays defined more accurately as "efficiency of investment." This efficiency relates the total prospective yield of a new capital good over its lifetime to its original supply price. It can be defined as that rate of discounting the aggregate of future yields which makes that aggregate equal to the supply price of the capital good bought.

One advantage of this concept lies in the fact that it measures profitability in the same formal manner as the major cost item: interest, namely, as a percentage of so much per annum. Obviously it will pay investors to add to their stock of capital goods so long as the rate of discounted future yields exceeds the current rate at which money can be borrowed. And the limit to further investment must lie where the—decreasing—marginal efficiency of such investment approximates equality with the rate of interest, in this roundabout way making the latter a codeterminant of output and employment.

As was already indicated, these aggregate variables, convenient because they are easily measurable, are themselves the result of more fundamental factors, partly psychological and partly institutional ones (246–247). Among the former we have, first, the "propensity to consume," namely, the manner in which typical income earners divide their receipts between expenditure for consumer goods and "additions to their stock of wealth." A second is the "state of long-term expectations" relative to the future yield of capital assets. A third is the attitude toward "liquidity," which expresses itself in the demand for money balances. As basic institutional factors Keynes postulates, on the one hand, the "wage unit," that is, the money wage offered for "an hour's employment of ordinary labor" (41) and, on the other hand, the quantity of money as supplied by the banking system.

It is these five factors which, together with the constants enumerated earlier—i.e., tastes, technology, etc.—ultimately determine the short-term motion of the system, and thus the level of output and employment "at any time." Here we have the skeleton of a "general" theory in the meaning of neo-classical methodology. It indeed provides an "engine for the discovery of concrete truth," without itself proclaiming any such concrete truth. It merely establishes a few functional relations placed in the framework of certain data, without prejudging the precise behavior of the respective functions. In order to advance toward "concrete truth," that is to say, in order to derive particular levels of output and employment and particular motions of the system, we must specify the functions and assign definite values to the parameters, for instance, by postulating that consumption rises in such and such proportion with income. But in doing so we descend to a lower level of abstraction, deciding for one among a number of logical alternatives: we construct a "special" theory.

Though a clear distinction between one "general" and several "special" theories of income and employment is implicit in the Keynesian model, his explicit formulations have blurred the issue. He starts out by bestowing on his "arguments and conclusion" the label of a "general" theory to be contrasted with the "special case" presented by classical and neo-classical teaching (3). But as we shall presently see, the concrete truth which is derived from his arguments and conclusions by no means *includes* that special case, as should be expected from a truly general theory. Rather he tries to refute that teaching on the basis of premises which, as we shall presently see, are not more general but radically different from major premises of the inherited doctrine.

At the same time it is a merit of Keynes's approach that it permits us to abstract from his propositions the analytical skeleton of a truly "general" theory, namely, a set of necessary, though not sufficient, conditions for the determination of output and employment. To the extent to which this set is complete and its items prove to be empirically verifiable it does fulfill the methodological requirements of "pure" theory. What this amounts to will become clear when we investigate what states and processes can actually be derived from the set of general conditions postulated by Keynes.

4. *The General Model in Motion*

For this purpose we shall have to arrange the analytical building blocks: data and independent variables, in such a manner that they reveal all possible feedback mechanisms which assure regular and continuous motions of the system. To do so we must again, as was necessary in the analysis of Smith and Marx, break into the self-regulating process at some arbitrarily chosen point.

We choose as our starting point a situation of large unemployment coupled with idle stocks of other resources, in particular, of fixed and working capital and of monetary balances. For some reason to be spelled out later, we assume that a process of net investment is set in motion—a process which, as we already know, will continue up to the point where the new marginal efficiency of investment equals the then ruling rate of interest. In order to determine the actual amount by which investment will increase, we should know some specific facts which are not part of the "general" theory, such as the physical conditions of supply in the capital goods industries, the actual state of long-term expectations concerning the yield of capital assets, the degree of preference for liquid balances, and the quantity of money supplied by the banking system.

However, so long as we stick to our original assumption that *some* net investment will be undertaken, the circular mechanism is bound to continue its course. With an unchanging technique of production—one of our data—additional investment must increase employment and thereby aggregate income and, in all likelihood, consumption. Such additional demand for consumer goods will in its turn add to the demand for labor, capacity, and working capital, and the system finds itself on the way to progressive utilization of the available resources.

This is by no means to assert that a state of full utilization and, in particular, of full employment will be attained in this fashion. What will in fact happen—whether an approach to full employment, or the petering out of expansion at some level of under-employment, or even a downward reversal of the system's motion —again depends on additional assumptions of the special type. One of them concerns the precise value of the marginal propensity to consume, that is, the ratio between additional consumption and additional income. The larger this ratio, that is, the more of each new dollar earned that is spent on consumer goods, the stronger will be the effect of rising income on aggregate employment. Conversely, the smaller this ratio—the more of each dollar earned that is saved —the sooner will the cumulative effect be exhausted, unless further investment imparts new momentum to the upswing.

Again it is not possible to be categorical about investors' behavior in such a situation. But the fundamental variables permit us to stress certain obstacles which stand in the way of a continuous rise of investment. On the one hand, as more and more capital goods are produced, the prospective yield of additional increments is likely to fall, at least so long as all factors making for the growth of the system are assumed away. Therefore, unless the rate of interest falls at the same time and at a sufficiently rapid rate, the inducement to invest will probably decline.

At the same time, the cumulative upswing may well bring forces into operation which will raise rather than reduce the rate of interest. These forces are partly psychological, partly mechanical. The former relate to changes in expectations, which may stimulate the demand for liquid funds as the upswing proceeds. The latter concern the need for larger cash balances necessary to finance the transaction of increasing output, possibly coupled with a rise in wages and prices. Unless the monetary authorities deliberately adjust the supply of cash for this rising demand, the interest rate will rise and thus depress rather than stimulate investment.

We shall subsequently see that special assumptions concerning the behavior of the "wage unit" play a role in such skeptical evaluation of the chances of continuing investment. But the conditions outlined are realistically relevant, and offer as the most favorable prospect the gradual approach to some position of pseudo-equilibrium where "there is no inducement to employers as a whole either to expand or to contract employment" (27). In order to persist, however, such a state of "underemployment equilibrium" must not depress long-term expectations. Otherwise a "sudden collapse of the marginal efficiency of capital" (315) threatens, and the system may enter a downturn. A decline in the rate of investment will then create new unemployment accompanied with a fall in aggregate income and consumption, initiating a cumulative shrinkage to the point where aggregate demand for and aggregate supply of output are again equal.

The system is likely to hover about this depression level of an underemployment equilibrium until another stimulus arises making for the renewal of expansion. It is essential for the automatism of the feedback mechanism that this stimulus be intra-systemic, and this all the more so since all extra-systemic stimuli are excluded by the assumptions underlying the model. It is interesting to note that Keynes expects the marginal efficiency of investment to recover autonomously after an interval of stagnation, owing to the gradual absorption of surplus stocks of working capital and, above all, to the need for replacement of worn-out fixed capital. Thus like Marx he relates the time span, which separates the downturn from the revival of output and employment, to the "average durability of capital" (318). This interval may change with a change of technology, but the concatenation of downs and ups is assured by these physical requirements, and the short-term feedback loop is closed.

This is, briefly, what a "general" theory can teach us. It yields no more than a catalogue of possibilities. These include the classical state of full employment, a drift toward a more or less stable underemployment equilibrium, continuous fluctuations between some lower and some upper limit of employment, or even a tendency toward an inflationary state of overemployment. It does not and cannot tell us the "concrete truth" of what, in fact, will happen. But its five independent variables, selected from an indefinite number of possible economic relations by an intuitive process of true genius, offer an analytical frame of reference of considerable specificity into which most of the logical alternatives can be fitted.[5]

5. *Keynes's Special Theory*

Had Keynes been an orthodox neo-classicist, such a catalogue would have satisfied his aspirations. But his deeper interest in "concrete truth," that is, in the construction of a "system" on the lower level of abstraction on which a Smith or a Marx built his theories, comes into the open in his attempt to design a model for the "economic society in which we actually live" (3). For this purpose he had to specify the relevant functions and parameters in such a manner that the resulting motions approximated the actual course of the modern industrial process.

Taking first the institutional factors, he regards the supply of money as fixed. In other words, on whatever criteria the monetary authorities are supposed to orient their policy, the level of employment and output is not among them. Concerning the other institutional determinant—the wage unit—money wages are assumed to be rigid in the downward direction and stable in the upward direction over a considerable range of expanding employment, until boom prices reduce their real value "to an extreme degree" (13–15).

Turning to the so-called fundamental psychological factors, we begin with the "attitude to liquidity" or the demand for money. It

---

[5] A reservation is necessary, e.g., with respect to the Marxian version of underemployment. More about this in sec. 7 of this chapter.

is supposed to be positively related to changes in aggregate income and output and, for speculative reasons, negatively related to changes in the rate of interest. Thus it is bound to rise with rising employment and in the later stages of a bullish security market. The "expectation of future yields from capital assets," on the other hand, is said to vary inversely with the supply price of capital goods and the increasing competition among producers of such goods.

From these specifications of the psychological factors influencing the rate of investment, taking into account the fixity of money supply and the tendency of money wages to rise with the approach to full employment, we must conclude that, with a rising level of activity, the obstacles to merely *maintaining* the rate of investment multiply. At the same time the behavior of the third psychological variable—the marginal propensity to consume, as specified by Keynes—makes it necessary for the rate of investment not only to be maintained but to be raised, if full employment is ever to be reached. Were the marginal propensity to consume to rise with rising income, investment itself and the psychological factors which determine its progress could be relegated to a minor place. Alas, there governs, according to Keynes, a "fundamental psychological law" (29–30; 96–98; 251–252), according to which "men are disposed, as a rule and on the average, to increase their consumption as their income increases, but not by as much as the increase in their income" (96). The result is a gap between income and consumption which widens in the short run with rising employment, and from period to period with the general increase in a community's wealth. This gap must be filled by increasing investment if the system is not periodically to lapse into a state of underemployment.

It is this shape of the consumption function which, coupled with the psychological and institutional blocks to steady investment, forms the cornerstone of Keynes's "special" theory. It makes it inevitable that, with increasing employment, a deficiency in effective demand is created on the side of consumption, which cannot be perpetually compensated by rising investment because of the instability of long-term expectations and rising liquidity preference.

On the other hand—and here the true feedback character of the construct comes into the open—the shapes of the respective functions, psychological, institutional, and technological, are such as to prevent the downturn of income and employment from cumulating indefinitely. With falling income the consumption gap must gradually close, and the inevitable wear and tear of equipment will in due time improve again long-term expectations.

6. *Keynes's Special Theory and the Orthodox Model*

There is no better way of demonstrating the "special" character of Keynes's theory of employment than a confrontation of its major postulates with the postulates of the "classical" (3)—we had better say neo-classical—theory against which he argues. This will show that the latter can by no means be subsumed under the former, but is a logical alternative to it. Such a comparison will also help us in penetrating beyond what Keynes himself regards as fundamental factors, to the ultimate determinants of his "special" theory.

The major differences in the assumptions underlying the Keynesian and the neo-classical model have been extensively discussed in the literature.[6] Keynes himself has emphasized in the very title of the book what appeared decisive to him: the strategic role which the quantity of *money* plays in the determination of the size of the "real" variables of the system, and a function of the rate of *interest* different from that attributed to it by traditional theory. We shall see that neither are these the true points of distinction nor do the conclusions of Keynes's special theory really depend on them.

It is true, neo-classical and, for that matter, classical theory treated money as no more than a "veil," which was supposed to affect the general level of prices but not to have any influence on the "real" variables of the system, such as the volume of output and employment, or even the rate of interest. This was so because wage rates and unit prices were treated as entirely flexible, in both

[6] The pioneering work was done in a celebrated paper by J. R. Hicks, "Mr. Keynes and the Classics: A Suggested Interpretation," *Econometrica*, vol. 5 (1937), pp. 147–159. More extensively Franco Modigliani, "Liquidity Preference and the Theory of Money," *Econometrica*, vol. 12 (1944), pp. 45–88.

the upward and the downward direction, so that any "abundance" or "dearth" in money supply relative to the aggregate value of inputs and outputs would be quickly adjusted through upward or downward revisions of wages and prices. Moreover, the same mechanism was also to neutralize the effect of any changes in liquidity preference which plays such a central role in Keynes's theory of interest: such changes in the demand for cash would be met by inverse changes in the cost-price level.

Keynes has removed this mechanism by introducing a new hypothesis concerning the determination of the "wage unit." As was recorded before, one of his fundamental hypotheses states that wage rates as they exist in a state of underemployment are inflexible in the downward direction. This assumption necessarily makes the quantity of money a codeterminant of employment and output. Once the minimum level of wages and thus of prices is fixed, it becomes, as it were, a problem of simple arithmetic to calculate the maximum level of employment and output that can be transacted with a given stock of money. Only accidentally or through the planned adjustment of this stock can the automatic forces be released which, all other conditions given, will bring about full employment.

Of course, even increasing money supply can push the system into full utilization only if this additional supply is not itself sterilized by rising liquidity preference, that is, if expectations are favorable to additional investment and consumption. But the same argument can be applied to the neo-classical mechanism which adjusts the wage and price level to the existing money supply. It, too, operates only so long as it is not obstructed by unfavorable expectations which respond, say, to a fall in wages and prices by cutting down consumption and investment in the present, because a further fall is expected in the future.

To put it differently, the unorthodox conclusions which arise from the Keynesian model follow from two unorthodox assumptions, each one of which suffices to destroy the tendency toward equilibration at the full employment level. One postulates the partial immobility of a strategic variable: wage rates, an effect which may be further enhanced by imperfections of competition in the commodity markets. It is this hypothesis which raises the supply of money to the rank of an essential determinant of the level of employment, output, and real income. However, even if pure competition were to prevail in both the labor and the commodity market, automatic equilibration would still be obstructed if, contrary to another orthodox assumption, consumers and investors were to form elastic expectations of future prices and capital yields at critical points. This argument is clearly the stronger one, since even planned adjustments of the quantity of money could not mechanically overcome such behavioral intransigence.

However, to get to the root of the problem we must now inquire into the reasons which, even under a regime of pure competition in both the commodity and the factor market, might induce destabilizing expectations. In Keynesian terms we ask: why should consumers in a downswing expect a progressive fall of prices; why should investors expect an eventual fall in their yields from a steady increase in the output of capital goods, and last, but not least, why should anyone at any time desire to hold cash rather than yield-bearing securities?

In the language of the textbook the answer lies in the "short-run inelasticity of supply" of industrial output, and in the losses of current return and asset value which it threatens. While discussing the effect of expectations on employment (Chapter 5) Keynes himself has described the intricate relationship between inelasticity of supply and both short-term and long-term expectations. What he failed to do was to point out the ultimate reasons for the inelasticity of supply itself.

We have touched before on the crucial point,[7] but had better restate it once more. It relates to the structure of costs in industrial production and, in particular, to the large share of fixed costs in total costs. In such a setup a fall in demand which reduces price below average total costs will not necessarily reduce to zero the quantity supplied. Continuation of production is bound to create

[7] See chap. 3, sec. 4.

losses. But so long as price lies above average variable costs such losses are smaller than the losses which would arise from a complete shutdown. However, losses are losses, and the anticipation of their possible occurrence is likely to influence investment decisions and sales policy. It is true that once money capital is sunk in fixed costs "bygones are bygones," and it is a measure of a marketer's rationality to what extent he is willing to treat them as such. But it is equally rational for him to refrain from irreversible long-term commitments unless his long-term expectations are favorable.

We saw before that the length and irreversibility of such commitments are themselves related to the technical and financial organization of modern industry, to the size and specificity of its capital stocks, and to all other technical factors making for immobility. Therefore even if social immobilities—imperfect competition—are absent from the commodity and factor markets, the *technical immobility* built into the industrial system at best retards, at worst reverses the operation of the self-balancing feedback mechanism by expanding the expectational horizon and spreading uncertainty. It then depends on the strength of their gambling spirit and their attitude toward risk-taking whether producers and consumers respond to changes in market conditions by persisting in buying and selling or whether they prefer to break Say's Law by maximizing their cash balances.

To sum up, the neo-classical and the Keynesian theory of employment arrive at opposite conclusions, manifested in the state of the system which the autonomous forces of the market are supposed to establish: equilibrium at full employment or some pseudo-equilibrium of underemployment. This difference in conclusions is due to a difference in assumptions, but neither party to the dispute is fully aware of the true nature of the latter difference. Keynes attributes his conclusions mainly to fluctuations in liquidity preference and their influence on the rate of interest, to the joint operation of which is imputed the role of money as a codeterminant of the real magnitudes of the system. In fact, it is the rigidity of wages, as his neo-classical critics stress, which brings the quantity of money into play; without this hypothesis wage and price adjustments are, in principle, capable of accommodating any degree of liquidity preference, restoring both interest and money to their classical roles.

But closer examination reveals, and this transcends the neo-classical objections, that not even wage rigidity is a necessary premise for the Keynesian conclusions. All that is required to transform the equilibrating feedback mechanism into one that exhibits cyclical fluctuations is the presence, at strategic points of the process, of destabilizing expectations. Though he was the first to assign to expectations a major place in his analysis, Keynes yet failed to appreciate the full significance of this factor. Nor did he trace expectational instability to the technical organization of an industrial market, a fact which emerges as the ultimate foundation of Keynes's "concrete truth."

It has been stressed here again and again that orthodox theory is applicable only to the conditions of a perfectly competitive market. This excludes not only social immobility as manifested in rigid wage rates but also the technical immobility of a mature industrial system. For this reason, as an interpretation of "the world in which we live," the Keynesian model has on purely intuitive grounds the better of its rival. Whether it also stands the test of confrontation with the facts will be our next topic to explore.

7. Can Keynes's Special Theory of Employment be Verified?

Our inquiry has reached a decisive stage. Keynes's theorems concerning the level of employment and income at any time turn out to be a consistent body of propositions, capable of depicting a short-term feedback mechanism for the economic macro-process. These theorems have been derived, first, from a set of general hypotheses describing psychological and institutional factors which are supposed to govern the industrial core process and, second, from a number of special assumptions which make the strength and direction of the basic forces determinate. All that is necessary to raise this set of premises and the conclusions derived from them to the level of a predictive theory is confirmation by experience.

It is obvious that for us even more is at stake than the empirical success or failure of the "New Economics" of our time. If the Keynesian hypotheses can be confirmed, or at least escape disconfirmation, the traditional methodology, even if not the substantive assertions of traditional theory, can be upheld. Contrariwise, if the relevant facts should be in conflict with either major conclusions of the Keynesian construct or major premises on which it is built, the case for the traditional procedure has once again been lost, and the need for an altogether different approach gains in urgency.

The task of testing the Keynesian hypotheses is far from easy. One reason is, and it may come as a surprise, that empirical data with which the special model can be confronted are rather scanty. Not *any* set of statistical time series referring to some period in the history of the capitalist process will do. It is a question of comparing the *autonomous* motion of the market with the motion as postulated by the model. Therefore events following the Second World War must be disregarded, considering the extensive manipulation of the Western economies by all manners of public control. On the other hand, most data available for events preceding the First World War are unsuitable for a different reason. As Keynes himself points out (306–309), during the nineteenth century particular forces relating to the secular growth of Western industry overbalanced the forces on which the model centers. And indeed, defective as our information is about the nature of industrial fluctuations before 1914, what the statistical material reveals fits much better into the Wicksellian scheme of "overinvestment" than into the "underconsumption" model of Keynes.

Thus we are left with the interwar period. But considering the strong influence which external factors exerted on the course of events in Britain and Germany—a radical change in export conditions in one case, a boom based on short-term capital imports in the other—suitable observations which refer to a large industrial country are confined to the U.S. economy during the 1920's.

Fortunately for our purpose, there is a widely held opinion that the experience during the New Era leading up to the Great Depression fully confirms the Keynesian hypotheses, and there is no doubt that a particular interpretation of this experience was an important element in the development of Keynes's own thinking. Thus the testing ground chosen here should be acceptable to the champions of the "New Economics."[8]

We shall conduct this inquiry on two levels: first, by registering the empirical behavior of the three proximate variables, that is, aggregate consumption, aggregate investment, and the rate of interest; and, second, by forming some notion about the underlying "ultimate" determinants, namely, the three psychological propensities, the wage unit, and the quantity of money. This procedure will also throw some interesting light on the respective merits of direct and indirect testing in social analysis, discussed earlier.

On the first level Keynes's hypotheses come off with flying colors. Between 1923 and 1929 the consumption function had exactly the shape which Keynes predicted: it rose but its rate of increase declined steadily. Conversely, investment showed a rapid increase in its rate of growth during the very years when the rate of growth of consumption slackened, in this way maintaining and even raising the level of aggregate employment and output. And there is no doubt that it was a sharp reduction in the absolute size of investment which in the middle of 1929 brought the boom to a sudden end. As far as interest rates are concerned there is general agreement that, judged by traditional standards, they were at no point high during the entire upswing. Still, the authorities began to raise the rediscount rate from 1928 on, and it is difficult to disprove that the ruling rate was not actually too high relative to the expected future yield to be obtained from potential investment.

Encouraged by so much confirmation on the level of the proximate variables, we feel all the more disappointed when we proceed to the study of the ultimate factors. First of all and most important,

---

[8] The main source for the data referred to below is the *Statistical Abstract of the United States*. See further, F. Modigliani, *Fluctuations in the Savings Ratio*, in Studies of Income and Wealth (New York, 1948), vol. 11, pp. 371–443, for the behavior of private savings during the critical period; Stanley Lebergott, "Annual Estimates of Unemployment in the United States, 1900–52, in *Measurement and Behavior of Unemployment* (Princeton, 1957), pp. 213–238; and George J. Stigler, *Trends in Output and Employment* (New York: National Bureau of Economic Research, 1947), pp. 43–45 and Table C.

there is no indication whatever that *personal savings,* the crucial test for the new psychological law about consumers' behavior, rose systematically during the upswing. Even in absolute values, not to mention as a ratio of national income, personal savings fluctuated quite unsystematically and were, e.g., at the top of the boom in 1928 no higher than at the beginning of the revival in 1923. Nor do we find any systematic fall in *real wages* which might explain the considerable rise in profits in a manner compatible with other Keynesian premises. In fact, real wages rose from 1925 on, mainly as a consequence of another phenomenon which does not fit into the model: steadily falling prices.

Money wage rates, on the other hand, remained practically stable between 1925 and 1929, though real national income rose by almost 20 per cent. It was largely this stability in labor costs together with continuous technical improvements which sustained the marginal efficiency of investment up to the end of the boom. Nor was there any indication of rising *liquidity preference* before the breakdown or of dearth in the *quantity of money.* Rather it has become a standard accusation against the monetary authorities that they failed to contract the money supply in due time.

All in all a picture emerges that is undecipherable in Keynesian terms: a falling rate of increase in consumption associated with rising real wages but not with rising personal savings; increasing profits combined with falling prices; a rapid increase in output accompanied by constant wage rates and constant, if not falling, marginal costs. But the riddle begins to resolve itself if we look at the *employment* figures. They too remained practically constant over the whole period, a fact which is confirmed by the stability of aggregate payrolls. But *stable* employment by no means meant *full* employment. According to one estimate, unemployment during the period of 1923–1929 never fell below 10 per cent of the available supply of man-years; another estimate arrives at a lower figure, but still one that is almost twice as high as the unemployment percentage in comparable prewar boom years.[9]

But how was it then possible for output to rise? The answer is

---

[9] See Lebergott, *op. cit.,* pp. 215, 218.

most dramatically illustrated by output in manufacture, which rose during the critical period by 20 per cent whereas employment fell by 5 per cent—an obvious case of *labor-displacing technical progress*. There we have the crucial variable, consideration of which makes everything fall into place: a "reserve army" of labor prevented money wages from rising, while the technologically induced fall in prices concomitantly increased the buying power of the employed.[10]

Yet apparently competition was sufficiently imperfect to enable producers to retain a considerable part of their cost reductions as profits. Closer examination shows that such profits were very unequally distributed between consumer goods and capital goods industries. From 1928 on, that is, more than a year before the turn occurred, the former felt the pinch of slackening consumption in growing inventory accumulation.

It is difficult to say whether it was the gradual realization of a disproportion between the rates of increase in consumption and in investment, or the simultaneous troubles in agriculture, or over-speculation on the stock market, that was responsible for the date in 1929 when expectations were suddenly and drastically revised. But it is beyond any doubt that the "underconsumption" implied in the behavior of the consumption function was *forced* underconsumption owing to competitive pressure on the wage level, rather than the *voluntary* underconsumption which would have shown in a rise of personal savings. Thus the events leading up to the Great Depression are a confirmation of certain features of the Marxian model, and are completely at odds with the basic hypotheses of Keynes's special theory.

The reason for this failure is not far to seek. By assigning technology to the constants of his model Keynes has eliminated from his analysis a factor which, contrary to his surmise, plays a strategic role even within the short run. But at this point we are not so much

---

[10] The simultaneous technical revolution occurring in agriculture aggravated, and the rapidly expanding service industries partly compensated for, the technological unemployment in industry.

concerned with the practical consequences of our findings as with their methodological implications. First of all, the precarious nature of indirect testing has been demonstrated only too clearly. Had we confined our investigation to the proximate level of the macro-economic data for consumption and investment, as some econometric model builders do, a mistaken verdict amounting to a confirmation of the underlying psychological hypotheses would have been unavoidable. Only by confronting the behavioral variables themselves, in particular the savings function, with the statistical material was it possible to interpret the macro-economic resultants in such a manner that the true determinants came to light.

But an even more important result emerges for the substance of the General Theory. Its conflict with the experience of the 1920's and the alternative explanations offered for these events refute not only the "special" version but also the adequacy of the "general" framework from which the former is derived. For what has proved to be the strategic factor in determining the course of employment and output between 1923 and 1929, i.e., technical progress, is eliminated by assumption from the Keynesian model, by treating the "quantity and quality of available equipment" and the "existing technique" as constants.

Still, if this were the only defect of the Keynesian construct, the remedy would be at hand. Why not simply transform the state of technology from a constant into a variable, thus extending the general framework, and then assign to this variable plausible values which make its operation determinate? Unfortunately the lesson which Smith, on the one hand, and, on the other hand, Marx have taught us excludes such a simple solution. Not only is the direct employment effect of technical changes far from predictable, but even with a labor-displacing technology the ultimate consequences depend on the available "escapements" and, above all, on the secondary effect of such displacement on new investment. Moreover, by opening the core process to the stimulus of technical changes, are we not breaking through the postulated closure of the system, opening it to the play of extra-systemic variables? In a word, will not such an extension of the general framework, even if successful, transform the Keynesian short-term analysis into a theory of economic growth?

8. *The Keynesian Model and the Theory of Economic Growth*

Keynes himself has thrown out some hints about the manner in which the determinants of his short-term model can be used for the interpretation of the secular process of capitalist development. These remarks—the product of "historical generalization" rather than of "pure theory"—take the form of an aside tucked away in the last section of the last chapter of the book (306–309). This sketch has since been elaborated by the so-called "maturity" theorists among his disciples, in particular in the work of Alvin Hansen.

There it has been shown that a "general" theory of secular development can indeed be built on these foundations. All one need do for this purpose is to establish separate sets of premises by combining one of the several forms which the fundamental propensities can assume, with one type of wage policy and of monetary management. Assuming further that each such combination of forces remains active over several decades, one comes up with a catalogue of possible secular processes formally analogous with the catalogue of possible short-term movements discussed above.

Keynes himself is more interested in presenting the outlines of another "special" theory, which in his opinion explains the actual development of the Western economies over the century preceding the Great Depression. Through most of the nineteenth century changes in the wage unit are said to have been in accord with changes in productivity, while "monetary systems were . . . sufficiently fluid and sufficiently conservative to provide an average supply of money in terms of wage-units which allowed to prevail the lowest average rate of interest readily acceptable by wealth owners under the influence of their liquidity-preferences" (308). On these financial foundations "the growth of population and of invention, the opening-up of new lands, the state of confidence and the frequency of war . . . seem to have been sufficient, taken in conjunction with the propensity to consume, to establish a schedule of the marginal efficiency of capital which allowed a reasonably average level of employment . . ." (307). In sum, the relative weakness of unions maintained the wage-unit in balance with the relatively flexible monetary policy, while tremendous opportunities for national and international expansion kept long-term yield expectations and thus the level of investment high. At the same time the accumulation of wealth was gradual enough not to depress the propensity to consume unduly, with the over-all result of a level of employment which, though not stable, fluctuated about a relatively high average.

The contrasting picture of the 1930's and Keynes's predictions about the future are rather vague. He does, however, suggest that "today and presumably for the future the schedule of the marginal efficiency of capital is, for a variety of reasons, much lower than it was in the nineteenth century" (308), and is likely to remain below the minimum rate of interest still acceptable to wealth owners. The consequences for the autonomous operation of the system, though not explicitly stated, are unambiguous: the trend of investment is likely to lag behind what it was in the nineteenth century, and this at a time when the rate of increase in aggregate consumption must be expected to lag owing to the rise in national wealth. As a result the secular level of employment must fall far below what can be regarded as satisfactory from either the economic or the political point of view.

The critical change concerns the marginal efficiency of capital. Hansen and other "stagnationists" spelled out a variety of reasons which were supposed permanently to depress long-term expectations. Each one of the great investment opportunities of the nineteenth century was said to be running dry: population increase, territorial expansion, and possibly even innovations.

This maturity theory, an obvious outgrowth of the depression psychology of the 1930's, offers another warning against the fateful step which is taken whenever the valid but unspecified variables of a "general" theory are made determinate by assigning to them definite values obtained by necessarily inadequate generalizations of limited observations. In the present age of world-wide population explosion, of desperate clamoring for development capital, of expanding nuclear technology and automation, the obstacles to stability and full resource utilization are unlikely to arise from the lack of objective opportunities for investment. On the other hand, the negative forces which in fact today depress long-term expectations and deter investors from fully utilizing the existing opportunities—the cold war, the political unrest in the decolonized regions, and last but not least, the weakening "pressures" in the advanced countries—could hardly have been predicted when the General Theory was written.[11]

It is for all these reasons that more theoretical interest attaches to a quite different attempt at distilling from the basic determinants of the Keynesian model a theory of economic growth. This was done in the writings of Sir Roy Harrod and Professor Evsey Domar.[12] There the issue of growth is not raised as an afterthought, but is shown to be embedded in the very structure of the Keynesian theory. Or to state it more pointedly, the model which Keynes himself built on his analytical foundations is revealed as incomplete. What is really implied in his set of independent variables is, in Marshallian terms, a theory of the secular development of capital, output, and employment, a theory in which the short-term fluctuations in the utilization of a constant stock of resources—Keynes's immediate concern—have a subordinate place only.

In order to follow this reasoning we must focus on the critical variable: investment. Because of the shape which Keynes imposes on the consumption function, it is the rate of net investment which ultimately determines income and employment. But changes in investment are bound to change one of the basic stocks of resources—real capital—and are for this reason in conflict with the macrostatic framework of the analysis, according to which "the existing

[11] This statement needs to be qualified as far as the "psychological law" is concerned that is supposed to shape the marginal propensity to consume. There for the first time account is taken of at least one of the changes in the patterns of economic behavior which are characteristic for the rise of "wealthy societies." More about this presently.

[12] The pioneering step was taken by Harrod in his "Essay in Dynamic Theory," *Economic Journal,* vol. 49 (March, 1939), pp. 14–33.

quantity and quality of equipment" is to be regarded as "given." How to reconcile these contradictory positions?

As we see it now, Keynes has tried to compromise the issue. He takes into account only those consequences of capital formation which can indeed be labeled "short-term," since they do not affect the size of the operating stock of capital. He disregards others which do affect it. Thus he concentrates on the payments which are disbursed to the factors of production while new real capital is being built, and on the direct and indirect effect of these payments on income and employment. He excludes from the analysis, or mentions only in passing, all problems which an actual increase in the capital stock raises for the demand-supply constellation of a growing system, once the new real capital is *ready for use*.[13]

This is not the place to discuss the intricate problems which arise when both income-generating and capacity-creating effects of net investment are simultaneously considered.[14] The upshot of the discussion can be stated in one sentence. Whether the path of the system through time exhibits more or less violent fluctuations (possibly degenerating into secular underemployment or inflation) or whether it approaches equilibrium of the classical or the Keynesian type depends on whether aggregate demand falls behind, exceeds, or just matches the growing capacity for supply. The critical demand-supply constellation in its turn varies with the supply of labor, the rate of its employment and remuneration, the rate at which additional income will be spent, and last but not least, on the manner in which changes in technology affect all these variables.

These refinements of the original Keynesian model are important in their own right, and we shall revert to them.[15] But what do they

[13] Keynes stresses the depressing effect of additions to capital stock on the marginal efficiency of capital—another indication of the short-term or macrostatic nature of his analysis. For a growing system, in which the demand for real capital can increase *pari passu* with its supply, the proposition would be unwarranted in this categorical form.

[14] See, besides the original writings of R. F. Harrod, *Toward a Dynamic Economics* (London, 1948), and Evsey Domar, *Essays in the Theory of Economic Growth* (New York, 1957), the critical exposition in Henry J. Bruton, "Contemporary Theorizing on Economic Growth," in *Theories of Economic Growth*, ed. by Bert F. Hoselitz (Glencoe, Ill., 1960), esp. pp. 243–267.

[15] See chap. 11, subdivision C.

signify for the methodological status of the model itself? They can only strengthen our conviction that, even within the larger framework which includes the extra-systemic variables, conventional procedures cannot reach the level of "concrete truth." To admit this in no way belittles the achievements of the General Theory as an advance beyond orthodox tradition. It has fulfilled the promise of Neo-Classicism in presenting us with a pure theory of the economic core process, that is, with a catalogue of essential factors and of their *possible* interrelations which determine the course of that process in an industrial framework. What it has not been able to achieve was its major aim: empirically valid generalizations about the *actual* course of events.

These consequences have not been entirely lost on the executors of the Keynesian legacy. Their expositions abound with references to "warranted" rates of growth and to "requirements" concerning a particular behavior of investment and income. It was even said of these analyses that all they offer "are, properly speaking, theories of the requirements of steady growth at full employment. They make no assertions with respect to the likely development of capital formation over time."[16] Though this verdict probably goes too far —in particular Harrod's intentions are predictive—it is true that the only definite conclusions which can be drawn from these growth models are instrumental ones referring to the conditions which make an equilibrium path possible. In the absence of these conditions anything may happen, and what will happen is as uncertain as is the empirical realization of the equilibrium conditions themselves.

9. The "Political Economics" in the General Theory

No account of Keynes's accomplishments is complete which does not properly evaluate his innovations in the psychological substructure of economic motion. It was he who for the first time gave the volatility of expectations its due in shaping overt behavior. It is

---

[16] See M. Abramovitz, "Economics of Growth," in *A Survey of Contemporary Economics* (Homewood, Ill., 1952), vol. II, p. 170, note 78.

true, when discussing the "propensities" which dominate the bargaining transactions of buyers and sellers, he holds to the traditional extremum principle. But in combining this monistic action directive with a large variety of possible expectations, he could allow for a wide spectrum of empirical behavior patterns. And the actual propensity to consume which he imputes to income receivers when they decide between present and future consumption transcends the temporal limitations of the extremum principle or of the equivalent utility principle. In the interest of accumulating wealth they may let go of present opportunities for minimization of consumption expenditure.

But such realistic differentiation of a variable, which traditionally has been treated as single-valued, merely adds to the obstacles which stand in the way of predictive theory. There is only one substantive conclusion which is compatible with such a variety of possible behavior patterns, and can thus be stated with near certainty: in an industrial market left to the uncontrolled devices of the micro-units, the state of full employment will be realized only by chance and, if so, will not be maintained for any length of time.

Now, this is an insight of, possibly, small theoretical interest but of great practical importance. To quote once more J. S. Mill, though "insufficient for prediction," it is "most valuable for guidance." But to turn it to such account one must abandon the position of a detached observer of that which is and become the promoter of a state to be accomplished. By postulating a state of full employment as the overriding *macro-goal* Keynes has taken this decisive step, thereby giving to his analytical findings quite a novel meaning. All the obstacles to the attainment of the postulated goal, which his "special" theory discloses, can now be turned into so many reasons for active interference with the autonomous course of events.

The General Theory in its entirety is a strange mixture of Pure and Political Economics, with the latter emphasis growing as the argument proceeds. But it would be wrong to interpret all the policy proposals designed to achieve and maintain full employment as part of a genuine Political Economics, that is, as planned modifications of a defective intra-systemic mechanism. Most of them fall in the category of traditional policies, which confine themselves to controlling the environment of the core process. This is true of both his monetary and his tax proposals. They are to remove institutional hindrances to keeping the rate of interest at a level conducive to investment, and to raising mass consumption. To that extent Keynes is right in stressing the "moderately conservative" nature of his reform ideas (377). But the situation changes, and the "revolutionary" implications of the analysis emerge, when rather than opening new channels for, and blocking dangerous paths to, spontaneous micro-behavior, such behavior itself is made the object of policy.

The decisive passage runs as follows: "In conditions of *laissez-faire* the avoidance of wide fluctuations in employment may . . . prove impossible without a far-reaching change in the psychology of investment markets *such as there is no reason to expect*. I conclude that the duty of ordering the current volume of investment cannot safely be left in private hands" (320; my italics).

We are at this point not concerned with the practical consequences of a "somewhat comprehensive socialization of investment which will prove the only means of securing an approximation to full employment" (378). The theoretical implications are no less far-reaching. They can be stated metaphorically in this way: In Keynes's judgment the behavioral patterns of certain economic actors have been found wanting. And he has given up hope that even a radical rearrangement of the stage sets will improve this part of the performance. Thus he calls a new actor onto the stage whose acting is supposed to give expression to the true meaning of the play, and even to compensate for the failings of the original cast.

Stated in the specific terms of the problem at hand, full employment is postulated as the desirable goal of the aggregate market process. Scientific reasoning then infers a path which is likely to take the system to the postulated goal, and also definite patterns of micro-behavior which are compatible with the suitable path. However, confrontation of the analytical result with the observed facts discloses that the patterns likely to materialize in the real world do not agree with the goal-adequate ones. Therefore new patterns must be established—a task of governmental Control. No longer restricted to their traditional task as watchmen and manipulators of the framework of the market, the public authorities are now entrusted with actual market functions, such as investing and consuming according to the requirements of the system's stability. Such trust is justifiable, not only because this new marketer is powerful enough to overrule opposing forces but also because he has no fixed "propensities" of his own which could conflict with his pursuit of the appropriate path.

Certainly this is a conclusion which radically differs from the conclusions which Walras drew from his rudimentary instrumentalism. He was concerned with the conditions for the establishment of compatible *micro-behavior,* being firmly convinced that a regime of laissez-faire was after all the best guarantee for the realization of equilibrium. Keynes's heresy lies in the renunciation of this belief, and in the appeal to a collectivist force which is to make up for the "misbehavior" of the individualist agents.

However, the difference between Walras and Keynes is not confined to the respective "means" which are regarded as suitable for the achievement of the postulated goal—it includes the nature of the goal itself. What is the reason, we must ask, that made Keynes choose "full employment" rather than the traditional "equilibrium" as the supreme macro-goal of a modern industrial society? Though a necessary property of equilibrium, when understood as a welfare concept, full employment by no means exhausts the conditions required to establish, e.g., the equilibrium which defines a Pareto optimum, the latter being equally concerned with a consumption optimum.

The answer to this question has a theoretical as well as a practical aspect. In the former context it points to the relative and historical character of the traditional welfare norm, and thus invites a critical inquiry into the nature of economic goals generally. As a practical proposition it emphasizes the fact that, at the present juncture, the productive application of all human resources may do more to promote the "good life" than "fuller satiation" of consumers with goods and services would do.

This is by no means an arbitrary interpretation of Keynes's intent. He was quite outspoken about what, in his opinion, was at stake when he offered his alternative to neo-classical orthodoxy "as the only practicable means of avoiding the destruction of existing economic forms"—we may well add: of the fabric of Western society—"in its entirety" (380).

PART FOUR

ASPECTS OF A SCIENCE
OF POLITICAL ECONOMICS

10

Instrumental Inference

1. *The Lesson of the History of Economic Analysis*

Part Two of this essay has been concerned with elaborating a scientific alternative to traditional Economics, labeled Political Economics. For clarification's sake it was then considered expedient to emphasize the differences between these two conceptual schemes and, in particular, between the hypothetico-deductive method conventionally applied and an instrumental-deductive method peculiar to Political Economics. Such emphasis could easily create the impression that the approach advocated here was a product of methodological speculation, entirely divorced from the body of knowledge accumulated over the past two centuries. Nothing could be further from the truth, and our account of some of the major turning points in the history of economic analysis should have dispelled any such notions.

In fact, Political Economics, in the sense of an integral theory which tries to relate the economic core process to the dominant factors of the sociopolitical environment, is as old as the archetype of traditional theory: Adam Smith's system of equilibrium growth. And even the instrumental-deductive method is anything but a novel analytical technique. True, its instrumental component was explicitly recognized only recently, and then under quite different labels.[1] But again some of its roots can be traced back to the *Wealth of Nations,* and we discovered recurrent indications of this pro-

[1] For some specific references, see appendix to this chapter.

cedure in subsequent stages of doctrinal evolution, culminating in the implicit instrumentalism of Keynes's reasoning. What still remains to be done is explicit systematization of these fragments.

However, even if most of the building blocks are available, the systematic construction of a Political Economics is a major task, and one that far transcends the scope of this study. In the remaining space we must confine ourselves to outlining what amounts to little more than a program of research. Thus the present chapter will be devoted to a more detailed exposition of the analytical procedure of Political Economics and, especially, its instrumental part. This will be followed by the application of this research technique to some topical issues. A few comments on the nature and origin of the macro-goals which are to guide both theory and practice in a regime of organized capitalism will bring our inquiry to its conclusion.

As a point of departure it may be useful once more to restate the place of Political Economics in the evolution of economic reasoning. In spite of its affinity with some unorthodox views, its rise and scientific function are closely even if negatively associated with the dominant trend in the history of economic analysis. This trend was defined earlier as the progressive erosion of an originally deterministic system. The original system itself, fully elaborated by Smith, is a perfect replica of the extended hybrid model which formalizes the main substantive propositions of traditional theory.[2]

What the historical survey in Part Three has added to our earlier methodological considerations is the insight that all features of this model were not retained unaltered in the post-classical stages of doctrinal development. Some of these features, especially those which refer to the nexus between extra- and intra-systemic factors and to the autonomy of the core process, were abandoned altogether by Mill and the neo-classicists, while others, such as atomism conservation and even the extremum principle, underwent significant modifications. Thus, at first sight, one might even wonder whether the hybrid model can really be treated as the paradigm of traditional scientific reasoning.

---

[2] See chap. 4, sec. 8.

The ultimate proof for its paradigmatic significance is the consequences for laws of motion (and thus for prediction) which follow from relinquishing or modifying any of its properties. Though such changes were introduced in order to approximate theory more closely to reality, their main effect was one of progressively destroying analytical determinacy, winding up with the neo-classical catalogue of equi-possible states and processes. To put it differently, the propositions of traditional Economics in all its stages of development contain genuine theory precisely to the extent to which they can be translated into the terms of the hybrid model.

For this reason the rudiments of a Political Economics and its instrumental technique can be interpreted as attempts at countering the growing incapacity of traditional Economics to penetrate into "concrete truth." At the same time such revisionist tendencies received support from the increasing need of economic practice for informed guidance in an order the operation of which could no longer be entrusted to decentralized decision-making alone.

On this background the task of the new Political Economics can now be defined. It consists, first, in recapturing with the help of instrumental-deductive analysis the formal determinacy of classical reasoning. Second, Political Economics is to devise, on the basis of its theorems, a public policy capable of shaping the actual performance of an industrial market system in accord with the macrogoals which inform the instrumental part of the analysis. Still more briefly, by an act of goal-setting and another act of policy-framing, Political Economics aims to achieve for economic science as well as for economic practice what classical Economics had expected to result from automatic feedback relations within the core process and between the core process and its environment.

2. The Instrumental-Deductive Method

The methodological program for a Political Economics, as it was formulated earlier,[3] can be summarized as follows: Social economies being organized entities, all economic theory is based—ex-

---

[3] See chap. 5, secs. 4–6.

plicitly or, as in traditional Economics, implicitly—on rules of rightness which assure the good working order of the organization. These rules are given concrete form in the configuration of the micro-units of the system and in the operational principles governing their motion, and are themselves oriented on some macro-goal which the good working order of the system is to accomplish. It is such centering of the analytical work on some collective goal extrinsically established which is one of the two features of the theory that bestow on it a "political" character. The other is the coalescence of theory with political practice.

However, configuration and operational principles vary with the content of the macro-goal. Therefore they cannot be taken for granted and treated as axiomatic premises from which the states and motions of the system are to be deduced, as is the case with the traditional procedure. Rather it is the first task of a Political Economics to determine those organizational rules which are appropriate to the realization of a given macro-goal. This is its *instrumental* part, based on regressive inference from an end to the means, or from a given effect to a suitable cause or causes.

After these causes have been discovered, the *deductive* part of the theory can be constructed as a progressive inference from cause to effect. More specifically, the results of instrumental analysis—suitable configuration and suitable operational principles—now serve as major premises from which, together with the minor premises which spell out specific initial conditions, specific explanations and predictions can be deduced in a conventional syllogism.

When it comes to the *testing* of the theorems thus established another peculiarity of Political Economics manifests itself: what was earlier called its "three-pronged" nature. This is to point to the fact that empirically valid—not merely logically correct—statements can be derived from regressive and progressive inference only to the extent to which political action based on instrumental analysis succeeds in approximating reality to the conditions of goal adequacy. In a general way one may speak here of verification by "indirect" testing, because the premises of progressive inference—the product of instrumental analysis—can be confirmed or disconfirmed only by confronting the resulting theorems with experience. But the object of experience is not facts "passively" observed. Before it can serve as a testing ground, the social realm of experience must first be reorganized in accord with the findings of the theory, and the theory proves true only if political action can *make* it true.[4]

It stands to reason that, once the major premises for the deductive part of the theory are known, procedure in Political Economics does not differ from the traditional way of economic reasoning. What does differ and therefore needs explanation is the instrumental part, in which these premises are established. The remainder of this and most of the subsequent chapter will be devoted to this task.

3. *The Search for Causes*

Instrumental analysis being an inferential procedure, the first step consists in defining the "knowns," and the "unknowns" which are to be derived from the former. Earlier we enumerated four sets of *knowns:* (1) a macro-goal usually specified by optimization criteria, (2) the initial state of the system under investigation, (3) pertinent laws of nature and engineering rules, including those psychological laws which link specific behavior to specific motivations, and (4) certain empirical generalizations which establish a tentative relationship between economic motivations and relevant environmental influences, in particular, political control.

The *unknowns* to be inferred are, on the one hand, the goal-adequate configuration of the micro-units and, on the other hand, the operational principles which are to govern their motion. They can be further specified as (1) suitable paths over which the system moves toward the macro-goal, (2) patterns of behavior suitable

---

[4] On the methodological significance of "action" as a component of "theory," see chap. 5, sec. 6. For the rest of this chapter we are going to study the processes of inference independently of any practical consequences, and therefore in ignorance of their confirmability. To be precise, we should then speak only of hypotheses and not of theorems. But this warning should render the looser terminology used above innocuous.

to keep the system on the suitable path, (3) motivations suitable to generate suitable behavior, and (4) political controls suitable to stimulate suitable motivations.

The precise role which each one of these items plays in the process of regressive inference can be best demonstrated by concrete examples. This will be the main purpose of subsequently studying instrumental analysis in operation. However, it may be useful as an introduction to such application to clarify the meaning which is to be attached to some of the concepts employed. Moreover, we cannot even start to apply instrumental analysis before we fully understand in what sense the knowns are "given" to us or, what amounts to the same thing, from what sources we draw our data.

THE KNOWNS

(1) THE MACRO-GOAL. In traditional theory the macro-goal or terminal state of the system is the major unknown to the determination of which the theoretical enterprise is directed. It is one of the two distinguishing features of instrumental analysis that the terminal state now becomes a datum, the other being the transposition of behavior and motivations into unknowns. This "inversion of the problem"[5]—deriving the path and the relevant forces of motion from a comparison of the terminal with the initial state, rather than deriving path and terminal state from the initial state with the help of a known law of motion—gives to the macro-goal the strategic place in the inferential process.

There are, in principle, two ways of defining the terminal state. One consists in spelling out all the physical magnitudes—in market systems also the price magnitudes—which describe those properties of the system in which the macro-goal materializes. In Tinbergen's terminology[6] this amounts to postulating the numerical values of the "target variables." In doing so we implicitly describe the quali-

---

[5] The expression is taken from J. Tinbergen, *On the Theory of Economic Policy* (Amsterdam, 1952), p. 14. See also appendix to this chapter.

[6] Chap. 2 of this book.

tative nature of the goal: whether it refers to aggregate output and its composition, to the level of employment or the rate of growth, to the order of distribution or the ratio between domestic and foreign trade, or to any combination of these or other target variables. And by fixing the numerical values we also decide on the optimization criteria of the terminal state: a definite level of output or employment, a specific rate of growth or ratio of distributional shares is postulated as welfare optimum.

Such prescription of the numerical structure of the terminal state is indispensable whenever empirical cases are studied with the practical aim of framing policy measures. If, however, we are interested only in establishing a general notion of suitable adjustment paths and behavior patterns, it suffices to postulate the qualitative nature of the target variables and of certain criteria of optimization, such as a Pareto optimum or full resource utilization or, to mention what under modern conditions is a rather eccentric goal: minimization of change. In order to retain the literary form of exposition we shall, in the subsequent discussion of concrete problems, confine ourselves to such qualitative determination of the macro-goal.

Conventionally the source of a datum is seen in observation, or in an assumption the content of which is, at least in principle, accessible to observation. This is not true of the terminal state in instrumental analysis. It is introduced as a mental construct the content of which may *become* an object of observation once effective controls reshape actual events in accord with the requirements established by the theory. Failing this there may never be anything "real" which corresponds to it. Thus within the confines of *economic* analysis the macro-goal appears as a discretionary postulate, neither the content nor the origin of which seems to be subject to any rules. This raises serious problems which we shall take up in the concluding chapter. We shall then realize that the choice of an economic macro-goal is anything but arbitrary, once such choice is related to more general criteria of social action.

(2) THE INITIAL STATE. Whatever the source of knowledge concerning the terminal state, in searching for the properties which define the initial state we seem definitely to be referred to observa-

tion. But will simple perception of actual facts and events supply us with a tractable datum?

We need not enter into an epistemological dispute whether immediate experience, with its "mixture of heterogeneous circumstances seemingly inseparably interwoven and confused" (Ernst Cassirer), is at all a subject of knowledge. There is a more specific reason why a criterion is required which can guide us in our observations. It was said earlier that the major inferences of instrumental analysis arise from a comparison between the terminal and the initial state. Such comparison is possible only if the same properties of the system are registered for both states, so that the physical and value magnitudes for the same variables can be set against each other. Thus it is the order of the terminal state—the primary datum —which directs observation of the initial state and helps us select from the "heterogeneous and confused circumstances" those which are relevant to our problem.

For this reason the definition of the initial state varies according to whether a particular level of resource utilization or a specific rate of growth or ratio of distribution, etc. is postulated as macrogoal. Fortunately quite a number of these state variables overlap, and there are, e.g., certain common characteristics of all initial states which we encounter in the study of production problems. Since the examples to be discussed fall in this category, it may be useful to list some of these features.

When seen in this context the initial state can be defined by the aggregate of available resources, the degree of their utilization, and the technical and social relations which govern such utilization. In all activities which involve processes of production, such as adjustment of supply to changes in demand or changes in the degree of resource utilization or economic growth, the *technical* relations are of primary significance. They refer to the physical arrangements by which resources can be combined as inputs, to the sequence of stages of production through which natural resources are transformed into finished goods, and to the coordination of the main sectors of production which assures steady replacement and, if necessary, expansion of material resources.

The pertinent *social* relations concern, first of all, the order of decision-making, centralized or decentralized or some combination of these polar forms. Closely associated with the order of decision-making are the prevailing systems of communication and sanction. Other types of social relations, such as the order of ownership in the means of production or the centralized or decentralized disposal of output, play a major role in the analysis of distribution problems.

The technical and social relations determining a particular initial state operate as *constraints* on the motion of the system toward the postulated terminal state. The more rigid the prevailing social and technical organization the smaller is the number of potential paths, and the more determinate the instrumental solution. Conversely, the weaker the constraints the larger is the totality of feasible movements and the greater the prospect of attaining the goal. Contrary to a general presumption we shall discover that the combination of decentralized decision-making with industrial technology—the social and technical relations typical for modern markets—imposes heavier constraints on goal-adequate motion than does a market economy applying a pre-industrial technology or an industrial organization governed by centralized decision-making.

Perhaps the most challenging instrumental problems arise from a "disturbance" of a given order of the system, say of a stationary or dynamic equilibrium. Such disturbances may be due to a change in any one of the system's basic variables, such as the quantity or quality of resources, the productivity of their combination, the order of tastes, etc., or even to a change in environmental conditions: monetary policy, tariff regulations, etc. In such cases the initial state must be defined inclusive of the disturbing factor.

The Unknowns

(3) THE ADJUSTMENT PATH AS A SEQUENCE OF CONFIGURATIONS. When the concept of configuration was first introduced,[7] it was to emphasize the structured as opposed to the random arrangement of the parts in an organized system. In an economic system, as we

[7] See chap. 4, sec. 5.

remember, the basic configuration concerns the arrangement of the activities of the micro-units in a circular flow. In this flow or sequence of activities resources are steadily transformed into outputs, some of which leave the flow in the form of consumption goods while others return to it as inputs serving the replacement and expansion of the capital stock. In market systems this physical or technical flow is supplemented by a steady money flow, which appears in circular succession as incomes—expenditures—business receipts—business outlays which again turn into incomes. It is this money flow that bestows on the sequence of technical activities the character of market transactions, and the good working order of the market is conditional on the perfect coordination of both flows.

As an unknown of instrumental analysis the configuration of the system takes on a wider meaning. There it refers to the succession of states which is suitable to transform the initial into the terminal state. This succession of states, which is the true definition of the "path," is thus the configuration of a *process*. And the task of instrumental analysis becomes one of inferring the course of this process from the knowledge of its take-off point and its terminus, combined with the knowledge of the pertinent laws of nature and engineering rules which govern all physical transformations.

The terminal configuration is given whenever the numerical values of the target variables are spelled out. If the macro-goal is defined only in terms of the quality of the target variables and the optimization criteria, the terminal configuration must first be derived therefrom.[8] The initial configuration, on the other hand, from which the path takes its departure is given with the technical and social relations discussed before. And the path itself, the dynamics of configuration, appears then as a sequence of structured states, each stage describing the physical and price relations between the state variables: inputs and outputs in the aggregate and for relevant sectoral subdivisions, employment and incomes, savings and investments, etc. From stage to stage these variables undergo expansion or contraction in the aggregate, or relative

---

[8] When discussing in chap. 11 the instrumental analysis of Macro-Equilibrium we shall have occasion to show how such a configuration can be derived.

shifts, until they assume the configuration of the terminal state.

It was said before that the number of possible paths is a function of the constraints imposed by the technical and social relations of the initial state. Only in rare cases are these constraints so severe that one single path is left open. As a rule the terminal state can be reached over a variety of paths.[9] But even then analysis can be made fully determinate by introducing additional criteria for what is to be regarded as the optimum path. Such "path criteria" form, then, together with the allocational, distributional, etc. criteria for the terminal state, a more comprehensive set of optimization criteria.

(4) THE SUITABLE "FORCES." If we were to study physical processes, the changes in the configuration of the state variables during successive stages of the adjustment path would be the major subject of research. In the context of a social analysis the study of paths is only preliminary to a more fundamental plane of inquiry. It concerns the "forces" which are suitable to initiate and sustain motion along the suitable path. From our earlier discussion we know that such force analysis moves on two levels: the level of behavior and the level of motivations, especially of action directives and expectations.

If path analysis is governed by the technical relations of the initial state, force analysis is dominated by the social relations, in particular by the prevailing order of decision-making. In this connection it is, at first sight, not obvious that force analysis plays any significant role in a fully centralized system. There the decision-makers and their subordinate functionaries are directly charged with the realization of macro-goals. Once path analysis has revealed to them the sequence of suitable changes in the state variables, their cognitive problem is solved. And no purposive problem can arise so long as planners and executants identify with the goals of the Plan.

However, since even a system of monolithic collectivism remains a social system in which the micro-units pursue goals of their own, such identification can at best be taken for granted for the framers of the Plan. A purposive problem concerning action directives re-

[9] This, incidentally, is the reason why we speak of "suitability" conditions rather than of "requirements."

mains with regard to the functionaries, and to that extent the behavioral and motivational issues pose themselves also under these
conditions. That they hold pride of place in all market systems has
been demonstrated over and over again, and the inference of suitable action directives and expectations from the knowledge of suitable behavior patterns—themselves inferred from the configuration
of the path—is in the center of instrumental market analysis.

(5) THE SUITABLE CONTROLS. Instrumental analysis of suitable
controls has a place only in the study of pure market systems or of
mixed systems like organized capitalism. In fully centralized systems,
total Control is the main feature of the social relations in the initial
state and, as we already indicated, is the social technique with the
help of which the system is moved along the suitable path. Control
enters as a special problem only where the social relations in the
initial state give the decisions of the micro-units sufficient leeway
for a legitimate conflict to arise between actual micro-behavior and
such micro-behavior as is suitable for the attainment of the macro-
goal. It is then the task of measures of Control, as the term was defined earlier,[10] to adjust micro-behavior to the macro-requirements,
or to supplement it by compensatory macro-action (public demand
or public investment), or, in the extreme case, to supplant it altogether by central decision-making (nationalization).

We have repeatedly stressed the tentative nature of all propositions which concern the "suitability" of specific measures of Control for the adjustment of motivational and behavioral patterns.
Within these limitations it is a legitimate task for instrumental analysis to infer—from the knowledge of the initial state, the findings
of path and force analysis and certain empirical generalizations
about the influence of controls on motivations—the set of alternative measures suitable to attain the terminal state. But the choice
between such alternative measures, which cannot be avoided if a
practical policy is to be formed, falls, in principle, outside such
analysis. Whether, e.g., the macro-goal shall be realized by giving
the widest possible scope to decentralized decision-making, or
whether and to what extent central decision-making is to take its

---

[10] See chap. 5, sec. 5.

place, is a choice that parallels the setting of the macro-goal itself. And the standards by which this choice is made may well be included in the optimization criteria of the latter.[11]

However, that does not mean that such standards can be chosen irrespective of other data of the analysis, especially of the social relations prevailing in the initial state. Two examples will illustrate what is at stake. There is no logical contradiction if the planning board of a fully collectivized system prescribes a production program which meets all requirements of a Pareto optimum in the sense of satisfying the tastes of all its micro-units. But in the absence of a price system the practical difficulties are probably insuperable. Thus the suitable measure to be taken for the attainment of this goal is the introduction of a price system, that is, a radical transformation of the initial configuration of the system. Conversely, an issue which will occupy us subsequently, balanced growth, may prove incompatible with a system of decentralized decision-making, even if these decisions are subject to sporadic measures of public Control. Only ongoing planning of the strategic movements may prove effective for the purpose, again at the price of a sweeping change in the original order of social relations. Keynes's insistence on "comprehensive socialization of investment" as a condition for assuring full employment is another case in point.

The instances cited can be interpreted in a different manner. All macro-goals are not necessarily compatible with the prevailing social relations and, in particular, with the prevailing order of decision-making. Therefore one may be forced to choose between abandoning the existing socioeconomic order or the goal. We shall revert to this dilemma in our concluding observations.

Appendix

It would be worth while to study in detail the relationship in which instrumental analysis stands to other "goal-oriented" analytical techniques that have been elaborated in recent years. Such a survey would conclusively demonstrate that Political Economics

[11] See the earlier discussion of this issue in chap. 5, sec. 5.

tallies well with the most advanced procedures in economic inquiry, and may perhaps serve as focus for the systematization of these ventures. For lack of space we must confine ourselves to a few general remarks.

Among the techniques that come to mind are: modern Welfare Economics; Activity Analysis with its major branches of Linear Programming, Input-Output Analysis, and Operations Research; Tinbergen's "Theory of Economic Policy"; and the so-called "Economic Projections" as, e.g., developed by Gerhard Colm under the aegis of the National Planning Association in Washington, D.C.[12]

What all these techniques have in common with instrumental analysis is their concern with determining the means for the achievement of given ends—in the language of Welfare Economics: with the "optimum methods for producing a given 'commodity menu' " (Reder); in the language of Linear Programming: with the maximization or minimization of some "objective function" limited by the existence of certain "constraints" (Dantzig); or with determining, as in Input-Output analysis, the levels of inputs and outputs of all industries contributing to the production of a postulated "bill of goods" (Leontief).

On the other hand, in contrast with Political Economics as here defined, most of these approaches have a strong technocratic if not collectivist bias, at least to the extent to which they deal with macroeconomic problems. Only this particular bias can, for instance, explain the almost exclusive concern with the configuration of the terminal state to the disregard of the adjustment paths and of the goal-adequate behavioral and motivational forces. In other words, the presumption is that, once the technical arrangements compatible with producing the commodity menu or the bill of goods are

[12] For special references see Kenneth E. Boulding, "Welfare Economics," *loc. cit.;* A. P. Lerner, *The Economics of Control* (New York, 1944); R. Dorfman, P. A. Samuelson, and R. M. Solow, *Linear Programming and Economic Analysis* (New York, 1958); W. W. Leontief, *The Structure of the American Economy* (2nd ed., New York, 1951); J. Tinbergen, *On the Theory of Economic Policy* (1952), and *Centralization and Decentralization in Economic Policy* (Amsterdam, 1954); *The American Economy in 1960* (Washington, 1962), and subsequent publications of the National Planning Association.

known, the sociopsychological problem of inducing the micro-units to act accordingly is implicitly solved.

At the same time, some of those techniques are capable of tackling a problem the solution of which is a precondition for the practical application of instrumental analysis. For didactic reasons we have so far assumed that the aspirations of an economic community can always be compounded in one macro-goal, and that the available resources are always sufficient to assure its attainment. This assumption is not unrealistic if, e.g., full employment or a certain order of distribution is postulated. The situation changes if more than one goal is pursued, e.g., a certain rate of growth combined with a stated minimum level below which consumption is not to fall. In such cases an inquiry into the *compatibility of goals* must precede the instrumental analysis of paths and forces. Activity Analysis and also Tinbergen's Theory of Economic Policy are valuable tools for testing the consistency of multiple macro-goals, and thus for the definition of a feasible terminal state from which instrumental analysis must take its bearings.

11

Instrumental Inference in Operation

1. *The Test Cases*

Instrumental analysis is to discover the particular set of causes that are suitable for the realization of some postulated effect. As such its scope of application is universal, and practically any economic problem can be subjected to its scrutiny. In now selecting a few test cases our criterion will be twofold. On the one hand, the topics discussed should be analytically illuminating; on the other hand, they should prove relevant for some of the practical tasks which confront the modern industrial systems.

Under both aspects, Stabilization and Balancing of Growth or, more specifically, the establishment of full resource utilization and the achievement of the continuous and efficient absorption of newly available resources, hold pride of place. These issues are today the major concern both of scientific observers and of framers of policy in mature as well as in developing countries, and are so irrespective of whether their regimes incline toward centralized or decentralized decision-making. In addition, in any system dominated by or aspiring to an industrial technology, Stabilization and Balancing of Growth pose the kinds of problems for the solution of which only a Political Economics applying the instrumental technique of analysis can provide answers.

But before proceeding any further a warning must be sounded. Even if we are going to discuss topics of crucial importance, the manner in which we can treat them here does not lend itself to direct practical application. Once more it must be emphasized that our purpose is didactic, and that no more is intended than a demonstration of some principles of instrumental reasoning within a highly simplified frame of reference. We shall, for instance, assume for all our test cases the validity of the extremum principle as the common action directive of marketers, and concentrate on the discovery of suitable expectations and of the control measures suitable to influence actual expectations in the desirable direction. Moreover, we shall assume, for the major part of the analysis, a closed system.

To assume otherwise would force us in each case to present a bewildering number of alternatives, or to spell out in full detail the specific values for all target variables and for the relevant data of the initial state, including path criteria, institutional constraints, and any other intra- and extra-systemic factor that could affect the final outcome. Not only is this a task for the technical specialist, but it is more than doubtful whether the necessary analytical spadework has already been accomplished on which such a theoretical edifice could be built. In contrast with an enterprise of this scope, all we aim at is the demonstration of a *modus operandi*.

A. MACRO-EQUILIBRIUM

2. *Stationary Equilibrium as Analytical Framework*

Stabilization and Balancing of Growth are attainable macro-goals, irrespective of whether the initial state of the system is one of equilibrium or of disequilibrium. In the former case the task consists in maintaining an existing state of full resource utilization or a steady rate of growth; in the latter case it is a question of transforming a state of underutilization into one of full utilization or of adjusting the structure of a system to changes in the rate of growth. In either case an equilibrating macro-state is a convenient framework for our investigations. This is obvious when equilibrium prevails to begin with. But even when disturbances of various kinds create an initial disequilibrium, the relations among the critical variables can best be gauged as deviations from their equilibrium values.

Under practical aspects one may still wonder whether *stationary* equilibrium is the proper frame of reference. Though the attempt has been made to conceive pre-industrial as well as capital-saturated market economies in this image,[1] all real economic movements during the past two centuries have occurred as parts of a comprehensive growth process. Still, in dealing with short-run problems it can be useful even in empirical work to abstract from secular motion. To do so here will greatly simplify exposition and, when studying growth itself, we can easily transform our frame of reference into one of dynamic equilibrium.

We have so far spoken of stationary and dynamic equilibria as convenient arrangements of our data. Actually these states of the aggregate are themselves instructive subjects for instrumental analysis. The very fact that structural changes are absent from such equilibria makes them an ideal testing ground for the conditions suitable to *maintain* an established network of economic relations.

3. *A Stationary Model of Industrial Production*

One unique advantage of stationary analysis lies in the fact that the terminal state is identical with the initial state. Therefore once the configuration of the former is postulated that of the latter is also given. But in postulating the terminal state we must describe stationary equilibrium in terms of the particular variables in which the macro-goal is to materialize.

We know already that stationary equilibrium when interpreted as a macro-goal coincides with a Pareto optimum.[2] As such it embodies allocational, distributional, and efficiency criteria, the last-named understood as referring to the rate and productivity of resource utilization. When we earlier discussed the Law of Supply

[1] See J. A. Schumpeter, *Theory of Economic Development* (Cambridge, Mass., 1934), chaps. 1 and 2; J. M. Keynes, *General Theory*, p. 220.
[2] See chap. 2, sec. 3.

and Demand,[3] the allocational aspect of such equilibrium was emphasized. Now, in view of the subsequent application of our findings to the problems of Stabilization and Balancing of Growth, the production aspect and, in particular, the efficiency of resource utilization are in the foreground, and the configuration of the terminal state must be specified accordingly.

Under the *efficiency aspect* stationary equilibrium can be defined as the permanent, full, and technically optimal utilization of employment-seeking resources. The qualification of resources as "seeking employment" is to exclude the notion that efficiency requires utilization of labor and real capital up to the technical *maximum*. In other words, "voluntary nonutilization"[4] is fully compatible with the concept of full utilization as here applied. This also takes care of natural resources potentially "available" below and above the ground, but not offered for utilization in the given situation.

What, then, is the precise configuration of the relevant variables in which the efficiency of resource utilization in stationary equilibrium manifests itself? To determine it we start from the most general property of our macro-goal, namely, the fact that stationary equilibrium is to be the result of *production,* that is, of the transformation of suitable inputs into a set of outputs which agree with some postulated basket of consumer goods. The inputs can be subdivided into the conventional categories of factors of productions, and consist on the most primitive level of technology of nothing but stocks of labor and natural resources. On the level of industrial technology with which we are concerned, we must add two stocks of real capital goods: equipment goods and working capital goods, the latter representing outputs in different stages of completion. By combining portions of these four stocks according to the pertinent laws of nature and engineering rules, the actual process of production is performed and temporary provision attained.

So far the entire productive effort is devoted to the production of consumer goods. This is bound to change when we introduce the

---

[3] *Ibid.,* sec. 2.
[4] See for an equivalent concept Keynes's notion of "voluntary unemployment," in the *General Theory,* p. 6.

additional requirement of *permanency* of production. Such permanency is assured only if the four stocks of resources are themselves continually replenished to make up for the wear and tear which production involves.

However, the manner of such replenishment differs greatly for the different stocks, as does its effect on the configuration of the production flow. The need for replacing the "used-up" parts of the stocks of labor and natural resources has no effect at all on this configuration. As far as the steady supply of labor is concerned, we may treat it as a sociological datum the explanation of which falls outside the realm of Economics. Or we may with the classical writers consider the output of consumer goods as the input which restores the labor force. In either case the structure of production as so far described is adequate. The same is true of the replacement of natural resources. They are nature's bounty which, in principle, cannot be replaced by human activity, and must be treated as a datum.

The situation is quite different for the two stocks of real capital. They become available only in the form of outputs of the production flow itself, and therefore affect its structure considerably. Whereas temporary provision can be achieved by channeling all inputs into one productive "sector" yielding consumer goods, permanent production requires a second sector in which equipment goods are produced and steadily reproduced.[5]

In illustrating this bisectoral configuration of a stationary production equilibrium we assume for simplicity's sake that there is only one consumer goods, bread. It is continually produced through the continual inputs of labor and equipment goods—plows, flour mills, baking ovens—both of which combine in transforming natural resources progressively into wheat—flour—bread. Labor and the natural resources, which we leave unspecified at the moment, are

---

[5] For the reproduction of working capital goods no special "sector" is required. They are really natural resources in the process of being transformed into finished goods, and as such appear in both sectors on successive "stages" of production, issuing in either finished consumer or finished equipment goods. The proper coordination of these production stages within each production sector poses interesting problems for instrumental analysis which, however, cannot be taken up in the present context.

to be regarded as data. The equipment goods, on the other hand, must themselves be continually reproduced pro rata of their wear and tear. This occurs in another production flow, which combines other units of labor and natural resources such as iron ores with other types of equipment goods (extraction machinery, blast furnaces, steel mills, machine tools), resulting in the plows, flour mills, etc. necessary for replacement.

However, we have not really solved our problem of maintaining continuity of production. The equipment goods applied as inputs in the equipment goods sector—extractive machinery, steel mills, etc.—must on their part be continually reproduced if continual provision with bread is to be assured. Thus it seems that we must introduce a third sector of production in which the equipment goods capable of making steel mills, etc. are produced. Still, why stop there? If this "third-level" equipment good in turn requires an equipment good for its production—and nowhere in an industrial system is there anything produced without the use of some equipment goods—we are faced with what appears as an infinite regress. What makes the situation even more puzzling is the fact that this logical paradox is in practice solved every day, as the permanency of actual industrial production flows convincingly proves.

Fortunately there is also a simple theoretical solution, and one which well demonstrates the significance of engineering rules in instrumental analysis. What is at stake can be grasped most easily if we return once more to what happens in the consumer goods sector where our object of final provision—bread—is produced. In discussing it above we left the substance of the required natural resources undetermined. In now spelling it out a clue will be found for the solution of our equipment goods puzzle.

One of the natural resources required for the production of bread is obviously soil or, adopting the most advanced technology, water. Still it is not the only natural resource. We can imagine dispensing with plows and, perhaps, even human labor, and yet raising wheat, but we cannot imagine dispensing with another input so far not mentioned: seed-wheat. But what is seed-wheat, and how is it obtained? It so happens that it is physically identical with the semifinished output bread-wheat, and it is a moot question whether it can really be called a natural resource. But whatever the correct classification may be, seed-wheat not only is indispensable but it possesses an outstanding quality which is absent from flour and bread, from plows and mills and ovens: the power of self-reproduction. Differently stated, seed-wheat as an input is capable of producing two types of outputs: bread-wheat as a potential consumer good and seed-wheat as its own replacement good.

The seeming paradox in the replacement of equipment goods can be resolved along similar lines. If there is an equipment good which, by application of suitable engineering rules, is capable of both producing other equipment goods and also reproducing itself, the infinite regress is replaced by a circular motion. What we actually find is not one such mechanical instrument, but a comprehensive group which is defined as machine tools. In conjunction and combined with labor and working capital goods such as steel, machine tools are the progenitors of all other machinery *and also of themselves*. For the physical maintenance of an industrial regime of production they play the same strategic role as seed-wheat plays in agriculture, and the reproductive system plays in the maintenance of organic life.[6]

The consequences of this discovery for the construction of a model of industrial production are reassuring. Far from being forced to complicate the model by the addition of ever more sectors, we can, in principle, content ourselves with the original two. However, for reasons which will appear when we discuss Growth, it will be convenient to subdivide the equipment goods sector into two sectors: one producing the equipment—henceforth called secondary equipment—which is required to produce consumer goods, and another one producing the implements which we call primary

[6] For details and also for a more technical exposition of the problems discussed in subdivision A, see my paper on "A Structural Model of Production," *Social Research* (June, 1952), pp. 135–176. The earliest reference to the "power of self-reproduction" on the part of machines, which I have been able to discover, is in Samuel Butler's *Erewhon* (London, 1872), chap. XXIV. The notion was formally introduced into Economics by Marx. For the further history of the problem, see my paper quoted above in this note.

equipment, required to produce both secondary and primary equipment.

What we have so far accomplished is a description of the structural requirements for a permanent flow of industrial production. However, the optimization criteria for our equilibrium goal as stated above include also the postulate of *full and technically optimal utilization of resources.*

In the foregoing the three sectors producing consumer goods, secondary equipment, and primary equipment appear organized in such a manner that output of each sector in a given period is at least large enough to replace the resources worn out in that period, hence production can continue at the same level in the subsequent period. But within the constraints so far established it may well happen that, e.g., more secondary equipment is produced in one period than is subsequently required. In that case part of the available equipment stock will go unused, and the criterion of full utilization is violated. To prevent this another constraint must be introduced: the quantity and quality of current outputs in each sector must *equal* the inputs required in the subsequent period.

We are finally in a position to spell out the configuration of a stationary production flow in precise terms. Beginning with primary equipment, the output of such goods in sector I during any one period must be equal to the combined wear and tear of such equipment, operating in the equipment goods sectors I and II during that period, and must thus be just sufficient to restore full productive capacity in these two sectors during the next period. The output of secondary equipment in sector II during any one period must on its part equal the wear and tear of such equipment operating in the consumer goods sector III, whereas the output of consumer goods during that period must suffice to satisfy the demands of the human factors operating in all three sectors during the subsequent period.[7]

---

[7] This is an occasion on which the language of simple mathematics proves much superior to literary exposition. We can very easily formulate the configuration of a stationary production flow in three equations. By denoting the

4. *The Suitable Path and the Suitable Forces*

By translating the macro-goal "stationary equilibrium" into a set of structural relations we have obtained an exact description of the terminal state. But since this terminal state is identical with the initial state, the question arises as to the meaning which can still be attributed to the notion of a *path* connecting the two states. The answer has already been indicated in the changing role—from outputs to inputs—which identical goods play in two subsequent periods. But it must now be shown through what processes of inter-sectoral relocations stationary equilibrium is continuously maintained.

In demonstrating these relocation processes we make use of the analogy of triangular trade relations between three countries, treating each sector as a trading unit. Then we can say that the consumer goods sector retains part of its current output for the provision of its human factors in the next period, while it offers the remainder as exports to the sector producing secondary equipment. On its part it is compensated by the import of the total output of that sector. The secondary equipment goods sector in turn must use part of its imports of consumer goods for the provision of its human factors, offering the remainder to the primary equipment goods sector from which it imports the necessary replacement of its own equipment goods. The primary equipment goods sector finally

---

period outputs of the three sectors as a, b, c, respectively, and by denoting the period input of labor as n, and that of equipment as f, we obtain

$$\text{Sector I} \quad a(1) = f_a(2) + f_b(2)$$
$$\text{Sector II} \quad b(1) = f_c(2)$$
$$\text{Sector III} \quad c(1) = n_a(2) + n_b(2) + n_c(2),$$

where the figures in parentheses refer to periods, and the subscripts indicate the sectors in which the outputs of period (1) are used in period (2). Of course, inputs and outputs can be "equated" in this manner only if there is merely one type of output in each sector. Where we have, as in reality, a number of physically different outputs in each sector, consolidation in one magnitude and equalization of inputs and outputs poses an index problem. A price system it is the most efficient technique for its solution, and we can interpret our variables in all market economies as price-sum magnitudes.

uses its imports of consumer goods for the provision of its human factors, and replaces the wear and tear of its equipment stock from the remainder of its own output.[8] Thus stationary equilibrium as a continuous process is conditional on the continuous equilibration of the intersectoral trade balances.

Turning to the *forces* which are suitable to maintain this equilibrating motion and, in particular, the required intersectoral relocations, we must now introduce as a further datum the prevailing social relations and, especially, the predominant type of decision-making. There is a good reason why we can confine ourselves to studying the polar cases of complete centralization and complete decentralization, disregarding all mixed systems. The reason lies in the fact that, once the equilibrium path has been established—a dynamic problem which is not now under investigation—suitable behavior is more or less assured by routinization. This excludes the need for any special measures of control, and thus for any socio-economic organization which could exert such control.

Still, the question can be raised: what are the suitable forces that will return the system to the equilibrium path, if it is accidentally displaced from it? This amounts to an inquiry into the forces which make stationary equilibrium "stable."[9]

In a system governed by centralized decision-making the appropriate behavior is determined once path analysis has determined the suitable movements, and therewith solved all cognitive problems. There remains, as we saw,[10] the purposive problem of inducing suitable action directives in the executants of the collective Plan.

[8] Again three equations derived from those set down in note 7 will make the "triangular trade" fully transparent:

$$f_c(2) = b(1)$$
$$= c(1) - n_c(2)$$
$$= n_a(2) + n_b(2)$$
$$f_b(2) = a(1) - f_a(2)$$
$$= c(1) - n_b(2) - n_c(2)$$
$$= n_a(2)$$

[9] See the reference to stability in chap. 4, sec. 4.
[10] See chap. 10, sec. 3.

But this is a political and administrative task to which economic analysis has nothing to contribute.

Much more is to be said about the stability conditions of a market equilibrium. Since the strategic movements were above defined as sectoral relocations within the aggregate of the production process, one might be tempted to subsume them under the category of shifts and to subject them to the behavioral rules as formulated in the reinterpreted Law of Supply and Demand.[11] That this would be a grave fallacy can easily be shown by a simple example. Suppose the "accidental displacement" consists in a rise of demand for secondary equipment above its equilibrium level, followed by a rise in its price. According to the rules of the Law of Supply and Demand, the equilibrating response would be an increase in supply. Since, however, demand for the good in question has not "really" increased, such a response on the part of the sellers, rather than restoring equilibrium, would transform the temporary disturbance into a permanent distortion of the sectoral relations. The only suitable response is to keep supply on the equilibrium level. What motivations can assure such behavior?

Since we assume the validity of the extremum principle, the critical factor is sellers' expectations. We remember that the cognitive motivations suitable to bring about a response in accord with the Law of Supply and Demand were positively elastic quantity expectations and price expectations of less than unit elasticity.[12] But in order to assure stability, that is, return to the original position of equilibrium, sellers' quantity expectations as well as their price expectations must have zero elasticity. More concretely, sellers must expect that buyers will reduce demand and price offers before the procurement period for additional output is completed.

Though our example has little practical significance—stationary equilibrium being more or less an imaginary construct—its theoretical significance is very great indeed. We meet here with a case in which the motivational compound suitable for maintaining goal-adequate behavior radically differs from the combination that ad-

[11] See chap. 5, sec. 4.
[12] See chap. 2, sec. 2.

justs supply to changes in demand. In other words, even if the same action directive operates, it is by no means the same type of expectations which, under different circumstances, assures the good working order of the system. It is this association of specific operational principles with specific macro-goals which makes instrumental analysis the foundation of Political Economics.

B. STABILIZATION

5. *The Suitable Path*

Macro-equilibrium is easily maintained in pure market systems as well as in fully collectivized systems. Absence of any disturbances permits perfect routinization of behavior and, for all practical purposes, makes force analysis redundant.[13] Contrariwise, Stabilization in the sense defined above, namely, the establishment rather than merely the maintenance of full resource utilization, is a major task of Control in a mixed system.

A collectivist system can be seriously destabilized only if the path analysis of the planners is faulty or the executants are incompetent or disloyal, or if uncontrollable extra-systemic events intervene. And the remedy can then only be improved path analysis and more effective political and administrative supervision. A pure industrial market system, on the other hand, is constantly exposed to lapses in resource utilization which the uncontrolled responses of the micro-units are incapable of overcoming. It is a basic Keynesian tenet that only controlled market systems can cope with this problem. This tenet will now be translated into instrumental terms. For this purpose we must, first of all, define the terminal and the initial state, and derive from them a path suitable for Stabilization.

To simplify our exposition we postulate as our *terminal state* a stationary macro-equilibrium as defined above. This means that we disregard the allocational and distributional criteria necessary to

---

[13] It is this easy compatibility of macro-equilibrium with laissez-faire that has made equilibrium analysis a preferred subject in classical and neo-classical theory.

make a Pareto optimum fully determinate, and confine our optimization criterion to the critical variable of resource utilization. Even in this respect we simplify further by postulating only *permanent* and *full* resource utilization, taking technical efficiency for granted.[14]

How must we define the *initial state* of disequilibrium so as to obtain an adequate take-off point for the Stabilization path? Obviously it must be a state in which part of all types of available resources, in particular of labor and capital, is idle.[15] As a first approximation it will be assumed that the "ratio of idleness" is the same for all resources and that the same ratio applies to money, the idle or "hoarded" part of which is measured by the difference between money actively circulating in macro-equilibrium and the money circulating in the state of underutilization. We further assume that the units of each resource, employed or idle, are of equal technical efficiency.

Now, if we want to trace a determinate path we must invest the initial state with a tendency to endure. In other words, intra-systemic forces must be at work which will prevent the system from moving toward more or toward less utilization of resources. We deal here with a "pseudo-equilibrium" corresponding to the under-employment equilibria described by Keynes.[16] What, then, is the sequence of configurations suitable to transform this initial state into a macro-equilibrium?

This path has been extensively discussed in the literature in connection with the "multiplier" concept. Following the precedent set

[14] It should be noted that this definition of the macro-goal fully agrees with Keynes's postulate of full employment. He goes even further than the proposition in the text. Not only does he exclude the study of resource allocation and of distribution from his analysis, but he is prepared to accept the allocational and distributional results of a full employment equilibrium as "optimal." See *General Theory*, pp. 378–379.

[15] If merely one type of resources is partly idle, whereas the other is fully utilized, equilibrium can be attained only through an increase in quantity or a change in quality of the complementary scarce resource—a problem of Growth. This view of the matter excludes a solution offered by neo-classical theory, namely, through the so-called marginal productivity mechanism. More about this in the appendix to sec. 8 of this chapter.

[16] See chap. 9, sec. 4. We speak of "endurance" rather than of "stability" because, in technical terms, pseudo-equilibrium is "neutral" and not "stable."

in the original Keynesian formulation[17] the initiation of this path is in the popular mind associated with acts of Control, such as public investment or other forms of public spending. There are sound reasons for such a notion, but they can be appreciated only after it has been demonstrated that, under modern conditions, the autonomous decisions of the micro-units are unlikely by themselves to achieve the same effect. Therefore we are going to describe the suitable path in true instrumental fashion irrespective of the particular constellation of forces which, in the end, will prove the only suitable one to keep the system to that path.

The first step must be an addition to the level of aggregate demand that prevails in pseudo-equilibrium, an addition which may be directed to either finished goods or resources. In order to develop into a process of Stabilization, this stimulus must be met by the following sequence of responses: a rise in resource employment and aggregate factor remuneration—a rise in aggregate output and income—a further rise in demand owing to the increase in aggregate income, and so on in successive rounds of expansion. The multiplier itself is the coefficient which expresses the magnifying effect on resource utilization aggregate output and income, which the primary addition to demand causes. Each such addition implies an act of "dishoarding," that is, an addition to the flow of money actively circulating. For this reason the original stimulus has rightly been defined as additional "spending," and this all the more so as the total effect of each addition to demand depends on the level of spending maintained during the secondary, tertiary, etc. stages in the multiplying process.

Macro-equilibrium is reached when successive additions to demand including their multiplying effects have gradually absorbed all idle resources. In order to stabilize the system at this point additional spending must cease. The number of additional acts of primary spending required to achieve Stabilization depends on the magnitude of the individual additions, the level of secondary etc. spending and, of course, on the size of the ratio of idleness. In the

---

[17] See *General Theory*, chap. 10. For a simple exposition see A. P. Lerner, *Economics of Employment* (New York, 1951), chap. 17.

ideal case this ratio diminishes in each round proportionally for all resources including money, and reaches the zero level for all of them simultaneously.[18]

6. *The Suitable Micro-Forces*

Once we know the sequence of state configurations in which the path manifests itself, suitable behavior consists in applying the appropriate engineering rules and in manipulating the system of price signals in accord with the path requirements. The critical issue is the motivational patterns which are to induce such behavior. Since we take the extremum incentive for granted, attention centers on suitable expectations.

To ascertain such expectations we must distinguish between the primary stimulus of an increase in demand and the sequence of price-quantity responses which form the actual process of expansion. The former issue, namely, how to break out of the repetitive circular flow of pseudo-equilibrium, is the crux of the matter. So we must ask: first, what type of expectations is suitable to raise demand for goods or for factors above the prevailing level and, second, what evaluation of the field of action in the light of the extremum

[18] Needless to say, in practice the process of Stabilization is much more complex. First of all, the technical efficiencies of individual resource units differ considerably in the real world. As a consequence, underutilization is bound to reduce prices below the average costs of marginal firms operating in macro-equilibrium. This makes it necessary to add to the process of quantity stabilization a price adjustment process, during which prices must be gradually raised to the point where, in macro-equilibrium, they again equal minimum average costs of marginal firms. Secondly, the ratios of idleness are hardly ever the same for all resources. Complete absorption of the more plentiful resources is then impeded by the "bottlenecks" created after the absorption of the scarcer ones, a dilemma which only an additional process of Growth can overcome (see note 15 of this chapter).

The process of Stabilization itself may be retarded by possible changes in the multiplier, owing to "leakages" of spending. There is further the retarding effect of rising prices for inputs and outputs as the consequence of bottlenecks. On the other hand, full utilization may be speeded up if the "accelerator" goes into operation, namely, the stimulation of additional investment as a consequence of the rise in demand.

All these modifications—themselves proper subjects for Control—are disregarded here in order to focus attention on the principal barrier to autonomous Stabilization: behavioral and, especially, expectational blocks.

principle is likely to induce such expectations? It stands to reason that these "expansion-inducing" expectations must differ from those which govern the initial state. To pinpoint the difference we must first define those expectations which make pseudo-equilibrium endure.

This is easily done because the expectations sustaining pseudo-equilibrium are the same as those which maintain genuine Macro-Equilibrium[19]: i.e., the elasticity of both quantity and price expectations must be zero. This amounts to postulating that buyers and sellers are supposed to expect the supply and demand quantities and respective prices obtaining in the present to continue unchanged in the future. And it is important to realize that not only will pseudo-equilibrium be steadily reinforced by the behavior resulting from such expectations but, conversely, these expectations in turn will be steadily confirmed and strengthened by their own behavioral consequences.

We know that only some increase in aggregate demand can break up this enduring state. Such increases can now be defined more precisely as due either to consumers spending beyond their current income or to producers spending beyond their current receipts. The former possibility is objectively limited by the size of private "hoards" and the access to consumer credit. But even where such a margin for additional consumer spending exists, there are no subjective inducements to make use of them. In view of the presence of idle resources, the factors employed cannot expect an increase in the price of their services. Therefore, when evaluated under the aspect of maximizing income and minimizing expenditure, pseudo-equilibrium reduces to zero the elasticity not only of their quantity and price expectations but also of their income expectations, thus barring any change in behavior which would reduce their assets or increase their debts.

However, the crucial issue is *producers'* behavior. In the prevailing state of "depression" they hardly meet with any objective blocks to additional spending, having considerable amounts of idle business funds at their disposal and easy access to credit. What sub-

---

[19] See sec. 4 of this chapter.

jective considerations should prevent them from mobilizing these
financial resources for the purpose of expanding output?

In ascertaining the expectations suitable for output expansion
we can again fall back on knowledge acquired earlier.[20] Given the
extremum incentive, such behavior presupposes positive elasticity
of quantity and price expectations. In substantive terms, the potential producer must expect that demand and, if possible, prices
for his output will rise. Incompatible as this type of expectation is
with pseudo-equilibrium, may not the producer justly anticipate
that his own actions will bring about a change that vindicates them
after all? More specifically, will not expansion of supply, by employing additional resources and disbursing additional income payments among them, create the compensating demand?

The answer to this question reveals at one and the same time
a structural weakness of decentralized decision-making, and the precise function which public control fulfills in the process of Stabilization. The critical issue was discussed earlier under the heading of
"solidarity" of investment decisions."[21] It was then stressed that a
specific act of autonomous investment, that is, investment undertaken in anticipation of a future rise in demand rather than in
response to a present rise, will prove profitable only if it is accompanied by a series of complementary investments. Only in that
case can an individual investor expect that sufficient demand will
be forthcoming for his future output, because the additional factors
employed and receiving remuneration in any one firm will become
additional customers for all the others.

What is true of autonomous investment is more generally true
of any act of autonomous output expansion. The expectation of
rising sales on the part of one producer, which alone can induce
him to expand, will be confirmed by subsequent events only if output and factor remuneration are simultaneously expanded by all or,
at least, by a large segment of the community of producers. Otherwise individual expansions are bound to create oversupply leading
to losses, because the factors additionally employed in any single

[20] See chaps. 2 and 3.
[21] See chap. 3, sec. 6.

line of production will normally spend only a small fraction of their incomes on their own output. Unless such solidarity of expansion is assured or some extra-systemic source of demand is opened, the elasticity of producers' quantity and price expectations is bound to stay on the zero level and, in the interest of loss minimization, pseudo-equilibrium will endure.

There is no prospect for such solidarity of autonomous expansion in an uncontrolled market, because there is no signal system which could thus coordinate decentralized decision-making. On the contrary, the more perfect the market the less capable is an individual marketer of conveying his *intentions* to his competitors. Price variations, the only signal system available, register only *completed actions*. This makes them a perfect guide for compensatory responses to stimuli actually emitted. But price changes cannot offer information that would *evoke* the kind of stimulus required for Stabilization, information, namely, about the future responses with which such a stimulus, once it has been emitted, is likely to meet.

It is for this reason that, once pseudo-equilibrium prevails, only extra-systemic stimuli can raise the level of activity. In the past it was left to the fortuitous escapements which autonomous Growth provided, to fulfill this function and thus to determine the timing and the strength of revival from stagnation.[22] To minimize the interim as well as the ratio of underutilization is today a task for public Control.

7. *The Suitable Controls*

There is no better example than Stabilization to demonstrate the true function of Control in an industrial market system. This function is to strengthen rather than to supplant the interplay of decentralized decision-making. Therefore in the ideal case public Control is temporary only, and withdraws as soon as micro-behavior has assumed the stabilizing pattern. More precisely, the task of Control is to arouse in marketers positive quantity and price expectations by actually raising the level of demand.

[22] See chap. 3, secs. 2 and 4.

This at any rate must be the primary concern of public spending, to which other consequences of such spending, e.g., the usefulness of public works or the welfare effect of unemployment benefits, are subordinate. The guiding idea has metaphorically been defined as "pump-priming," and if the pump to be primed is understood as marketers' motivations, the simile is aptly chosen. The priming then consists in creating, outside of the prevailing intra-systemic network of market relations, a demand stimulus to which marketers can respond in multiplier fashion. And the decisive change is that, once such an extra-systemic stimulus is emitted, there is no longer any need for solidarity of action. The secondary effect of public demand, namely, the creation of additional income and expenditure, establishes conditions from which any individual marketer can draw benefit, irrespective of the action of others.

How long and in what amounts priming must continue depends on the long-term effect which the multiplier process exerts on expectations. If positive expectations persist and spread, the "pump" will begin to operate and autonomous expansion will take over. Otherwise public spending must continue at an increasing rate until the progressive rise in resource employment, income, and expenditure does create the suitable expectations—if it ever does.

This last reservation is called for in view of the contingent nature of the relationship between specific controls and specific motivations, which has been stressed repeatedly. This contingency must certainly caution us against ascribing to public spending a mechanical effect on resource utilization.[23] Far from being a problem of simple arithmetics, the actual effect is incalculable *ex ante,* and may even be negative if, owing to the rise of negative expectations, the public addition to spending is overbalanced by reduction of private spending. One historical experience of this kind made during the early years of the New Deal was quoted above,[24] and the

---

[23] Such an interpretation, which has sometimes been read into Keynes's account of the Stabilization process, shares the main weakness of traditional theory, namely, the disregard of expectations as an independent force. For an example, see A. P. Lerner, "Functional Finance," *Social Research* (1943), pp. 38–51.

[24] See chap. 3, sec. 6.

question arises how such an emergency can be met, short of making spending permanent at an increasing scale and of thus progressively curtailing the scope for decentralized decision-making.

The solution can only lie in the introduction of what may be called "secondary controls." Supplementary to primary Control, which tries to influence expectations indirectly by improving the objective conditions of demand, such secondary controls are directly concerned with shaping expectations in a manner suitable for Stabilization. Their aim can be defined as the formation of an enlightened public opinion capable of understanding the function of primary Control and also the economic and social advantages which suitable micro-responses are certain to confer on all strata of marketers.

In developing these secondary controls, a principal responsibility falls to economic science. Dispelling faulty notions about the inflationary effect of public spending in conditions of underutilization or about the consequences of a rising public debt is more than an exercise in pedagogy. When presented in full awareness of the subtle relationship between public and private action, the Political Economics of Stabilization can be a major factor in shaping both policy stimuli and micro-responses according to the requirements of the good working order of the system. If today we have reason to anticipate a more cooperative reaction on the part of the business community to actions of primary Control than was the case thirty years ago, this is partly due to the more enlightened instruction on matters economic, which the present generation of business leaders have received during their college days.

At the same time it is clear that the role of government in devising and carrying out secondary controls is a limited one. The lion's share falls to all the agencies engaged in forming public opinion, from the media of mass communication, the organizations of business and labor, the utterances of statesmen and parliamentarians, to the popular literature on Economics.[25] But in order to gauge the effectiveness of these secondary controls, the authorities responsible

[25] For an instructive example, see Robert L. Heilbroner and Peter L. Bernstein, *A Primer on Government Spending* (New York, 1963).

for primary Control had better adopt the rule of "incremental-ism,"[26] that is, "time" and "dose" the expansion of public spending with an eye to the nature of private responses. This is fully compatible with an initial push strong enough to raise demand above the threshold of stagnation, and with stand-by measures of more comprehensive Control in case suitable private responses fail to materialize. But so long as pump-priming is preferred to socialization of spending, an incremental policy of demand regulation offers the most favorable prospect.

C. BALANCING OF GROWTH

8. *Is Growth a Subject for Economic Theory?*

As we remember, with the abandonment of all extra-systemic feedback mechanisms by Mill and his contemporaries, Growth ceased to be a topic for traditional analysis. It took almost a century until, in the wake of the Keynesian Revolution, new attempts were made to recapture for theory a realm of experience that had been a major concern for a Smith or a Marx.[27] But even today opinions divide over the question of whether the secular evolution of economic systems is a legitimate subject for "law-like" generalizations, not to say for prediction. It almost looks as if the study of economic growth were to become the center of a new "Methodenstreit," in which model constructing theorists vie with historically and sociologically minded "empiricists."

Before we take sides in this dispute we must look at the objections which the empiricists raise against any theoretical approach to the problem. These objections are implied in the manner in which is formulated the task which the study of economic growth is to accomplish. In the words of one representative champion of this view the task consists in

---

[26] For a discussion of a policy of incrementalism, see Charles N. Lindblohm, "Policy Analysis," *American Economic Review,* vol. 48 (1958), pp. 298–312.
[27] See the references to the work of Messrs. Harrod and Domar in chap. 9, sec. 8.

explaining long-term changes in . . . the immediate determinants of the level of output (to wit: the supply of resources . . . the state of the arts, the organizations of markets, the legal framework of economic life, and the psychological attributes of the population) . . . and the influence of such changes on output.[28]

But in order to construct a theory from such findings we must proceed to

the distillation of dependable uniformities from a process of cumulative change. A dependable law implies some stable system of structural characteristics (tastes, propensities, motives, physical obstacles, organization, law, etc.) which cause a set of recognizable tendencies to emerge in the relations among variables. Social structure, however, is notoriously in flux . . . the longer the period, the less likely are we to find the degree of stability we need. . . .

The study of growth, therefore, stands closer to history than do other economic subjects. . . . If the economics of growth attains the rank it ought to have in our subject, we should expect to see history, geography, and sociology take a prominent place in the training of economists in the future.[29]

One may well be skeptical about the practical prospects of ever seeing so formidable a program carried out. But as the task is defined by Professor Abramovitz, one can indeed conceive of no other procedure but a "synthesis" of all the relevant findings which the specialist branches of social research have unearthed and are still going to unearth. Even so we shall most likely never come up with "dependable uniformities," but at best with a taxonomic survey of what happened in the past and may happen in the future.[30] Thus the fate of an economic *theory* of growth hangs in the balance until its task can be formulated in a manner that yields a problem the solution of which is at the same time crucial for empirical growth processes and also amenable to analytical treatment.

[28] See M. Abramovitz, "Economics of Growth," in *A Survey of Contemporary Economics*, vol. II, (Homewood, Ill., 1952) pp. 134–135. See also the writings of S. Kuznets, W. A. Lewis, and W. W. Rostow.

[29] *Ibid.*, pp. 177–178.

[30] For an attempt to catalogue our present knowledge in this manner, see W. A. Lewis, *The Theory of Economic Growth* (Homewood, Ill., 1955). Admirable as its content is, the title of the book is ill chosen.

There is indeed such a problem, and to discover it we only need to spell out the reason why the more comprehensive task—namely, that of arriving at valid generalizations for *all* the determinants of the level of output—is so difficult to accomplish. The reason is that almost all these determinants are themselves the result of forces which operate outside of the economic realm. Since we can no longer fall back on the classical solution according to which changes in the determinants of economic motion can be related to changes in that very motion, these "outside" determinants must be treated as genuine data, about the behavior of which Economics has nothing to say. Stated differently, we must reconcile ourselves to the fact that, in general, the determinants of output are causes but not effects of the level and change in output.

However, there is one exception to this. As our discussion of the industrial structure of production has reminded us,[31] there is one factor of production for which the classical hypothesis is true: *real capital*. Being an output as well as an input, the size and variations of the capital stock are intra-economic phenomena, open to the discovery of "dependable uniformities." And it is contingent on the role of the factor capital in shaping the actual processes of growth whether these uniformities are important enough to serve as a foundation for an economic theory of growth.

To call any one factor fundamental makes sense

only if, from the almost infinite chain of causation, one selects a particularly significant intermediate link, namely that link in which the effects of all the more basic causes are collected as if in the focal point of a lens.[32]

If it could be shown that the quantity and quality of the stock of real capital and its changes through time form just such a "link" with the other determinants of growth, an economic theory of growth might be constructed after all. Though by no means covering the entire ground which the empiricists have mapped out for us, such a theory could provide an analytical core around which

[31] See secs. 3 and 4 of this chapter.
[32] See Eugen von Boehm-Bawerk, "Wert, Kosten und Grenznutzen," *Conrad's Jahrbuecher* (1892), 3. Folge, vol. III, pp. 353–354 (my translation).

sociological and historical studies of other growth-inducing factors might group themselves.

A significant witness to this conception has recently arisen. W. W. Rostow, himself a protagonist of the empiricist approach, concludes a survey of the many preconditions for the "take-off" of a stagnant pre-industrial society into sustained industrialization with these words:

> . . . the *essence* of the transition can be described legitimately as the rise in the rate of investment to a level which regularly, substantially and perceptibly outstrips population growth; although when this is said, it carries no implication that the rise in the investment rate is an *ultimate* cause.[33]

The key position in economic development which is there assigned to investment (or, as we prefer to say, to the formation of real capital) is due to the fact that real capital is the central channel through which the secular process, at least of an industrial system, is affected by all other determinants, be they changes in population, the exploitation of natural resources, the level of technology, or even changes in savings habits or in entrepreneurial outlook.

Of course, most if not all of these factors themselves cooperate in maintaining, expanding, and contracting the prevailing stock of such capital, and thus in providing the pathway through which their further influence is channeled. However—this is really the strategic point—the technical capability of the system to respond to changes in extra-systemic determinants is at any moment *limited* by the quantity and quality of the intra-systemic factor "real capital." To put it differently, whatever the stimuli of growth and their provenance, only a theory of the formation, maintenance, and liquidation of real capital can explain the possible responses of the system to such stimuli. The *economic* theory of growth thus largely coincides with the theory of capital formation.

---

[33] See W. W. Rostow, *The Stages of Economic Growth* (Cambridge, England, 1960), p. 21 (italics added). See also B. Higgins, *Economic Development* (New York, 1959), pp. 204–205. To simplify exposition, investment will be defined here as an addition to the stock of *material* capital, to the exclusion of all investment in "human" capital through education and research.

However, in order to place our argument in the proper context, an important proviso must be added. Capital formation is a fundamental requirement for economic growth whenever absorptive capacity is scarce, that is, when the available capital stock is fully utilized. In other words, our view of the matter is correct only for economic systems in which either collectivist planning or public Control of market movements has succeeded in stabilizing resource utilization. If part of the available capacity stands idle, Growth merges with the process of Stabilization, and is to be analyzed along similar lines.

We have here one of the reasons why the study of unorganized capitalism could do without an explicit theory of growth. On the one hand, cyclical fluctuations kept the industrial system in a state of underutilization for much of the time. On the other hand, the automatic escapements discussed earlier offered periodic stimuli of demand, providing temporary utilization not only for the pre-existing stock of resources but also for the increments of population and the improvements in productivity.

There we meet with a veritable paradox. Industrial fluctuations, by causing underutilization of existing capacity, somehow facilitated the process of growth. The modern policy of Stabilization, by trying to avoid waste of current resources, creates a capital bottleneck when it comes to absorbing newly accruing ones. A fate which has always retarded the development of pre-industrial societies, is now also overtaking mature industrial systems, at least to the extent to which they succeed in stabilizing their current activities. It is in this highly topical context that our statement of the problem must be read.

Appendix

Emphasis on the central role of capital formation in all industrial growth processes seems to conflict with a major tenet of neo-classical theory: *the marginal productivity theorem.* Contrary to the position adopted here which asserts that in the absence of idle capacity an increment in labor supply or a change in technology can be absorbed only if complementary real capital is formed, neoclassical theory insists that, in principle, any quantity of other resources can be employed on a given stock of "pure capital." All that is necessary is to adjust the physical form of such capital to the changing employment requirements, and to equate the remuneration of factors with their marginal productivities.

Now, it is certainly true that at any time there exist a number of technical combinations between labor and equipment, with the help of which a given output can be produced. And it is equally true that, given the extremum incentive, the optimum combination seen from the aspect of the investor is determined by the relative prices of labor and capital. Therefore, in *setting up* a business a fall in money wages, which an increment of labor may generate, is likely to affect the choice of factor combination. However, at any moment when an increment of labor appears in the market the large majority of firms have *sunk* their money capital into a specific type of plant and equipment. Unless amortization of the real capital in use is far progressed, and unless the wage reduction is regarded as permanent, scrapping the available equipment in favor of one which bears the same value but has a higher employment capacity would grossly violate the extremum principle and has, in fact, never been recorded.

One might, however, think of other alternatives more easy to accomplish because they leave the physical form of the capital in use unaltered. After all, the theoretical configuration of equilibrium does not require that the available capital stock be utilized to the maximum of its capacity,[34] nor is it in normal practice so utilized. Therefore it seems to be technically feasible, by *"overutilizing" existing equipment* beyond the point of minimum average costs, to absorb a certain increment of labor. In particular, introducing a two- or three-shift system might go a long way in such absorption.

It must be admitted that, in certain branches such as farming or retailing, expansion of employment on the given capital stock

[34] See sec. 3 of this chapter.

is possible even within one and the same shift. On the other hand, in most manufacturing industries the margin for such expansion is very small indeed or, what amounts to the same thing, the marginal productivity of labor will quickly approach zero. And as far as the introduction of additional shifts is concerned, it must be remembered that such overutilization of equipment rapidly raises "user costs" as a consequence of the rising physical wear and tear. Replacement, however, depends on a proportional expansion of output in the equipment goods industries, some of which like iron and steel already work in three shifts.

In sum, the arguments adduced against the need for real capital formation under conditions of growth are valid only for small changes, in particular for so-called "once-over changes" in which a fixed quantity of labor or a given technical progress is to be absorbed over an indefinite period. They lose relevance if, as is usual, growth stimuli are continuous, demanding a continuous rise in capacity. (For a definitive treatment of the problem, see Leif Johansen, "Substitution versus Fixed Production Coefficients in the Theory of Economic Growth."[35])

Reference must finally be made to the *post-Keynesian version* of a theory of growth, as it has been elaborated in the work of Messrs. Harrod and Domar. By building their models on the assumption of "fixed production coefficients," they side with our view of the matter in treating the existing capital stock as more or less inflexible over its lifetime. However, they derive from this common premise a radically different conclusion. For them the bottleneck is not the limited capacity of the available capital stock, but the relative scarcity of the complementary factors labor and productivity improvements. As a consequence the steadiness of growth is said to be periodically threatened by idleness of capacity, which destabilizes even current activity unless it is counteracted by public policy.

This divergent conclusion is bound up with the Keynesian premise of a tendency toward "oversaving," which allegedly bedevils wealthy societies. As we saw earlier,[36] there has been little evidence

[35] *Econometrica*, April 1959, pp. 157–176.
[36] See chap. 9, sec. 7.

for such a tendency in the past and, considering the contemporary atomic and cybernetic revolutions, even less so for the foreseeable future. And the major growth venture of our time, the industrialization of backward regions, is certainly threatened by shortage rather than by surplus of real capital.[37] Still, whichever way the empirical evidence may point, in the post-Keynesian theory of growth as in our own conception, the stock of real capital forms the analytical core.

9. What is Meant by Balancing of Growth?

In identifying the core of the *economic* theory of growth with the analysis of changes in real capital, we seem to limit the scope of this theory drastically. In fact, however, such an analysis is capable of dealing with most of the issues that are conventionally included in the study of economic growth, even if it examines them only under the particular aspects of intra-systemic responses to a variety of extra-systemic stimuli. It is true that the latter, namely, changes in labor supply, productivity, etc., are not themselves subjected to analysis but treated as data. But even so we come up with a large catalogue of combinations, each one of which reflects an empirically relevant case.

In the remainder of this chapter we shall confine our attention almost exclusively to but one of these cases, albeit a central one: the effect of population and productivity increases on the growth of employment and output in mature countries. Our focus will again be the paths and forces suitable to attain a stated macrogoal. As such goal we postulate the Balancing of Growth, and our first task is to give this concept a precise and instrumentally apposite meaning.

Balancing of Growth was earlier defined as the achievement of continuous and efficient absorption of newly accruing resources, and it was emphasized that this achievement might require a change in the system's structure. This definition leaves it open whether, in an industrial market economy, such absorption can

[37] See sec. 14 of this chapter.

be brought about by the spontaneous operation of micro-forces, or whether it calls for public Control. As we did in the discussion of Stabilization, we postpone the answer until we know more about suitable paths and forces. However, we must now state explicitly what is to be meant by "continuous" and "efficient" absorption. *Efficient* absorption of resource increments is achieved when the system approximates some order of equilibrium as earlier defined, that is, when the newly entering resources are utilized permanently, fully, and in technically optimal fashion. However, in defining the meaning of *continuous* absorption we cannot fall back on earlier considerations. Rather we meet here with a problem that is intrinsic to the phenomenon of growth itself.

There is in principle no objection to treating an isolated batch of immigrants or the introduction of a particular innovation as a growth stimulus, even if both events lack the character of continuity and if conventionally such a process of "once-over" growth is treated as deviation from and return to stationary equilibrium.[38] However, in reality even such once-over changes occur in the wider framework of a continuously growing system, exposed to the impact of, e.g., a continuous rise in population or continuous technical reorganizations of production.

It is to this wider frame of reference that the concept of Balancing of Growth refers. What the intra-systemic responses are to "balance" are the possible disturbances evoked by such continuous influx of resource increments. There is little to worry about, as we shall see, so long as such growth stimuli are *steady*, that is, arise at a constant rate. The situation is quite different if, as in the majority of practical instances, one or more of these stimuli *vary* over time. Then the Balancing of Growth, that is, the establishment of permanent full and technically optimal utilization of resources, poses difficult adjustment problems—the true testing ground for the productive efficiency of any economic system under the stresses of growth.

The achievement of such a balance was above subsumed under

[38] See R. F. Harrod, *Toward a Dynamic Economics*, p. 7.

the notion of equilibrium. But whenever the process of growth is continuous, equilibrium cannot be conceived as a "permanent state," as was possible in the context of stationary analysis. It is itself no more than a passing phase in an ongoing process, or rather a succession of such phases, and will therefore be denoted as *dynamic equilibrium*. Dynamic equilibrium is, then, the specific configuration in which our macro-goal materializes, and our next task is to describe its relevant features.

10. *Dynamic Equilibrium: Configuration, Paths, Forces*

The features of dynamic equilibrium, which are essential for growth analysis, can be described most aptly if they are contrasted with the structural characteristics of stationary equilibrium. As we remember, the prime condition for maintaining a stationary structure of production is a tripartite sectoral organization of the system, and a distribution of inputs over the three sectors such as to assure a constant output of consumer and equipment goods over time. This implies, in particular, equality between the output of the equipment goods sectors in one period and the input of equipment goods in the subsequent period in accord with the replacement needs of all sectors. Since the aggregate supply of each type of extra-systemic resource is assumed as constant, the absolute magnitudes of the outputs also remain constant, and the time profile of the system is one of uniformity.

Contrariwise, the time profile of dynamic equilibrium is one of steady change. This means that one or more extra-systemic resources flow into the system at a steady rate, to be steadily used as inputs for a steadily increasing aggregate output. What is the suitable *configuration* (sectoral organization and resource distribution) that assures such steadiness of growth?

To simplify the description we shall assume, to begin with, that only one extra-systemic resource increases steadily: labor. Then to achieve in every period of expansion dynamic equilibrium, that is, the full and efficient absorption of the labor increment, the process of production must perform two functions. First, it must assure provisioning of the resources actually employed including the replacement of used-up real capital—a function identical with the stationary function. Second, in each successive period it must provide the real capital necessary to employ the steadily accruing increment of labor at the prevailing level of technical efficiency—the dynamic function. To fulfill both functions, of the aggregate of resources employed in any one period more must now be engaged in producing real capital and less in producing consumer goods than would be the case if the same quantity of resources were employed in stationary equilibrium.

As a consequence the intersectoral order of production must differ from that prevailing under stationary conditions. It will be instructive to illustrate this by a numerical example for either order of production. For this purpose we must assume definite values for three strategic magnitudes. Two of them, the average ratio of the value of capital stock to its associated output and the average rate of depreciation, are properties of a stationary as well as of a dynamic structure of production. We set them at 3 and 1/15, respectively, values which agree fairly well with those typical for a mature industrial economy.

From these data the stationary percentage distribution of inputs and outputs over sectors I, II, and III, producing primary equipment, secondary equipment, and consumer goods, respectively, can be calculated as 4:16:80. In order to ascertain the intersectoral shifts necessary to attain a dynamic equilibrium, another datum must be numerically fixed: the rate of the labor increment steadily to be absorbed. Setting it at 5 per cent, we obtain a dynamic distribution of inputs and outputs over the three sectors in the order of 12:23:65.[39]

Before we comment on the difference between the two production structures we shall give our dynamic example a more realistic interpretation. To this end we add to the influx of labor steady

[39] For the method of calculation and, more generally, for a technical exposition of the problems discussed in this subdivision, see my "Structural Analysis of Real Capital Formation" in *Capital Formation and Economic Growth* (Princeton, 1955), pp. 581–634, in particular secs. 12 and 24.

improvements in the level of productivity. But if they are not to disturb dynamic equilibrium these technical changes must be of the so-called "neutral" type. Specifically, they must not change the prevailing capital-labor ratio, that is, on balance neither be capital-saving nor labor-saving. Though neutral technical progress raises the real output of the average combination of labor and real capital from period to period, the average employment ratio of capital remains constant. If it were to change, the prevailing intersectoral ratios would have to be adjusted each time to the new requirement of either more or less capital per capita of employed workers—a typical problem of Balancing of Growth to be discussed below.

With this proviso the assumed 5 per cent growth rate can now be interpreted as the sum of two dynamic stimuli, for instance, of an annual influx of 1 to 1½ per cent of additional labor and an annual rise in productivity of between 3½ and 4 per cent. This well coincides with the growth as postulated by several bodies of experts for the United States economy over the decade of the sixties.[40]

Examining now more closely the configuration of a dynamic equilibrium as above illustrated, we find that, compared with a stationary equilibrium employing the same quantity of resources, the two equipment goods sectors together have increased by 75 per cent, whereas the consumer goods sector has shrunk almost by 20 per cent. But the two equipment goods sectors have by no means expanded at the same rate. Inputs for and outputs of secondary equipment have risen by less than one half above the stationary level, while those of primary equipment lie three times above that level. This is not surprising when we remember that sector I must satisfy the increased requirements for replacement as well as for expansion in both equipment goods sectors.[41]

[40] See, e.g., Rockefeller Brothers Fund, *The Challenge to America: Its Economic and Social Aspects* (New York, 1958), and Annual Report of the President's Council of Economic Advisers, 1962.

[41] It may again clarify matters if, in analogy with the three equations in which the configuration of stationary equilibrium was described (see note 7), the interrelations of the dynamic sectors from period to period are also expressed symbolically. We distinguish dynamic from stationary variables by a prime sign. Moreover, the capital stocks operating in the three sectors must

It is now easy to derive from these dynamic sector relations the *path* suitable to maintain dynamic equilibrium through time. We meet with another triangular process of intersectoral relocations,[42] modified by the need for steady additions to the capital stock in each sector. Assuming again the same initial aggregate of resources in dynamic as well as in stationary equilibrium, we now find that the consumer goods sector exports to the sector producing secondary equipment a larger share of a smaller output, to be compensated by the import not only of its smaller replacement requirements but also of an addition to its equipment stock. Sector II in turn re-exports a larger share of its imports of consumer goods to sector I than it does under stationary conditions, to receive as imports besides replacement goods also an addition to its capital stock. The greatly expanded sector I finally retains a much larger share of its current output to provide for its own growth.

What are the *forces* that maintain this dynamic equilibrium and, in particular, perform these intersectoral relocations? The answer is an almost literal restatement of what we found as valid for the maintenance of stationary equilibrium. Once dynamic equilibrium has been established, barring an extra-systemic change in the growth stimuli, the steady motion of the system can be entrusted to routinized behavior, irrespective of whether we deal with a collectivist or a market order. At the same time the stability of dynamic equilibrium in a market system is assured so long as, under the guidance of the extremum incentive, quantity expectations of buyers and sellers have unit elasticity, whereas their price expectations have zero elasticity. In other words, they are to expect that the existing

---

now be introduced as additional variables, denoted by the capitalized letters F'_a, F'_b, F'_c.

We then obtain

$$\text{Sector I } \quad a'(1) = f'_a(2) + f'_b(2) + \triangle\ F'_a(2) + \triangle\ F'_b(2)$$
$$\text{Sector II } \quad b'(1) = f'_c(2) + \triangle\ F'_c(2)$$
$$\text{Sector III } \quad c'(1) = n'_a(2) + n'_b(2) + n'_c(2)$$

where, for the same initial aggregate of resources, a' and b' are larger, and c' is smaller, than the corresponding stationary magnitudes a, b, and c.

[42] See sec. 4 of this chapter.

rate of increase in employment and output will be maintained, and that unit prices of commodities and factors will remain constant.[43] Since behavior in accord with these expectations will steadily make them come true, dynamic equilibrium can be regarded as definitely stable so long as actual expectations assume the goal-adequate form.[44]

11. *Changes in the Rate of Growth: the Suitable Path*

Balancing of Growth is achieved through such responses to the rate of growth of extra-systemic stimuli (in particular, labor supply and productivity) as will either maintain the old or establish a new dynamic equilibrium. The configuration of the latter, as described above, will serve as the definition of the terminal order. So long as we move in dynamic equilibrium through time, the initial order is structurally identical with the terminal and, as we saw, growth balance can be maintained through the routine behavior of planners or marketers. A real problem of balancing arises, however,

---

[43] Among the factors determining dynamic equilibrium are savings. Therefore the same expectational conditions are valid for the rate of savings and investments and their respective prices: interest and profit. Constancy of prices requires, of course, an increase in the active flow of money proportional to the increase in real output, a requirement which a routinized monetary policy can easily fulfill.

[44] This result conflicts with the majority opinion in the literature, as originally expressed by Harrod in *Toward a Dynamic Economics,* Lecture Three. For a lucid presentation of this view, see K. K. Kurihara, *Introduction to Keynesian Dynamics* (New York, 1956), chap. 13.

This is not the place to enter into a detailed discussion of the problems involved. The ultimate point at issue is the proper conception of the industrial structure of production. By using a two-sector model in which the two equipment goods sectors are merged into one investment sector, Harrod and his followers cannot help missing the critical relationship. If, e.g., aggregate savings rise or fall, all other variables remaining unchanged (Professor Kurihara's example, *op. cit.,* pp. 203–206), they deduce not only a corresponding change in the output of secondary equipment goods but of *all* equipment goods, initiating a cumulative deflation or inflation. Their defective frame of reference conceals the fact that, with a steady rate of growth of resources, such an intra-systemic change of the consumption-saving ratio will change output of *primary* equipment *inversely* with that of *secondary* equipment, thus restoring dynamic equilibrium. Only a tripartite model of the structure of production reveals these compensatory sectoral movements, and with them the general "peristalsis" of a system undergoing growth.

if the initial order of the system deviates from dynamic equilibrium because of an increase or a decrease in the rate of growth of labor supply and (or) productivity.

This is the problem to which we now turn. In order to give the exposition a flavor of realism, we start out from the present situation in the United States. As we mentioned earlier,[45] since the middle fifties the American economy has been suffering from underutilization of resources, and a controversy has been going on as to whether we are confronted with a failure of Stabilization, namely, of fully employing currently available resources, or with an insufficient rate of growth, that is, with a failure of the system to absorb newly accruing resources. What speaks for the latter diagnosis is the striking fact that, contrary to what is typical for destabilizing recessions, aggregate output and employment have been rising at an average of about 3 per cent, even if the potential performance of the system under steady and full utilization of resources is estimated at about 5 per cent.

For our didactic purposes it is irrelevant whether and to what extent destabilization, that is, idleness of currently available capacity and labor, participates in causing the actual underutilization of manpower and the slackening of technical improvements. In accord with the proviso stated above[46] we will assume that all apparently idle capacity is technically inferior, so that the economically serviceable capital stock can be treated as by and large fully utilized. We are then faced with a genuine problem of growth, and the instrumental question directs itself to the path and the forces suitable to raise the rate of growth of employment and output from the actual level of 3 per cent to the potential level of 5 per cent.

We know that the core of the problem is capital formation. In order to ascertain the capital requirements for the balancing of influx and absorption of resources at the new rate, we shall again make use of our tripartite model of the structure of production. We retain the coefficients for the capital-output ratio and the rate of de-

---

[45] See chap. 3, sec. 6.
[46] See sec. 8 of this chapter.

preciation assumed above,[47] and arrive at the following sectoral percentage ratios of inputs and outputs for the different growth rates:

Growth Rate	0	3%	5%	8%
Percentage Input and Output in				
Sector I	4	8.5	12	20
Sector II	16	20.5	23	25
Sector III	80	71.	65	55

Interest centers on the changes in the combined output of equipment goods in sectors I and II. If the growth rate is to rise from 3 per cent to 5 per cent, the *annual output* necessary for the replacement and expansion of the total capital stock must rise from 29 per cent to 35 per cent of total output, that is, by over one-fifth. However, this figure does not tell us by what percentage the total capital *stock* in operation at the rate of 3 per cent must increase in order to attain the size required steadily to sustain a growth rate of 5 per cent. To establish this figure we must remember that, according to our assumption, three units of capital are required to produce one unit of output. Therefore, to *produce* the necessary addition to capital *stock* in the two equipment goods sectors, an expansion of *output* in sector I is required equal to more than twice the total annual output of this sector at the old growth rate.[48] In other words, to bring about an expansion of the employment capacity of the system sufficient to absorb steadily a 5 per cent increment of labor and neutral technical improvements, an *intermediate process of once-over growth* must be set in motion, during which the necessary addition is gradually built up. This can be done only if, in the interval, the output of consumer goods is reduced so as to free resources, and in particular the scarce resource "real capital" which can carry out this expansion.

The contortions which the structure of production would have

47 See sec. 10 of this chapter.

48 For the technique of calculation, see my monograph on *Structural Analysis,* sec. 24, cited in note 19 of this chapter.

to undergo during this process of real capital formation are highly complex. For a precise exposition of this path of once-over growth the reader must again be referred to the monograph cited above.[49] But in a general way three major phases can be distinguished in this path. First, output of consumer goods must be reduced in order to reduce the replacement and expansion needs for secondary equipment. This now makes it possible in a second phase to utilize part of the capital stock in the two equipment goods sectors which hitherto served to maintain and expand the capital stock in the consumer goods sector, for the expansion of the key resource: primary equipment. Once the stock of primary equipment has risen to the size required to sustain the higher growth rate, the stock of secondary equipment can also be expanded and absorption can begin.

In order to end up in a terminal order of balanced growth, balanced, namely, at the higher rate, the addition to capacity thus constructed must be neither larger nor smaller than the new increment of labor and productivity require. Both overbuilding and underbuilding of real capital unbalance the system, with dire consequences for its stability, presently to be discussed.

But before proceeding to the study of the forces which will bring about equilibration or disequilibration, another problem must be faced which still concerns the adjustment path itself. We have so far assumed that the technical improvements, which contribute to the rise in the growth rate, are of the neutral type, that is, are neither capital- nor labor-saving. This is a very unrealistic assumption, which must be abandoned if we are to understand the true dynamics of economic growth. Not only are most innovations non-neutral in one or the other respect, but there has been a clear bias over the past century and a half in favor of labor-saving technical changes. And considering the two major advances in technology

[49] See *Structural Analysis* secs. 14–20. Incidentally, in the elaboration of the intersectoral shifts necessary to form real capital outside of dynamic equilibrium lies the empirical significance of the technique of once-over growth analysis. At the same time the "advantages" of idle capacity, when seen in the light of changes in the rate of growth, are forcefully brought home to us. They spare the system the complicated structural shifts which, as we shall presently see, are beyond the cognitive range of decentralized decision-units.

which are going to dominate the coming era of industrial evolution —atomic energy and automation—this bias is certain to be enhanced.

Such a technological trend, however, is bound to create a new dilemma. Not only will capital per capita have to rise considerably, but any addition to capacity, originally built with the aim of absorbing a rising labor increment, is now likely itself to displace labor on a large scale. If Balancing of Growth is to be achieved under such conditions, new capacity must be built to absorb the technologically unemployed. The rate of growth of the total capital stock sufficient to accommodate a physical increment of labor amounting to, say, 1½ per cent plus the primary *and secondary* requirements of the new technology, may well have to rise to 6, 7, or even 8 per cent.

Anticipating in the coming decade a much more rapid advance of automation, we tentatively assume that the U.S. economy will require a growth rate of total capacity of some 8 per cent to balance the rate of increase of employment-seeking workers and of capital-requiring improvements. This incidentally is the rate at which the most intensely developing countries, such as the Soviet Union and Mexico, have grown over the past decades. As the figures show in the preceding table this will imply a more than 50 per cent increase in the current output of equipment goods, and an increase in the capital stock necessary to produce this additional output by the equivalent of six times the annual output of such goods at the 3 per cent growth rate. Even if a corresponding rise in productivity will facilitate the physical task of such output expansion, it will by no means simplify the concomitant behavioral and motivational adjustments, which are our next problem.

12. *Changes in the Rate of Growth: the Suitable Forces*

To describe in full detail the patterns and changes in patterns of behavior and motivations on which successful adjustment to a higher rate of growth depends, would require a special monograph. All we can do here is to highlight certain strategic decisions which must be taken during the major phases of the process of capital formation. In particular we shall try to establish the expectational patterns which, given the extremum incentive, are suitable to induce decisions favorable to the Balancing of Growth. In each phase different problems confront a collectivist and a free market system. It will be instructive to consider them side by side.

As we can infer from our path analysis, the main behavioral problem during the *first phase* of capital formation in a state of full capacity utilization is to bring about a reduction of current consumption, which will free capacity in the sector hitherto producing secondary equipment. For a collectivist system, in which the planners are aware of the path requirements, measures of command, such as rationing or the imposition of a sales tax, will easily solve this problem. This is so, at least, so long as the new level of consumption lies still far enough above the subsistence level to maintain the physical fitness and the working morale of the population.

The situation is quite different in a free market system in which the choice between consumption and saving is left to the spontaneous decisions of the micro-units. Since the initial order is an equilibrium, even if a pseudo-equilibrium with idle labor and gaps in technical efficiency, intended savings are currently equal to intended investment, and the level of consumption is fixed. Only through additional voluntary savings or through forced savings induced by increasing business loans can consumption be reduced and capacity be freed. To assume that the propensity to save on the part of individual income receivers varies spontaneously in proportion with the macro-goals of growth puts too much of a burden on the doctrine of preestablished harmony. Whether, on the other hand, potential investors are willing to increase their borrowing depends on the state of expectations in which they find themselves under prevailing conditions.

This issue is best considered in the context of the *second phase* of adjustment. Again a centrally planned economy finds little difficulty in utilizing for the expansion of primary equipment output the capacities which the reduction of consumption has indirectly freed in the sector hitherto producing secondary equipment. Contrariwise, even if additional savings and credit facilities are available, the individual investor in a free market economy is confronted with a very difficult decision. Once again the investment required is of the autonomous type, present prices and sales giving no indication of either the magnitude or the direction of any additional demand. We know that prevailing expectations, which have so far supported a 3 per cent growth rate, possess unit quantity and zero price elasticity.[50] In order to induce a decision to form additional real capital, they must both assume positive elasticity, that is, an increase in demand for final output and, possibly, an increase in its unit price must be expected. Is it likely that evaluation of the prevailing state of affairs in the light of the extremum incentive will transform expectations accordingly?

To come up with the correct answer we must distinguish between the stimulus of increasing labor supply and the stimuli which technical improvements emit. In the former case we are again beset by the "solidarity dilemma": only simultaneous investment decisions of all or most producers will create a market for the output of each one of them. All the arguments adduced against the spontaneous initiation of a process of Stabilization[51] apply here with equal force. They are even strengthened in view of the fall in the present demand for consumer goods. Expectations inducing additional investment must actually have negative elasticity, that is, the present fall in demand and prices must be regarded as only temporary to be followed by a rise above the earlier equilibrium level.

The expectational conditions are quite different if opportunities for cost-reducing innovations open up. In this case the profitability of individual investments is independent of what other investors do, since the new technology assures its user of competitive superiority even in a nonexpanding market. There is, then, good reason to assume that expectations will turn in the right direction.

Summing up our results for the second phase of capital formation, one can state that, in principle, a centrally planned system will pass it successfully. The same is true in a free market system for

[50] See sec. 10 of this chapter.
[51] See sec. 6 of this chapter.

the absorption of technical stimuli, whereas the stimulus of a mere increase in labor supply is unlikely to find a goal-adequate response. What about the *third phase,* in which the new equipment is actually built? Is it likely to conform to the requirements of the new growth rate, in both size and type? Or must we anticipate overbuilding or underbuilding of the new capital stock, again unbalancing the system and, possibly, even destabilizing its circular flow altogether?

Again there is, in principle, no reason why planners in a collectivist system, in full awareness of the size and type of additional equipment required, should commit gross errors of overbuilding or underbuilding, at least, to the extent to which their decisions are based on a correct analysis of the adjustment path. In a free market system, on the other hand, a new growth balance can be achieved only by accident. Even if all potential investors were to take a positive decision during the second phase, there is no signal system that would inform them of the size and type of investment actually required. Nor is there any tie-up between the required rise in the rate of growth and the rise in aggregate savings, the unplanned result of many independent savings decisions.

Under these conditions some overbuilding or underbuilding of the new capital stock is practically unavoidable. And the superiority of the technical stimulus during the second phase turns now into a grave shortcoming, at least when the technical improvement is of the labor-saving type. Even if the process of capital formation were to culminate in an addition to capital stock exactly in line with the postulated growth goal, secondary displacement would now change the growth goal itself, requiring still more capital formation. This is the reason why underbuilding is the more probable danger, whenever the major growth stimulus is a strong innovation of the kind which automation represents.

One can maintain that underbuilding is in general the lesser evil. Though it fails to absorb the total of accruing resources, it is generally compatible with a pseudo-equilibrium of retarded growth, an analogue to the condition in which the American economy seems to find itself at present. The much greater perils of overbuilding lie in the devaluation of excess capacity, followed by a general reduction of investment with the deflationary consequences of a downward multiplier effect. This is the reason why a fall in the rate of growth reducing demand for existing capacity was rightly regarded by the pessimistic wing of the Keynesian School as a threat also to Stabilization. Though their empirical premises have proved wrong, their theoretical reasoning seems irrefutable.

13. *Changes in the Rate of Growth: Suitable Controls*

When discussing Stabilization it was pointed out that the true function of public Control in an industrial market economy is to support rather than to supplant decentralized decision-making. And the ideal case, for which Stabilization is a perfect paradigm, is one in which the role of Control is only temporary, to be taken over in due course by goal-adequate behavior on the part of the micro-units themselves.[52]

The only controls which appear suitable to help marketers successfully take the hurdles that stand in the way of spontaneous Balancing of Growth are of an entirely different nature. If the system is continuously to approach dynamic equilibrium, that is, if the supply of real capital is currently to meet the demand stemming from employment-seeking labor and from innovations ready for profitable use, the process of capital formation must be subjected to *ongoing Control* in each phase. This is not the place to outline a comprehensive prospectus for a policy of controlling economic growth. All we can do here is to comment briefly on the different types of Control which are required at different stages of the adjustment process.

There are at least three areas in which public Control must currently modify, if not altogether take over, the decision-making of the micro-units. One refers to the balancing of aggregate savings with the requirements of investment. The other concerns the creation of an expectational climate conducive to positive investment decisions. The third is the promotion of goal-adequate formation of

[52] See sec. 7 of this chapter.

real capital, in particular the prevention of either over- or under-building of the capital stock.

The *Control of savings* is, in principle, the easiest of the three tasks. Once a definite rate of growth has been decided upon—a public decision on a macro-goal about which more will be said below[53]—the required volume of aggregate savings, and especially the necessary increase or decrease in savings, can be calculated. It will then be largely a task for monetary and fiscal controls to bring actual savings in agreement with required savings, in the extreme case by taxing consumption or expanding public services, as circumstances may demand.

It is much more difficult to *influence business expectations* by public policy, especially when the solidarity dilemma cautions against unilateral ventures. Informed public discussion of the growth goal, tax relief for timely investment, perhaps the development of an insurance system against certain risks may help to create the required expectations displaying negative elasticity. But in the end it may be necessary for the controlling authorities to stand by with a comprehensive program of public investment, both to create a demand stimulus and, if necessary, to bring about the Balancing of Growth even against the resistance of the private sector of the economy.

Lastly, *goal-adequate expansion of the capital stock* is to some extent assured once actual savings are equated with required investments. Still, it may be necessary to provide for the absorption of technological unemployment by a well-timed program of public investment, or by other measures of productive relief, such as retraining for higher skills or shifting to service industries. Compensatory investment is likely to be in the center, and in this respect it is imperative to dispel a popular illusion.

An almost unanimous opinion has it that growth is the universal remedy for unemployment, and that moving forward on the technological frontier is the best assurance of balanced growth. The truth is that only "neutral" growth, that is, investment that does not itself create secondary unemployment, has this balancing effect. Neutral

[53] See chap. 12.

investment, however, promises by no means the highest returns to private investors. It is for this reason that compensation of technological unemployment is primarily a task for public investment unconstrained by extremum incentives. Thus the progressive expansion of the public sector, currently advocated for the better satisfaction of communal demands, fulfills a complementary function in the Balancing of Growth. There is, of course, an alternative, but one which is hardly more pleasing to traditional views: the direct Control of private investment, at least to the extent to which its secondary effect is labor-displacing.

14. *The "Take-off" into Industrialization*

At first sight, there seems hardly to be any connection between the growth issues that confront mature industrial countries and the very peculiar problems with which a pre-industrial economy has to struggle in starting on the road to industrial development. Not only does its institutional and cultural environment radically differ from either a modern collectivist order or any form of organized or unorganized capitalism, but it differs in a way which may make fundamental political transformation if not revolution a precondition for development.[54] The dominant intra-systemic forces—the action directives and final micro-goals—seem to foster social inertia rather than change, since they are as a rule of the homeostatic type. Therefore perhaps the most important policy decision to make before any development plan can be devised is to choose between accepting the prevailing motivational patterns, and trying to use them for new goals,[55] and modifying them by means of educational and institutional reform in the direction of extremum incentives.

And yet when all this is admitted there remains the core problem emphasized in Rostow's statement quoted above: the quintessential rise of the rate of investment. And there can be little doubt about

[54] For a sober evaluation of this problem, see Robert L. Heilbroner, *The Great Ascent* (New York, 1962).

[55] Burma seems to fall in this category. See E. Hagen, "The Allocation of Investment in Underdeveloped Countries: The Case of Burma," in *Investment Criteria for Economic Growth* (Cambridge, Mass., 1955).

the relative functions of centralized and decentralized decision-making in lifting a pre-industrial economy out of the pseudo-equilibrium of stagnation. Whatever the role of private entrepreneurs may be in later stages of development, the initially prevailing attitude of the masses of the population toward work consumption and saving and the general lack of large-scale economic organization throw the responsibility for the "big push" upon domestic and foreign planning authorities.

It is not to the status of the pioneers of economic development but to their investment objectives that our foregoing analysis has something to contribute. This brings us back to our discussion of the industrial structure of production. A model of its basic configuration was then built up through a sequence of analytical steps. Starting out with one sector supplying consumer goods, we were compelled in the interest of permanence of provision to add a second sector in which the periodic needs for replacing the real capital used in the consumer goods sector were satisfied. But even this extension of productive organization did not yet assure the self-balancing of the system through time. For this purpose a third sector had to be added, providing for the periodic replacement of the real capital operating in both equipment goods sectors.

What then appeared as a *logical* sequence can well serve as an image, even if a crude one, of the *historical* stages through which a pre-industrial society must move on its way to industrial maturity. When interpreted in this sense the schema highlights some of the major obstacles any primitive society must overcome when embarking on economic development.

As was already indicated, the economic circular flow of contemporary pre-industrial societies can be conceived as a state of pseudo-equilibrium, in which large quantities of manpower and natural resources are unutilized or are utilized below the efficiency level attainable even under primitive conditions. The central problem of the Take-off into growth is then to bring these unused resources into utilization at a gradually rising level of technical efficiency. In terms of the categories of our industrial schema almost the entire stock of active resources is, to begin with, engaged in producing consumer goods. Replacement of the simple tools used up in the process is mainly a by-product of the current activity of the households, even if some specialized metalworking crafts can be considered as rudiments of an equipment goods sector.

The major task of increasing investment can, then, be defined as, first, providing consumer goods production (starting with agriculture) with more and more efficient implements and, second, the gradual building up of equipment goods sectors capable of providing for both replacement and expansion of production.

Considering the international "gradient" of industrial production, which places regions on very different stages of development side by side, this formulation of the problem is, of course, oversimplified. During long periods of development it is not only feasible, but in the interest of economizing available resources it may be desirable, that a country satisfy its needs for productive equipment through imports. Still in the present climate of international tensions the striving for early structural self-sufficiency—a state which is quite compatible with international division of labor in raw materials and finished specialties—may have a better justification than the spokesmen of the mature economies are always willing to admit. Certainly the collectivist giants of the modern world, the Soviet Union and Communist China, have geared their development policies from the very outset to the achievement of such self-sufficiency. And the very efficient nucleus of both secondary and primary equipment goods production, which Imperial Russia had built up during the decades preceding the First World War (supported by large imports of primary equipment during the 1920's) goes a long way to explain the rapid industrialization of the Soviet Union.

What all these historical experiences emphasize coincides with the main conclusion of theoretical analysis: as a rule no pre-industrial region, considering its production structure and the ensuing subsistence level of provision, is capable of lifting itself by its own efforts out of its pseudo-equilibrium of stagnation. Capital imports are a structural necessity for a successful Take-off, and it is no accident that the issue of world-wide development became the focus of international economic policy only after some regions of the globe had achieved the level of industrial maturity required for the support of the universal "revolution of expectations."

In conclusion, a brief comment is in order on a particular aspect of the macro-goal that is only vaguely defined by the terms of accelerated development or industrialization. An interesting controversy has arisen about the role which Balancing of Growth is to play in the aspirations of the policy-makers both inside and outside a developing region. Against the majority opinion affirming that balanced growth in the sense defined earlier is an indicator of successful development, Professor Hirschman has recently stressed the stimulating effect which *lack of balance* is likely to have on incentives of both public planners and entrepreneurs.[56]

If this discussion is not to bog down in semantic confusion, we must distinguish between the ultimate macro-goal toward which every economic system, mature or in process of development, is to strive and the intermediate goals adequate to certain stages of development. As far as the former is concerned, Hirschman seems to agree with the opinion of the majority.[57] This does not exclude "tensions, disproportions, and disequilibria" from exerting a creative function at certain stages of growth. But when we face up to the limited success which even the strongest efforts of balancing economic development are likely to achieve in most of the regions concerned we need hardly worry about too little disequilibrium. Whether its effect on incentives and behavior will be as favorable as Hirschman expects depends on the manner in which environmental conditions in a given case affect motivations, a notoriously tenuous relationship as has been pointed out here repeatedly. But the controversy has a different aspect. It again raises the crucial issue of criteria for the choice of macro-goals in Political Economics, an issue which we can no longer evade.

---

[56] See Albert O. Hirschman, *The Strategy of Economic Development* (New Haven, 1958), esp. chaps. 3 and 4. For the opposite view, e.g., Ragnar Nurske, *Problems of Capital Formation in Underdeveloped Countries* (Oxford, 1953).
[57] *Op. cit.,* p. 92.

12

The Vindication of Goals

1. *A Retrospective View.*

We are approaching the end of our journey. Our study of three test cases has demonstrated that Political Economics and, in particular, its instrumental part is an operational procedure. It enables us to demonstrate, for any one macro-goal or any consistent set of macro-goals, the conditions—structural, behavioral, and motivational—which assure goal attainment. Moreover, in all instances in which actual behavior and motivations differ from goal-adequate ones, it informs us of measures of public Control suitable to bring about the necessary conformance of these dynamic forces.

Up to this point we move in the realm of scientific thinking. However, before the findings of instrumental analysis can be developed into a genuine theory, collective action must intervene. That is, whenever actual forces deviate from the suitable ones, the appropriate measures of Control must actually be put into practice. Only after reality has been transformed through such action can the instrumental inferences serve as major premises in a deductive syllogism and the ensuing conclusions be empirically tested.

There is, however, one special case in which this intermediate step of reality-transforming action can be dispensed with. This is the case in which action directives and expectations of the micro-units *spontaneously* conform to those which are suitable to achieve one particular goal, namely, the state of macro-equilibrium earlier defined as Pareto optimum.[1]

[1] See chap. 2, sec. 3, and chap. 5, sec. 3.

It is to this special set of circumstances that traditional theory refers. But we have been forced to realize that this set of circumstances is special not only from the analytical but also from the historical aspect. In other words, the particular environmental conditions which assured such conformity of actual with goal-adequate behavior prevailed only during a passing phase in the evolution of modern capitalism. So did the empirical validity of the theorems derived from the corresponding premises. As a consequence, one can say that the step from Traditional to Political Economics is an advance from a special to a general rule for the acquisition of economic knowledge. Or stated differently, Traditional Economics is contained in Political Economics as a limiting case.

An additional point is worth emphasizing once more. Considering the vast plurality of possible macro-goals, the body of theorems which Political Economics yields is much larger and much more complex than the theorems stated by traditional theory. But such complexity by no means prejudices the determinacy of either the instrumental or the deductive part of the analysis. So long as the postulated set of macro-goals is internally consistent and is compatible with the available stock of resources, we can in each instance prescribe a specific policy as suitable for goal achievement. Moreover, within the limits set by human spontaneity, we can also predict the states and processes which arise from the application of such a policy.

It is this neutrality of the research technique of Political Economics that permits us to treat the macro-goal pursued as a datum rather than as a problem. In his capacity as a citizen or as a social philosopher the economist may certainly take an interest in the nature of a particular macro-goal, but it does not concern him professionally. Once again, the analogy suggests itself between the economist and the engineer, both of whom are to design "machinery" for purposes which are no business of theirs.

However this very analogy alerts us to certain limitations of such goal neutrality. The engineer can roam freely only within the limits set by the laws of nature and engineering rules, and must for this reason decline the commission to build a perpetuum mobile. We stressed repeatedly that the same constraints are valid in the economic realm.[2] But there they do not exhaust the factors which curb discretionary choice of macro-goals. An additional constraint is introduced by the social character of a sphere of activity in which attainment of any macro-goal is conditional on an irreducible minimum of spontaneous consent on the part of the micro-units. In other words, no macro-goal can be pursued by any authority claiming to act on behalf of the "whole," if it is totally repudiated by the "parts."[3]

Recognition of this limitation does not yield a criterion for the choice of "suitable" *final* macro-goals, be they terminal states or processes. But it introduces as an indispensable precondition for the attainment of the latter a specific *modal* macro-goal, that is, a specific mode in which the final macro-goals are to be selected. This modal macro-goal concerns the order of decision-making. Negatively formulated, it postulates that effective decision-making can never be fully centralized. The positive formulation is less determinate. It states that whatever substantive macro-goals an economic society may want to pursue, their realization depends on a "minimum" of decentralized decision-making being granted to the micro-units. What this minimum is varies from society to society; it is likely to rise with the level of civilization and technology.

If we were to content ourselves with this conclusion, our exposition would, up to the very end, stay within the safe limits of instrumental-deductive reasoning. It is true, we have now restricted the range of legitimate macro-goals to those which are not altogether repudiated by the micro-units. Still, a minimum of decentralized decision-making—the organizational technique by which minimum consent or, at the very least, indifference on the part of the micro-units is established—can well be interpreted as just another requirement or suitability condition for the attainment of the substantive end.

However, there is no denying that, implicitly and even explicitly, we have gone much further.[4] Not satisfied with the unquestionable

[2] See chap. 1, secs. 3 and 4, and chap. 5, sec. 4.
[3] See chap. 1, sec. 4.
[4] See chap. 5, sec. 5.

requirements of a "minimum," we have postulated a "maximum" of decentralized decision-making, namely, the preservation of market relations to the largest possible extent compatible with goal attainment. Our test cases have been investigated with this criterion in mind. But this is a criterion that cannot be justified by appeal to purely instrumental considerations of the kind so far discussed. It appears as a macro-goal in its own right. How can we vindicate its postulation?

2. Ends as Means

At first sight any attempt at vindicating a particular macro-goal must appear as overstepping the legitimate boundaries not only of Economics but of scientific inquiry generally. Will not such an enterprise inevitably carry us beyond the realm of facts and factual relations into a region in which value judgments and norms rule— a region in which the modern mind finds it difficult if not impossible to argue cogently?[5] In what follows we shall indeed draw near the critical boundary, but the road toward it leads through some safe territory well worth exploring.

We begin with a long overdue clarification of the very concept of a macro-goal. The terms "end" or "final" goal or the notion of a "terminal" state employed above are bound to create the impression that we are concerned with aims which can be attained once for all. That this is not so was implicitly shown in the kind of macro-goals on which we demonstrated the instrumental technique of inference. Equilibrium, Stabilization, or Balancing of Growth are ongoing processes which satisfy continuing wants and are sustained by continuing relationships and continuing operation of the underlying forces.[6]

[5] For a consistent exposition of modern "scientific value relativism," supported by a truly encyclopedic critique of the literature on the "intersubjective demonstrability" of norms, see Arnold Brecht, *Political Theory* (Princeton, 1959). The main initiator of the modern debate was, of course, Max Weber.
[6] See in this connection the illuminating discussion of "criteria of well-being," in Geoffrey Vickers, *The Undirected Society* (Toronto and London, 1959), chap. 2.

However, the "open" structure of most macro-goals shows not only in their time dimension. From the outset this inquiry laid great emphasis on the *modal* character of economic activity, stressing its lack of inherent ends, in contrast with other human activities —vital, interpersonal, political, scientific, etc.—to which such ends are intrinsic. This dichotomy between the "final" and the "modal," or between the world of ends and the world of means, is quite sharp if we distinguish economic from other activities. But it becomes blurred when we study the ends themselves more closely.

Far from presenting a random sample, human goals are interrelated and their *ensemble* displays what can be called a graded structure. Take a political goal such as the equality of all citizens before the law. The political scientist can accept this goal as a datum for his investigations, in the manner in which we accepted above the postulate of Balancing of Growth. Such a goal is, then, not itself subject to further scrutiny but serves as a known from which unknowns, in particular the political conditions for the realization of such equality, can be derived. However, a quite different question may be raised. This question is not concerned with the "how" but with the "why" of legal equality. In other words, the problem now is the ulterior purpose which such equality is to serve. The answer may be found in its effect on social stability, or on the contractual relations necessary for the effective operation of markets, or on the correspondence of political reality with professed principles of social ethics. As a consequence of this shift in the direction of inquiry, what served as a goal for Political Science becomes transformed into a "means" for a sociological, economic, or ethical investigation.

In this new role the original goal is not interchangeable with any other. Speaking in methodological terms, it can no longer be treated as a freely chosen premise; it is now a dependent variable fully determined by the new point of reference. The same is true for the macro-goals on which our economic test cases have been oriented, such as Balancing of Growth or Stabilization. They are certainly not intrinsic to the process of social provisioning, as Professor Hirschman's preference for a certain degree of "imbalance" or Schumpeter's advocacy of economic depressions as an instrument of "creative destruction" shows. But this is no reason why the choice between these alternatives should be a matter of flipping coins. It can be made determinate by using as a criterion a more distant goal to the realization of which the proximate economic goal is to contribute—in Hirschman's case the expected stimulating effect of imbalance on incentives; in Schumpeter's case the goal of strengthening the technologically progressive strata of society.

Two important conclusions follow from these considerations. First, there is for society at large as for the individual a *hierarchy of goals* in which the ends in one sphere of activity appear as means in another one. To that extent the intrinsic value of most final goals, which was stressed above over and against the extrinsic value of economic striving, is relative only. These goals require, as it were, the additional sanction of being able to serve as a suitable means. But it would be wrong to interpret such a hierarchy of goals as a "linear" relationship between different spheres of life with, say, economic activity representing the lowest rung of the ladder, above which social, political, aesthetic, scientific, etc. activities arrange themselves in a fixed order. The example in which equality before the law—a political goal—is shown as a suitable means for improving the efficiency of the market—an economic goal—has already indicated that the relations between different activity levels are highly complex and, as often as not, even circular.

However, and this is our second conclusion, within a *given* hierarchy the precise nature of these interrelations poses a genuinely scientific problem unencumbered by any value judgment or norm. And the research technique for the solution of such problems is again instrumental analysis. Though the context is now more comprehensive, the formal problem is again one of regressive inference —to establish, at any stage, the suitability or nonsuitability of a given goal as a means for the attainment of another goal higher up in the hierarchy.

Such broad applicability of instrumental analysis should not surprise us. It is true that the intrinsic means-oriented character of economic activity provides it with a natural home. But as a formal technique for the study of ends-means relations its validity extends over the whole range of social research. As such it is capable, within the limits of a given hierarchy of goals, of testing the compatibility of the individual items, and of thus determining the choice of the fitting goals.

We can go one step further. We can inquire into the *actual* hierarchy of goals which a given individual or group has adopted and we may try to ascertain the explicit or implicit reasons for that particular ranking of activities—a taxonomic enterprise in which given values and norms are treated as facts. But there the safe path ends. Whenever the hierarchies of different persons or groups clash, no method of scientific inquiry, as the concept is understood today, can offer criteria for the resolution of such conflicts. In fact, the critical borderline is already reached if a *commonly accepted hierarchy* of goals is to be *vindicated*. Inferential determination through instrumental analysis is possible only for goals which can be interpreted as a means to another goal. But there is in every hierarchy at least one goal that cannot be so interpreted: the apex of the pyramid.

We shall refrain from stepping over the borderline by asking, for instance, whether Reason or Revelation—Philosophy or Theology—can offer "intersubjectively demonstrable" criteria for the choice of such an apex or ultimate goal: the decision about a worldly *summum bonum*—the "good life." We have nothing to contribute to a debate in which two thousand years of arguing forward and backward have so far failed to move either side an inch. Our aims are much more modest. We shall be satisfied with a provisional yardstick capable of guiding one of our major decisions in the narrow realm of provisioning without foreclosing any answers to the larger question of "what life befits Man."[7]

---

[7] The predicament of modern Man when faced with this question has been well described in Hans Jonas, "The Practical Uses of Theory," in *Philosophy of the Social Sciences: A Reader,* ed. by Maurice Natanson (New York, 1963), esp. secs. VI–VIII.

3. A Means as an End

In a general way we have already postulated such a yardstick. It refers to the social mode in which the substantive macro-goals are to be chosen in a controlled economic system. Several times we expressed a clear preference for manipulative over command controls, in the interest of assuring the maximum extent of decentralized decision-making compatible with goal attainment. It is now our task to elaborate some of the implications of this postulate and, above all, to state the reason why this mode of decision-making should be preferred to others.

To come to grips with our problem we must avoid a misunderstanding. Were we to ask for no more than maximum micro-autonomy within the behavioral limits required for the attainment of *arbitrarily chosen* macro-goals, we would speak as the Oracle to the Lydian king. *Any* restriction of micro-autonomy up to the limit of full collectivization could be justified even if it were shown that the macro-goal selected—e.g., complete equalization of wealth and income, or a rate of growth which reduced present living standards to a subsistence level—ran counter to the strivings of a powerful minority or even the majority of the micro-units. One would merely have to demonstrate that this was the only mode of decision-making which assures goal realization. But our postulate implies much more, namely, the *elevation of micro-autonomy itself to the rank of a genuine goal.* This may well lead, in the examples cited, to a conflict between the postulated mode of economic action and the substantive goals postulated for the aggregate state of provisioning. There is only one way of avoiding such a conflict: we must restrict the choice of our substantive goals to such states and processes as can be brought into agreement with the strivings of the large majority of micro-units. How can we justify such restriction?

At this point our discussion about an ever-present hierarchy of goals becomes relevant. It has taught us that the goals dominating one sphere of human activity can be vindicated whenever they can be interpreted as suitable means for the achievement of a major goal in some other sphere which ranks higher in the total hierarchy. Now provided it can be shown that controlled micro-autonomy as defined above serves the attainment of an acknowledged *political* end, and that, furthermore, the political sphere ranks, under the given conditions, above the economic sphere, the choice of our postulate is no longer arbitrary. In specific terms, such micro-autonomy is vindicated if it is suitable to promote political freedom, and if such freedom takes precedence over any conceivable principle according to which production and distribution can be organized.

The first condition is easy to fulfill. To justify controlled economic micro-autonomy as a means suitable to promote political freedom, a distinction which has acquired fame in the context of Rousseau's Political Philosophy proves helpful: the distinction between the "will of all" and the "general will." In Rousseau's words, "the latter considers only the common interest, while the former takes private interests into account, and is no more than the sum of particular wills."[8] Whatever the relevance of this distinction may be for Man the Citizen, its importance for Man the Provider can hardly be exaggerated. It helps us to draw the line between economies controlled by command and others controlled by manipulation, and thus between collectivist and market systems.

In the light of this distinction micro-autonomy has the important function of releasing the will of all and of thus limiting the choice of macro-goals to those which do not violate the well-understood private interests of the large majority of the micro-units. As a matter of fact, this rule underlies the traditional formulation of a Pareto optimum to which we have frequently referred. Of greater importance in the present context is the fact that Stabilization and Balancing of Growth—the macro-goals figuring in our test cases —fulfill the same condition. By extending the opportunity for the utilization of present resources and by assuring the utilization of newly accruing ones at a rising rate of productivity, both these goals offer benefits all around to the ultimate detriment of no one.

[8] See J. J. Rousseau, *The Social Contract,* trans. by G. D. H. Cole (London, 1913), Book II, chap. III.

However, two qualifications are necessary to delineate the validity of our postulate. First, as was already stated, it is the *well-
understood interest* of the micro-units that must agree with the
macro-goal, rather than their crude strivings. This qualification distinguishes a regime subject to manipulative controls from a regime
of laissez-faire. To enlighten the individual marketer about his true
interests by reducing expectational uncertainty and by suitably patterning action directives is the very function of manipulative controls.

The second qualification raises graver problems. It brings home
to us that, however hard we may try to avoid choices based on
value judgments pure and simple, we cannot run away from an
ultimate decision as to the relative significance of the economic and
the political sphere or as to the ranking of rivalling political goals.

Pleading for nothing but Stabilization and Balancing of Growth
betrays a conservative attitude toward social change. It implicitly
denies the need for radical reform of the socioeconomic structure on
which organized capitalism is to build. But one need only remember
the vast "pockets of poverty" which disfigure the sight of even the
wealthiest nations to face the challenge of another macro-goal: redistribution of the claims on aggregate output. Moreover, as was already pointed out,[9] in many developing countries political transformation if not revolution appears as the very precondition for
economic growth.

Certainly such fundamental transformations are bound to violate
powerful private interests. Even if essential for the *future* establishment of economic *consensus* they do not agree with the present "will
of all." Under such conditions our rule is bound to fail, as does
Control by manipulation alone. Wealthy societies with a long tradition in decentralized decision-making may succeed, as the example of Britain shows, in accomplishing adjustment of their social
structures without surrendering the essentials of micro-autonomy.
Poor societies without such traditions are likely to sacrifice freedom
by adopting Control by command as the only conceivable organizational means for conquering destitution and exploitation—a turn

---

[9] See chap. 11, sec. 14.

toward restriction of micro-autonomy, of which we see the beginning but not the end. Nor is this the only source of anti-liberal tendencies in the noncommunist part of the world. The drift of the cybernetic revolution in modern technology is in the same direction of more and more highly centralized decision-making.

4. *A "Quarter Truth" as Provisional End*

These last considerations cut off the one remaining line of escape from the ultimate consequences of our reasoning. Even if not warranted on intrinsic grounds, micro-autonomy might yet be defended as criterion for goal selection if it were in accord with the historical trend. But the facts just cited point to the opposite conclusion: the prospects for "economic freedom," understood as individual decision-making sustained by manipulative controls, are doubtful everywhere. That this should be so at the very moment when the progress of technology holds out the promise of breaking the fetters of Nature's stinginess, and thus of assuring ever-widening strata of mankind "freedom from want," appears as a historical paradox. But the course of our inquiry has prepared us for it. From the outset it has been stressed that the balance between the technological and the social component is precarious in all socioeconomic systems. In a crude generalization one might say that up to the Industrial Revolution rigid social patterns shackled material progress. Since then the dynamics of technology have been progressively shaping social evolution.

Thus in affirming the autonomy of what is genuinely social and human against this technological trend we are hardly riding the wave of the future. Therefore, such affirmation amounts to the pronouncement of a *norm,* and as such represents a step over the critical boundary which separates scientific inquiry from the region of value judgments.

This need not prevent us from asking for the reasons which lie behind the decision for this particular norm. Alas, the answer is made burdensome because of the mist of error and cant which today confuses the meaning of freedom in every field of human endeavor. It is the noble banner under which the centuries-old struggle for emancipation—religious, political, national, social, economic, racial, and sexual—has been waged. But it also serves as a shield behind which political and racial suppression, economic exploitation and factionalism of every kind hide. The case is not improved by the hazy notions which champions of a so-called liberal political philosophy spread about the relationship between "freedom" and "order"—to be matched only by the authoritarian short cuts of some of their conservative opposite numbers.[10]

This is not the place to join in a debate which must lead to a point where argument ends and faith has the final say. So without any further attempt at rationalization be it admitted that liberty, as it has taken form in Western society, may well be no more than a "quarter truth." And yet it must be adopted as a "provisional value" if those among us who believe in absolute values are to be allowed to continue fighting for them.[11]

For the skeptically minded a more modest reason will do. He admits that micro-autonomy limited by nothing but manipulative controls is probably incompatible with particular stages in the socio-political or technological development of human provisioning. For this reason the organization of a controlled market cannot embody universal truth. Yet even so it remains a perpetual challenge to political practice. It is, in Bacon's words, one of the "inventions that may in some degree subdue and overcome the necessities and miseries of humanity" while leaving undefiled what through the ages has been upheld as the true image of Man.

---

[10] See for this problem my *The Price of Liberty* (London, 1937).
[11] See Albert Camus, *Resistance, Rebellion, and Death* (New York, 1961), pp. 72, 248.

PART FIVE

A POSTSCRIPT

Political Economics
in the Late Twentieth Century:

The Quintessence of Political Economics

The purpose of this Postscript, as I have outlined it in the Preface, is a limited one. First of all, I am going to examine the major propositions of the original text in the light of the *economic events* that have occurred since the book was originally published. Second, I shall deal with some of the objections that have been raised against the *theoretical foundation* and the *analytical technique* of the book. Finally, and this amounts indeed to a modification of my original views, I feel bound to reconsider the nature of the *macro-goals* that a realistic public policy based on the findings of a Political Economics can pursue in the coming decades.

To place these issues in the proper perspective, it may be useful once more to summarize the gist of a Political Economics in a few propositions:

1. The markets of industrial capitalism, when left to exclusive self-regulation, have for a long time lacked that minimum "orderliness" which is required both for satisfactory provisioning and for theoretical generalizing. The reason is that uncontrolled market movements have become too irregular to permit individual marketers to achieve the interlocking patterns of behavior on which stability of aggregate provisioning, full resource utilization, and balanced growth depend. At the same time, this defect at the level of action also forestalls, at the

level of theorizing, generalizations sufficiently reliable to support predictive statements.

2. As a consequence, these markets have been progressively subjected to public control, but neither aggregate output nor the general price level has as yet achieved a satisfactory degree of stability.

3. This failure must be attributed to the limited range of conventional market controls. These controls confine themselves to altering the *field of operation* of the micro-units—e.g., by raising or reducing taxes, interest rates, tariffs, etc.—without however directly controlling marketers' *responses*. I call these controls "primary."

4. If, in the interest of safeguarding the viability of a system based on decentralized decision-making, orderly states and processes are to be established, additional "secondary" controls need to be introduced. Their task consists in inducing responses, in particular expectations, on the part of the micro-units that are in accord with the requirements for stable provisioning and full resource utilization.

5. The first step in the search for secondary controls consists in specifying a consistent set of macro-goals in accord with the desired level and composition of aggregate output. From the knowledge of such macro-goals, of the initial state of the system, and of certain technological and psychological constraints, the goal-adequate movements of the system, goal-adequate patterns of behavior and motivations on the part of the micro-units, and finally, goal-adequate public controls can be determined with the help of a particular analytical technique, called here "instrumental inference."

6. The findings of instrumental inference concerning goal-adequate primary and secondary controls must then be applied as measures of economic policy. In this manner the actual motion of the system can be transformed into goal-adequate motion—the *practical* aim of Political Economics.

7. To the extent to which this transformation is successful and orderly states and processes are established, the necessary con-

dition is fulfilled for generalizing explanations and predictions —the *theoretical* aim of Political Economics.

The Factual Background

Against this background let me now examine whether the major economic events of the last twelve years, national and international, have reduced or enhanced the need for a reorientation of our conceptual and practical concerns in the direction of Political Economics.

In the discussion that followed the original publication[1] it was repeatedly asserted that rather than fostering tendencies toward increasing "disorder," certain developments during the last two generations have actually strengthened the stability of organized capitalism and the predictability of its movements. Compared with the era of unbridled competition, contemporary monopolistic and oligopolistic organization—in particular, administered wages and prices combined with the advance of professional management— was said to facilitate business planning and thus to render market relations more transparent. Admittedly the ensuing rigidities impeded speedy adjustment to changes, but they were supposed to make prediction easier. So does in this view the transformation of ownership control into the predominance of managerial control— in Professor Galbraith's terminology, the rise of a "technostructure."

Against such an optimistic evaluation of the structure of organized capitalism, I have stressed the multiplication of incentives beyond the narrow range of the extremum principle and the growing uncertainty of expectations—both developments to be traced back to the progressive extension of the "time horizon" of market transactions, which has even robbed the profit incentive of its determinacy.[2] Moreover, even if we accept the growing ability of the corporation to plan ahead, this argument limits itself to the level of the micro-analysis. The problem of stability and predicta-

[1] See *Emase,* especially Professor Henry C. Wallich's statement (pp. 156–58) and my Rejoinder (pp. 170–74) .
[2] See pp. 46–49 above, and *Emase,* pp. 11–14, 170–74.

bility is, however, macro-economic. It concerns the question "by what mechanism these individual plans can be expected to build up into a coherent whole."[3] The question is all the more justified as Galbraith himself admits that "there is no priori reason why the policy pursued by two mature corporations will be the same, for there is no reason to assume that the goals or the intensity of commitment to goals will be the same in any two cases."[4]

In addition, rising rates of unemployment, associated with rising rates of inflation as experienced during the recession of 1974-75, can rightly be attributed to rigidities caused by monopolistic organization on both sides of the social fence. Yet these are the very rigidities that my critics invoke as a stabilizing factor. Perhaps the ensuing maladjustments are now no worse than the disturbances that beset earlier stages in capitalist development. But this is no consolation in an age when the public refuses to tolerate a degree of instability that it once accepted as an Act of God.

Still, all these pros and cons remain in the realm of speculation. The only reliable basis for judging the degree of the present system's stability and the feasibility of macro-prediction is the actual course of the economic processes over the last thirty years and the success or failure of the forecasts related to it.

The touchstone for economic prediction is, of course, the forecaster's ability to anticipate whether a movement observed in the present will continue its direction or reverse it. In this respect the predictions pertaining to the two decades following the end of the Second World War have been surveyed above and have been found badly wanting.[5] Even the showpiece of later efforts—the Kennedy tax reduction of 1963—proved inconclusive because the upturn in investment preceded the tax reduction by a full year.

These negative results have been fully confirmed in a study based on Professor Lawrence R. Klein's Econometric Model for the United States, covering the years from 1953 to 1965. It shows that even the employment of elaborate theoretical and statistical tools

---

[3] Thus J. E. Meade in his review of Galbraith's *The New Industrial State*, *Economic Journal*, June 1968, pp. 372–92.

[4] See J. K. Galbraith, *The New Industrial State*, Boston, 1967, p. 195.

[5] See pp. 50—57 above.

does not yield satisfactory results. The study is actually concerned with "postdiction," because a system of simultaneous equations is tested ex post on statistical material available from observations of the past. Moreover, the results concern the very period that contained the data to which the model's equations were originally fitted. In spite of the favorable bias of this setup, the predictions of cyclical turning points have consistently proved wrong when made more than two quarters ahead.[6]

Now it must be admitted that the techniques applied in the building of econometric models have been much refined during the last decade. All the greater is the disappointment when we examine their forecasting record during the latest business recession. In the interest of objectivity, I quote a leading protagonist of econometric research.[7]

The 1970 recession was generally foreseen, but proved somewhat worse than the model estimates. . . . In the 1974 crisis, the forecasters—and business, partly because it believed them—made the most colossal forecasting errors since 1945. . . . The 1974 forecasts said that the economy would probably begin to recover in early 1975, though we did warn of the risk of the "deepest and most prolonged recession of the post-war period." . . . The economy, in fact, entered the worst crisis since World War II.[8]

What is interesting in this statement is not only the admission of failure but the reminder that, in 1974, business was offered two alternative and radically opposite forecasts—a technique that certainly improved the chances of being right! In fact, this technique of offering alternative forecasts seems to have become standard. It was repeated for 1976, and business was explicitly admonished to "be alert to the alternatives."[9] One cannot help wondering whether

[6] See *Survey of Current Business,* U.S. Department of Commerce, 46, no. 5 (May, 1966) , pp. 13–29.

[7] See Otto Eckstein, "Econometric Models and the Formation of Business Expectations," in *Challenge,* March–April 1976, pp. 12–19. Professor Eckstein is President of Data Resources, Inc.

[8] *Ibid.,* p. 17

[9] *Ibid.,* p. 18.

business needs the econometrician for such an alert. Moreover, whereas the scientific observer can rest content with sitting on the fence, business must decide now whether to act or not to act, well aware that its decision may affect the course of events, though ignorant in what direction.

I have stressed repeatedly that it is the irregularity of economic facts rather than any defects in the prevailing research methods that is responsible for the poor showing of the forecasts. For this reason it is instructive to learn the reasons to which an expert like Otto Eckstein attributes the recent failures. "The models failed because they did not properly allow for the full impact of the food and energy situation and the end of price controls. Nor could we believe that the Federal Reserve would press the economy steadily downward while it was sinking of its own."[10] In our terminology what ultimately vitiated the forecasts was the incalculable effect of extra-systemic forces on the intra-systemic behavior of producers and consumers.[11] But there is no reason whatsoever to expect a cessation of extra-systemic shocks in the future. Under such circumstances what the economic information services can do, and more and more are doing, is to provide an ongoing exploration of current events. As was anticipated here twelve years ago, ". . . prediction of the future will have to turn into a continuous re-examination of the present."[12]

Instrumental Inference Once More

Where does this leave us? Far from dismissing the aim of economic prediction as idle or even illegitimate, it is one of the basic tenets of this book that the ability to predict is the very precondition for investing the modern industrial systems with that minimum of order on which decentralized decision-making depends. This is

---

[10] *Ibid.*, p. 17.

[11] See pp. 49–50 above, and *Emase*, pp. 9–11.

[12] See p. 49 above. In a different context it was stated (p. 117 above) that only after the public controls of a Political Economics have established an orderly framework for the industrial process will the probabilistic techniques of modern econometrics find their proper place.

so because the prevailing tendency toward disorder, which, as we saw, recent events have strengthened, can be counteracted only by measures of public policy. But in order to devise suitable policies, we need a theory that can tell us the future effects of measures we employ today. However, so long as the observable facts from which the explanatory principles are to be abstracted lack that minimum of order which is the prerequisite for any scientific generalization, it seems impossible to construct such a theory.

It is from the horns of this dilemma that Political Economics tries to lift economic analysis. Thus it cannot be emphasized too strongly that Political Economics claims to be a theoretical science, logically at par with, even if methodologically different from, Traditional Economics, in which I include also the Marxian model. It is not a revival of Institutional Economics, which never transcends the "natural history stage" of descriptive inquiry—Political Economics is a deductive science. In accord with traditional theory, it tries to derive a past or a future state of the system from the knowledge of its initial conditions and a "law of motion." The difference between the two approaches concerns the manner in which such a law of motion and its ultimate determinants are established. In traditional theory they either emanate from a process of induction—from the generalization of observations relating to actual behavorial and motivational patterns—or they are postulated as constitutive definitions, as for instance the extremum principle is treated in Professor Friedman's "positive economics." In either case these generalizations or postulates serve as highest-level hypotheses and thus belong to the "knowns" of the deductive syllogism.

Contrariwise, Political Economics denies that, at least under the conditions of organized capitalism, either observations or constitutive definitions can result in such highest-level hypotheses. Rather, it insists that the forces—behavior and motivations—that rule economic motions and, in particular, changes of motion cannot be treated as known but fall themselves in the category of unknowns to be determined by analysis. Therefore a major task consists in devising an analytical technique suitable for such determination.

This technique—instrumental inference—has been described in detail in Chapters 5 and 10 above. It has revealed itself as a search procedure for discovering suitable means to a stipulated end. It falls in the category of "heuristics" or of what C. S. Peirce called "retroduction." It is "regressive" inference, starting from a "given" end—in our field a stipulated economic macro-goal—deriving therefrom paths suitable to attain the goal, and behavioral and motivational patterns suitable to set the system on a suitable path and keep it to it.

It is true that there are no formal rules analogous to the rules of deduction observance of which would safely guide us to the solution. We must "hit" on it by what Michael Polanyi has called a logical leap.[13] However, this is by no means a leap in the dark but one that is directed by the nature of the problem and by more or less rigid constraints that set narrow limits to the area where the solution can be found. Yet, as the critical responses to my earlier exposition[14] show, there are some issues that require further elucidation.

In fact, the major objections raised concern one and the same issue, namely the question whether instrumental inference can really dispense with the laws of positive economics. If not, my critics ask, what difference is there between instrumental and conventional economic reasoning?

(1) The problem arises, first of all, when we try to circumscribe the precise nature of the "constraints" that make instrumental inference determinate. I have defined them above as the pertinent laws of nature and engineering rules, including also those psychological laws that link a specific behavior to specific motivations.[15] Against this some of my critics insist that in order to trace out the implications of the macro-goal (s), we must employ, "in addition to laws drawn from the natural and psychological sciences, some of the laws or assumptions of 'positive' economics about the interrelationship of economic variables."[16]

[13] See his *Personal Knowledge, loc. cit.,* p. 123.
[14] See, e.g., *Emase,* p. 182–84.
[15] See Ch. 10 above, especially pp. 253 and 257–61.
[16] See Ernest Nagel in *Emase,* p. 64. Also Fritz Machlup, *ibid.,* pp. 125–26.

That this is not so, and that introduction of so-called "economic laws" into the nexus of instrumental inference would actually obstruct it, can be easily demonstrated. Let us assume a fully automated system in which all processes of production and distribution are servo-controlled to the point where human decision-making is limited to goal setting, that is, to decisions concerning the content of the output menu and the specific techniques to be applied, and to the acts of programming the computers. Once these preliminaries are completed there are obviously no sources left other than engineering rules and the underlying laws of nature from which the suitable structure of the path and the suitable operation of the active forces—in this setup exclusively "subhuman" forces—could be derived.

The insight imparted by this fiction is fully valid for our present economic organization, market as well as collectivist, in which human behavior does enter at strategic points. Given for such a system the identical output menu and the identical technology, it stands to reason that the behavior of the human agents must follow a path identical with that pursued by the automated system. Under no circumstances must it be ruled by laws of its own. Speaking quite generally, we can say that to be suitable behavior must be free to adjust itself to the varying requirements of different goals and different engineering rules. Far from aiding in the instrumental search, "extraneous" economic laws, even if they were to exist, would destroy what is essential in instrumental analysis—flexibility of behavior and motivations.[17]

(2) Of quite a different nature and well worth pondering is another objection. It concerns the last step in instrumental inference—the derivation of public controls suitable to transform actual motivational and behavioral patterns into goal-adequate ones. This is the decisive link that connects the imaginary world of the "suit-

---

[17] For further details, especially on the role which the institutional setup—a part of the initial conditions—plays in the instrumental inference, see *Emase*, pp. 24–25. There (pp. 19 and 176–77) I have also extended the brief comments stated on p. 263 above, on the feasibility and compatibility of several macro-goals pursued simultaneously.

able" with the practical world of the "real." Or, as it has been
stated in Chapter 5 above, only if we succeed, first, in analytically
deriving suitable controls and, second, in reorganizing the actual
economic process by applying those controls shall we finally "order"
the system in such a manner that a deductive syllogism, based on
a behavior pattern determined as suitable, will lead to confirmable
predictions. But, the critics ask, how can we be sure of the efficacy
of any control measure unless there are positive laws that relate specific measures to specific motivations?[18]

In the main body of the book, I have repeatedly taken note of
this problem[19] when I included among the "knowns" of instrumental inference "certain empirical generalizations which establish
a tentative relationship between motivations and relevant environmental influences, in particular, political control" (p. 253 above).
So the issue boils down to a precise specification of the nature of
those "empirical generalizations."

Now there is no doubt that my critics refer to laws or generalizations of "positive" economics.[20] However, we need only to spell out
some of the generalizations I have in mind in concrete terms to
realize that they have nothing whatsoever to do with the laws and
generalizations that positive economics claims as valid for the economic core process. Rather, the relationship between motivations
and environmental pressures—impersonal as well as deliberate ones

[18] See Gerhard Colm, "The Dismal Science and the Good Life," *The Reporter*,
July 15, 1965, pp. 56–58; Robert L. Heilbroner, "Is Economic Theory Possible?"
Social Research, Summer 1966, pp. 272–94, especially p. 292; Fritz Machlup, *Emase*,
pp. 125–26; T. W. Hutchison, "Economic Means and Social Ends," *Journal of Economic Literature*, June 1970, pp. 445–46, and in personal correspondence.

[19] See pp. 66–68, 142–43, 154–56, 253, 260–61 above. Also *Emase*, pp. 26–32, and
especially pp. 186–88.

[20] See, e.g., Colm, *loc. cit.* "How would 'instrumental analysis' work if we cannot
make any meaningful statement about the probable effect of the use of such instruments as tax reduction on consumer and business? Admittedly our *economic
knowledge* is pretty deficient. There is, however, no reason for exaggerating the
degree of ignorance."

Or Machlup, *loc. cit.*: "The questions regarding . . . the political controls designed to stimulate the right motivations cannot be answered except on the basis
of full knowledge of theoretical laws, institutional rules, and empirical generalizations about *economic relations*—that is, on the basis of *positive economics*"
(italics added) .

in the form of public controls—fall in the category of "social causation." In this respect I have referred to J. S. Mill's program of an "Ethology" or "Science of Character," designed to determine "the kind of character produced . . . by any set of circumstances, physical and moral."[21] In another context I have enlarged on these comments by stating that "it is not surprising that psychology has not yet presented us with any laws of social causation on which instrumental analysis could safely be based. However, this does not exclude a few empirical generalizations or rules of thumb that permit us to form an estimate of the probable effect of certain types of control on economic motivations. Thus it is safe to presume that the effect of control will be determinable and predictable whenever (1) the macro-goal at which control aims and the specific measures it takes coincide with the freely chosen micro-goals of the controlled, and (or) the sanctions imposed for non-compliance are severe and inescapable."[22] In the same context I have pointed out that it is, in principle, easier to control marketers' expectations than their action directives. This is so because such control, especally by spreading information about the future course of economic processes to be guaranteed by a goal-adequate economic policy, is bound to reduce uncertainty of expectations. And "every marketer is interested in improving his commonsense knowledge about his present and future field of action."

However, whatever form public controls may take—lenient, as in the case of improved information, or severe, as, e.g., in the case of wage and price controls—their effect is never mechanical. We deal now with a social and no longer with an engineering problem, with a challenge that can be accepted or rejected, even in the extreme case of coercion. In other words, the strength of the linkage between public controls and micro-motivations is proportionate with the degree to which the purpose of such controls is, first, *understood* and, second, *approved* by those who are to be controlled.[23]

---

21 See pp. 67—68 above.
22 See *Emase*, p. 29.
23 See p. 161 above, and *Emase*, p. 189. More recently, *The Path of Economic Growth*, p. 287.

From all this it should be clear that the empirical generalizations with the help of which goal-adequate public controls can be ascertained are a world apart from any alleged laws of economic behavior, such as the "law" of supply and demand. They belong in a much wider context, referring to the effect of any environmental stimulus on any type of social response, economic or otherwise. They are, in other words, the general rules on the observance of which the overall functioning of any society depends, traditional, market, or collectivist.

We can also express the difference between laws of positive economics and the generalizations that relate micro-motivations to public controls in methodological terms. The former—if they exist at all—are *intra*-systemic, that is, they concern the interrelations among economic variables. The latter are *extra*-systemic, associating the shape of one particular economic variable—motivations—with a specific political variable—control. As was said before, the latter link is tenuous because it can be arbitrarily broken in any given case. But general and continual rejection would signify more than failure of public control over the economy—it would amount to total anomie.

The Function of Public Controls

These considerations throw light on the distinction between primary and secondary controls, which plays an important role in the above summary.[24] I have described there the role of *primary controls*—the conventional measures of modern economic policy, such as tariffs, taxation, social legislation, but also the fiscal and monetary controls advocated by the "new economics" of Keynesian provenance—as altering the micro-units' field of operation without, however, deliberately controlling their responses. Now one might retort that, e.g., a change in the level of taxation or an increase in public spending during a depression implicitly also aims at altering micro-behavior through the effect on expectations. But such prediction relies upon the axiomatic role that the extremum prin-

[24] See also *Emase*, pp. 32–34, and especially pp. 188–90.

ciple plays in conventional theory and is therefore of questionable validity. It reduces the effect to a pseudo-mechanical relationship—tax reductions are supposed necessarily to increase aggregate spending, as public investment is supposed always to raise aggregate employment. That, in fact, there is no necessity in that relationship was shown only too clearly in the example of the public works program undertaken in this country during the Great Depression. As the reader was reminded earlier, the New Deal policy, rather than raising aggregate investment and employment, reduced both because of a simultaneous reduction of private investment.

In the present context this example is instructive in several respects. First of all, in counteracting the public stimulation of investment, private investors either did not understand their true interest, or they deliberately acted against their interest from political opposition—in either case violating the extremum principle. Second, it is unlikely that a similar act of "sabotage" would occur today. During the last generation social learning has progressed to the point where the influential strata of the business community have become convinced that in a depression an active fiscal policy fosters profit maximization. Third, comparison between the two historical situations throws light on the role of secondary controls.

Secondary controls have been defined above as a tool designed to induce such micro-behavior as is in accord with the requirements of goal attainment. They cover a wide spectrum, from one extreme of minimum intervention—improvement of information—through indicative planning, planning by command (wage, price, profit, and investment control), and compensatory action to neutralize goal-inadequate micro-behavior, to the other extreme of partial and total nationalization.

In the climate of today the newly acquired understanding and affirmation of the "new economics" on the part of business would probably permit us to dispense altogether with secondary controls if a typical depression were to be combatted with fiscal policy. On the other hand, during the "unenlightened" thirties only strict secondary controls—vast compensatory public investment, possibly coupled with control of private investment—would have assured the success of the primary controls. The same seems to be true of the recent "atypical" recession, in which rising rates of inflation combined with rising rates of unemployment. Certainly the primary control applied—tax reduction—has so far had only a limited success. At the time of this writing it seems more than unlikely that tolerable rates of inflation and unemployment can be restored without an incomes policy coupled with public investment, that is, without secondary controls.[25]

These comments should also dispel the notion that secondary controls are meant as substitutes for primary controls. They must be seen as standby measures, to go into effect whenever unsuitable micro-behavior threatens to obstruct the purpose of primary controls. This function should be predominant in the handling of future extra-systemic shocks. But nothing of what has been said here negates in any way our earlier warning about the tenuous nature of all extra-systemic regulation of the economic core process. This is especially true of the milder forms of secondary controls, defined above as "manipulating" controls. They are wholly dependent on a consensus of insight and will among controllers and controlled.

This does not mean that we must accept once and for all the degree of consensus as it obtains at any time. The acceptance of fiscal policy referred to above is only one instance of the continuous learning process that has characterized the history of capitalism over the last 150 years. It has taught, and continues to teach, the different strata of the economic community to embrace, or at least to live with, regulatory measures that economic theorists, no less

---

[25] My stress on the need for reconciling micro-behavior, especially of the decentralized production units, with public control has received support from an unexpected quarter. The recent Nobel Laureate, L. V. Kantorovich, writes in *Optimal Decisions in Economics*, Moscow, 1972, p. 206: "The system of optimal planning creates a theoretical basis for solving the problem of combining planning with incentives and initiative of enterprises . . . new forms of management have to be employed which combine planning with autonomous action of the (decentralized) units." I owe both the reference and the translation from the Russian to Professor Leon Smolinski, who edited the recent publication of Kantorovich's *Essays in Optimal Planning*, International Arts and Sciences Press, Inc., White Plains, N.Y., 1976. See also his Introduction to that volume, especially pp. XXV-XXVII.

than the men of practice, had once regarded as intolerable—from social legislation and progressive taxation to collective bargaining and fiscal control. Weakening of such consensus, on the other hand, would call for ever stricter measures of secondary control, raising the specter of autocratic coercion to compensate for the loss of spontaneous conformity. Such a development would in no way invalidate Political Economics and especially its theoretical part: instrumental inference. But it would affect the range of feasible macro-goals and of the means to be applied to their realization.

Political Economics in the Late Twentieth Century

Alas, these observations are far from academic. Rather, they point in the direction in which organized capitalism seems to be moving. Therefore they cannot help affecting our views of the aims Political Economics can and should pursue in the coming decades.

Insofar as I have discussed the factual background and the analytical procedure on which Political Economics builds, I have been able to uphold the position taken in the main body of the book. This is no longer possible when it comes to spelling out the nature of the macro-goals, realization of which is not only a necessary but also a sufficient condition for establishing and maintaining an orderly framework of the modern industrial system. My former statements on this issue appear to me in retrospect as much too "harmonistic." They lack awareness of three major problems that have since come to the fore: the ecological threats, the growing importance of a public economic sector, and last but not least, the need for "internationalizing" both primary and secondary controls.

(1) The reader will remember that I chose Stabilization and Balanced Growth as my test cases for demonstrating the uses of instrumental inference. I did so not only because of the analytical interest that attaches to these issues. Their resolution appeared to me at the time as the condition for the achievement of that minimum order on which the preservation of the fabric of Western society depends.[26] It seemed to accomplish what can be defined as

[26] See p. 319 above, and *Emase*, pp. 35–36.

a dynamic Pareto optimum, that is, a process of dynamic macro-equilibrium that yields, within the limits of a given state of distribution and of a given taste structure, the full and technically most efficient utilization of resources.

Not that I was totally blind to the deficiencies of aggregate provision that the limitations mentioned create even in the wealthiest nations. Still, as far as the prevailing distribution of income and wealth is concerned, I believed that it threatened stabilization and growth only in poor countries, especially during the early stages of their development. In the regions of industrial maturity, I expected that the very fact of continuing growth, by steadily raising everyone's standard of living in absolute terms, would for an indefinite period stifle socially disruptive demands for a change in the distributional shares. And in the interest of preserving the maximum "micro-autonomy" possible, I was willing to accept the prevailing taste structure as determining the qualitative form of the goods and services provided, including the division between present and future satisfaction.

I was quite conscious of the fact that such limitation of the macro-goals practically to be pursued expressed "a conservative attitude toward social change."[27] But it enabled me to formulate a program of reform that genuinely reconciled order with freedom. This seemed possible because, on the one hand, Stabilization and Balanced Growth—full utilization of present and newly accruing resources at a rising rate of productivity—offered benefits to all to the detriment of none. This assured, on the other hand, a degree of social consensus high enough for the controlling authority to confine itself to "controls by manipulation."

(2) Recognition of the *ecological triad*—population explosion, gradual exhaustion of essential material resources, and progressive deterioration of the environment—has radically changed this picture. It may be true that the sudden shock of realizing these threats has somehow misled public discussion into exaggerating the time scale and even the scope of these dangers. Still, while shunning all

---

[27] See p. 320 above, and *Emase*, p. 36.

speculations about impending doom and while acknowledging the technological potentialities of finding tolerable solutions, there is at this point no conceivable solution that would not imply a gradual reduction of the growth rate of the mature countries.

To see this we have to take into account the new international aspect of the problem of industrialization. Given the changing balance of political and military power not only between East and West but also between North and South, the chances are slim that the underdeveloped half of mankind will in the long run submit to Western industrial hegemony. However, simultaneous industrial progress in all regions of the globe may well be incompatible with the available and even the potential supply of natural resources. Even more important, the ecosphere may not be able to absorb the heat that the energy required for universal industrialization will emit. The answer can only be a gradual redistribution of the world's resources in favor of the non-Western regions—be it by agreement or, more likely, by economic if not military threats—resulting in a deceleration of Western economic expansion.

However—and now we are back at the beginning—such reduction of the rate of economic growth is bound to put out of action the safety valve that has up to now protected the income and wealth pyramid in the advanced countries. In other words, the present distributional shares can no longer be treated as constant—a development with drastic consequences for overall consensus and thus for control.

(3) The gradual shift of inputs and outputs from the so-called private sector of the economy to the *public sector* operates in the same direction. To the extent to which this shift is financed by taxation of the wealthier strata, it already represents an act of redistribution. Besides, it enforces a change in the prevailing taste structure—an effect that also accompanies some ecological policies, especially those related to protecting the environment. These are bound to raise the price of certain goods if they do not altogether prohibit their production.

However desirable such an imposed alteration of individual consumption patterns may appear from hygienic, aesthetic, and moral viewpoints, it is bound to interfere with the micro-autonomy of consumers and producers. Moreover, by reducing the funds available for private investment, it further reduces the general rate of growth of the goods economy, as measured by conventional standards.[28] And even if we were to apply more sophisticated measures of welfare—by necessity value laden and thus controversial—the prospect is dim that the broad masses of consumers will readily exchange the expected rise of their goods baskets for purer air, cleaner water, and better health. Rather, in order to maintain the level of their goods provision, they will call even more insistently for redistribution, thus further undermining what consensus still prevails.

The line of least resistance to such a call is inflation, more precisely, cost-push inflation. The recent history of the British economy is a striking example of the failure of this expedient. Stripped of all surface appearances, it amounts to substituting class struggle for efficient controls. In the United States the conflict has not yet assumed such intensity. But mounting pressure generated by a falling growth rate may well recommend this solution, however futile in the long run, to those who, in the name of liberty, prefer a free-for-all to strict secondary controls over wages, prices, and profits, based on a new "social contract."

(4) Difficult as the peaceful solution just indicated may appear on both political and administrative grounds—requiring a quantum leap in social learning—it is not altogether utopian. But it may well become so when we place the transformation to be achieved in the context of *international relations*.

In speaking of strict controls based on a new consensus, our frame of reference is naturally the nation state with an administrative machinery capable of planning and of dispensing rewards and penalties, built on a common tradition and on the unreflective bonds established by daily contacts, irrespective of conflicts of interest. But where is the political authority to control the transactions of multinational corporations? By what measures can we achieve that

---

[28] See David Smith, "Public Consumption and Economic Performance," *National Westminster Quarterly Review*, November 1975, pp. 7–30. Also, a forthcoming study by the Organization for Economic Cooperation in Paris.

minimum of international solidarity in employment policy, monetary and fiscal management, etc., on which the stabilization of all
but the wealthiest national economies depends? And how will even
the wealthiest nation insulate itself from external shocks such as
have shaken the United States during the last five years?

And even if we indulge the fancy that future calamities might
create a minimal consensus among the nations of the West, how
will they neutralize the disturbing impact of the rest of the world,
be it the communist countries or the underdeveloped regions,
whose future development, according to a recent United Nations
Report, rests with drastic measures of public policy based on fundamental social and institutional changes?[29] A country such as the
United States can perhaps withdraw into autarky, purchasing stability with a reduction in the standard of living, as the countries of
the Eastern bloc have been doing for decades. But how are regions
less favored by nature and technology to find their balance?

Conclusion

As an attempt to read the signs of the times, these reflections are
somber. But I must emphasize once more that they leave unimpaired the theoretical validity and the practical significance of a
Political Economics as opposed to traditional reasoning. Even if we
were to draw the radical conclusion that no regime short of global
autocracy was capable of establishing global "order," such an appraisal, however repugnant to our most deeply cherished values,
would not be refractory to instrumental analysis. As I have insisted
here again and again, the exploratory techniques of a Political
Economics are neutral to the socio-political structure of the economies studied.[30] But I have also pointed out that "all macro-goals
are not necessarily compatible with the prevailing social relations,"
that is, with the socio-political structure of the initial state. "Whenever a conflict arises, we are compelled to choose between abandon-

[29] See *The Future of the World Economy, United Nations,* 1976, ST/ESA/44,
[30] See especially Part Four, *passim,* above. And now even more explicitly in *The
Path of Economic Growth,* chaps. 3, 4, 7, and especially 16.

ing the goal or the existing order."[31]

The United Nations Report just referred to takes its stand on favoring radical changes in the socio-political structure of the developing nations. Many of us might hesitate to follow suit when a similar transformation is advocated for the structure of the countries of the West. They may well fear that changes other than gradual ones may threaten not only cultural but physical survival. But they must then realize that such hesitation implies the abandonment, for the time being, of all perfectionist plans, intra- and internationally. And indeed, the best that is feasible in the present state of transitional turmoil may be the achievement of a "tolerable degree of disorder."

[31] See p. 261 above, and *Emase*, p. 35.

Index of Names

(Numbers in **boldface** indicate principal references)

Index of Subjects

About the Author

Adolph Lowe is Professor Emeritus of Economics of the Graduate Faculty at the New School for Social Research and at the University of Frankfurt am Main. From 1919-24 Professor Lowe was Section Head in the Ministries of Labor and Economics of the Federal Republic of Germany and Head of the International Division of the Federal Statistical Bureau from 1924-26. He has been a member of the faculties of the University of Kiel where he was Director of Research at the Institute of World Economics, the University of Frankfurt am Main where he was Professor of Economics from 1913-33, and the University of Manchester, England, where he was Honorary Special Lecturer in Economics and Political Philosophy as well as Rockefeller Fellow from 1933-40. In 1941 he was appointed Professor of Economics at the New School and remained in that capacity until 1963. He was named Director of Research in the Institute of World Affairs in 1943 and held that post until 1951. Among his publications are *Unemployment and Criminality* (1914), *Legal Aspects of Economic Controls During War Time* (1918), *Economics and Sociology* (1935), *The Price of Liberty* (1937), *The Universities in Transformation* (1940), and *The Path of Economic Growth* (1976). *Economic Means and Social Ends, Essays in Political Economics,* edited by Robert L. Heilbroner, was published in 1969 in honor of Professor Lowe's 75th birthday.

DATE DUE

JUL 2 1981			